Commemorative Issue

Laura Ingersoll Secord
A Heroine and her Family

David F. Hemmings

(from the Dictionary of Canadian Biography Online
Courtesy of Libraries and Archives Canada
Also: Courtesy of Niagara Falls Public Library

Born on 13 Sep 1775 in Great Barrington, Massachusetts,
British North America, eldest daughter of Thomas Ingersoll
and Elizabeth Dewey.
Died 17Oct 1868, at Chippawa, Ontario, Canada.
Buried in Drummond Hill Cemetery.

2nd Edition

Note

The painting on the front of this book was taken from one by Mildred Peel who found a striking resemblance in bone and facial features between the model, Phoebe Grace Laskey (1878-1924), and the artist's opinion of Laura Ingersoll Secord in earlier times. Phoebe Laskey was the great great grand niece of Laura Ingersoll Secord and was later married to Robert Noble. Her grandmother was Phoebe Secord, a granddaughter of Major David T. Secord, one of Laura's husband James' older brothers. The Laura Secord Candy Shops Ltd. adopted the image for their marketing; the company started with a single store on Yonge Street in Toronto, Ontario.

Appreciation

The author would like to thank Melissa Bottomley, Manager
of the Laura Secord Homestead, and the Niagara Parks
Commission for their encouragement in the preparation of
this work; the Friends of Laura Secord,
Caroline Mitchell McCormick, Milton Secord,
Elaine Akre Smith, Sandra Smith DiNanni,
Susan Nelson Frey, Janet Smith Kellen,
Laura Secord Giles, Susan Dimock Mulligan, Barbara March,
Maggie Parnall, Eldrid Ingebjørg Mageli, Eva Klerk Gange,
and many family members in Canada, the United States,
Norway and Guatemala for their assistance with
Laura Secord's direct descendant information; and his wife
Dr. Diane Hemmings for her listening, editing and support
during this project.

The author is also grateful for the assistance provided by the
staff members at the Library & Archives of Canada,
Public Archives of Ontario, Brock University Special
Collections Library, Toronto Metropolitan Reference Library,
Chippawa Library, Niagara Falls Library, Ontario Historical
Society, Ontario Parliament Building, McMaster University
William Ready Library, Niagara-on-the-Lake Library; and
Sarah Maloney at the Niagara Historical Society for their
courtesy in allowing the reproductions of images and
documents, some of which are in this book.

Library and Archives Canada Cataloguing in Publication

Hemmings, David F.
    Laura Ingersoll Secord : a heroine and her family /
David F. Hemmings. – 2nd ed.

Commemorative issue.
Includes bibliographical references and index.
ISBN 978-0-9865772-4-6

    1. Secord, Laura, 1775-1868. 2. Secord, Laura, 1775-1868 –
Family. 3. Canada--History--War of 1812. I. Title.

FC443.S4H45 2013   971.03'4092   C2013-900297-9

Bygones Publishing
Niagara-on-the-Lake, Ontario L0S 1J0
www.bygonespublishing.com

Printed in Canada by Carruthers Printing, Smithville, Ontario.

Contents

Preface

In 1945, when my mother ended her service to the war effort at the end of World War II, only my father knew what she had done and neither of them talked about it for more than thirty years. Even though the definitive book on the British Special Operations Executive had been published in 1966, she was reticent to discuss her endeavours as a Major equipping spies to be parachuted in France, many of whom never returned.

This reluctance to discuss extraordinary endeavours is not unusual, regardless of the courage exhibited or the century in which the action occurred. Laura Ingersoll Secord's grandson, James Badeau Secord (1836-1899) of Niagara, the second son of Charles, wrote a letter in 1887 at Sarah Ann Curzon's request in which he described how humble Laura had been whenever she spoke within the family circle about her courageous deed in 1813. "My grandmother was of modest disposition, and did not care to have her exploit mentioned, as she did not think she had done anything extraordinary. She was the very last one to mention the affair, and unless asked would never say anything about it."

Women in front-line service, female civilians in espionage behind enemy lines, and covert reporters of enemy plans and positions had their roots in earlier wars. It was often these courageous and patriotic spies whose actions, after a period of scrutiny, were considered heroic and to the benefit of their country during a war. Being behind enemy lines provides a unique opportunity to know the plans or dispositions of the enemy and to attempt a means to convey that intelligence back to those who need it. Embarking on such endeavours are opportunities for previously-obscure, brave women to become heroines in their own time.

Gender and gentility had their place in Georgian and Victorian society. It was common in war-time for men to be sent to the front to defend their women, children and their country. The concept that women could perform acts of bravery and patriotic duty on the front line in a war was not in the psyche of the British Army, nor the male-dominated historians that wrote about their exploits. It was not until such women as Edith Louisa Cavell (a nurse) were shot for espionage in World War I that the world realized the full extent of possibilities for women in courageous front line actions. In 1920 the British Royal Warrant made provision for awards to women of the nursing and hospital services in wartime. Subsequently this was extended to other acts of extreme bravery. Yet no woman has yet won Britain's highest medal for valour – the Victoria Cross – although the potential remains.

The most significant issue for those behind enemy lines is the fear of reprisal or retribution on themselves or their families for an action against the enemy. In Niagara Township in the War of 1812-1814, there were less than one thousand civilians behind enemy lines and only for limited periods – in Queenston, St. David's and Niagara-on-the-Lake (Newark, or just Niagara). Most were women, children and old or infirm men left to fend for themselves in a countryside that harboured marauding Americans and their Indian scouts. However, remaining residents could not avoid being aware of military manoeuvres and inadvertent communication of plans from those whose houses had been plundered by uncontrolled armed enemy soldiers. And the issue of reprisal did not rest with the protagonist alone, but also with those sympathizers who were aware of their action. So, when Laura Secord walked to the DeCew house to disclose the primary evidence of American plans to move on the British outpost at Beaver Dams, Laura's sister-in-law Hannah Secord and other family members and friends had equal cause to be fearful of reprisal if Laura Secord were caught en route or the act discovered by an enemy force at a later date. Such is the possible trail of retribution in the uncertain world of a frontier township so close to the country's border that the enemy could invade at any time. It was particularly real in the 1812-14 War in which American forces were required to serve in a foreign land, with officers and men who took advantage of the opportunity for plunder and retribution without proper approval from their commanding generals.

Laura Ingersoll Secord's involvement in the War resulted in both danger and financial hardship to her family. For the immediate period following the War, the residents of Niagara Township concentrated on rebuilding their lives and their properties. Upper Canada remained under military law until 1818, when Lieutenant-Governor Sir Peregrine Maitland was appointed to sort out the War claims and re-establish civilian administration in the province. In the aftermath of the 1812-14 War, petitions were the standard approach of achieving some recompense for the individual or family who had suffered. For the Secords, these petitions were not primarily for commemoration, recognition or reward, but for family reimbursement in difficult times. Assertions of loyalty and sacrifice during a war became the basis for many claims on the Upper Canada state. However, the Secord's claims were in competition with those of many others in the colony for lands, patronage, appointments and war loss claims. Some petitions therefore had to be excluded in favour of others. In the period from 1815 to 1820, as before, loyalty was primarily a male concept, and so there was an absence of female images and femininity in the assessments. In this period James Secord's claims were likely therefore to get greater attention than those of his wife.

The particular problem for the Secords was James' crippling knee injury sustained at the Queenston Heights battle; this limited his motion for the rest of his life. The primary issue, after selling some of his land, was for James to generate enough income to sustain the family's economy, especially as their widowed daughters and grand-children relied on them for some assistance. Clearly, from the records, this family's income did not improve with the war; James could not profit from the war's outcome nor could he make substantial war claims. Some of the Secords' petitions were successful, but not particularly profitable, and some were rejected by the Upper Canada administration. However, in quieter days during the latter stage of her life, Laura Secord was able to live in modest comfort with the joy of two faithful daughters and two grand-daughters in the same household.

Laura Secord cannot be credited with saving Canada. That would exaggerate the importance of the Niagara peninsula in the defence of the nation. Individual acts of extreme courage and bravery do win battles, but wars are won by a combination of factors – typically economic, psychological and military. However, success at the Battle of Beaver Dams positioned the British and Canadian forces well for the remainder of 1813. Laura Secord was a key figure of outstanding courage and endurance; her deed merits the status of heroine. As the Globe declared: "the story of Laura Secord is too deeply seated in the Canadian mind to be removed now."

The 2nd Edition of this book follows the successful run of a book that had as much information from primary sources as was known in early 2010. As often happens after a book is published, more information comes to light – for this biography, it was emails from Norway and Guatemala and some diligent searches into family shoeboxes that have yielded enough exciting material and images to merit a new edition.

Two years of additional research have produced family photographs and interesting stories about Laura Secord's descendants. Two of these are reproduced in this edition. Sons of Dr. Clayton (Carlos) Forsythe Secord, a trailblazing medical missionary to Chichicastenango, Guatemala in 1900, have assisted in bringing their father's extraordinary story to this edition. Sincere thanks go also to Eldrid Ingebjørg Mageli and Laura's newly-identified family in Norway for the exciting "To Our Children" document, written in 1928 by Laura Secord's great-granddaughter for a wider audience, which sheds new light on the descendants of Laura Secord's eldest daughter Mary Lawrence Secord Trumble in Europe and the United States; relevant excerpts are included in this edition. Both sets of material have been accompanied by excellent photographs. Finally the book includes most of the descendants of Laura Ingersoll and James Secord, to the eighth generation, which is to the present day. The first four ancestral generations of Laura Ingersoll are also included. Any errors or omissions rest solely with the author.

The material in this book is based on primary sources and the portrayal of Laura Ingersoll Secord and her family is based on what is evident in letters and other available documents.

It is the author's hope that this book offers an accurate portrait of a national heroine, grounded in the original documents and considering the social, military and provincial administration environments of the time. This book addresses the realities that Laura Secord, her family and friends faced in the generation following the War, and considers the people in Laura Secord's life and those who came after her. It is not about the poetry, ballads, plays, and other mythification of her life and deeds; nor is it about the Laura Secord Candy Shops Ltd., which, in 1970, did a wonderful job of restoring the Laura Secord Homestead museum in Queenston to its current state. This book is written for the descendants and Friends of Laura Ingersoll Secord, as a record of the lives, deeds and events that form a balanced view of her contribution to Canada.

As far as possible the text is arranged in chronological order; however, there are some overlapping dates which could not be avoided without fragmentation. The author has incorporated many petitions, letters, promotion and plaque texts; some of the quoted documents have added punctuation for easier reading.

At the time of this publication, the Homestead has become an important attraction for the War of 1812 Bicentennial Celebrations, especially in June 2013, the 200th anniversary of Laura Secord's Walk. The community on both sides of the border is "celebrating 200 Years of Peace". The Niagara Parks Commission, current manager of the Laura Secord Homestead property in Queenston, Ontario, has recently completed an infrastructure initiative at the Homestead with funding received from the federal and provincial governments. A new visitors' centre has been constructed and a Methodist church structure moved one block onto the site with its exterior and interior reconstructed to an 1860 theme.

"A Village in a village", Queenston
Courtesy: Author's Collection

This Commemorative Issue recognizes the Bicentenary Anniversary of Laura Ingersoll Secord's brave Walk from the family Homestead on Partition Street in Queenston to the DeCew House in present-day Thorold on 22 June 1813 - a walk that will be retraced by thousands of hikers on Saturday, 22 June 2013. In the last two years the Friends of Laura Secord have been working diligently towards a celebration of our heroine's courage by establishing a Laura Secord Legacy Trail and managing a 32-kilometre hike, mostly along off-road paths that are as close to the original route as can be determined. The local municipalities have encouraged this activity to improve personal fitness for participants of all ages, and the City of St. Catharines named a downtown building in honour of Laura Secord in October 2012. The City of Ingersoll, Ontario and the Town of Great Barrington, Massachusetts have forged a heritage connection; and representatives from both have visited the Homestead - an example of the 200 years of peace that has been our history since the War of 1812.

A final note regarding terminology. It is now well accepted that the aboriginal populations of Upper and Lower Canada played a highly significant role in British victories during the War of 1812 - the battles of Detroit and Beaverdams, in particular, deserve special mention because they were both won almost entirely by aboriginal participation. The term used at the time of the War of 1812 was "Indian" rather than the current "Aboriginal" or "First Nations". As all the documents of the period during and around the War of 1812 use "Indians", the author will be using this term and earlier tribal names for consistency throughout this book. Some individual tribal names have also changed since that period.

Thomas Ingersoll and his Family

m(1) Elizabeth (Betsy) Dewey
    Children: Laura m. James Secord
            Elizabeth Franks m. Daniel (Rev.) Pickett
            Myra m. Julius (Jock) Hitchcock
            Abigail m. Guy Woodworth
m(2) Mercy (Mrs.) Smith
m(3) Sarah (Sally) Whiting
    Children: Charles Fortescue
        Charlotte
        Appy
        Thomas
        Samuel
        James
        Sarah

Thomas Ingersoll had 3 wives and 11 children.

The Early Years: 1775-1811

On 13 September 1775 in Great Barrington, Berkshire County, Massachusetts, British North America, 17-year old Elizabeth (Betsy) Dewey delivered her first child to her 26-year old husband Thomas Ingersoll, a storekeeper and Revolutionary War officer. Laura Ingersoll was small and fragile, but resilient and well cared for by her gentle mother. In the next eight years Elizabeth delivered three sisters for Laura – Elizabeth Franks, Myra and Abigail Ingersoll – all of whom survived to adulthood and marriage. Sadly, Elizabeth died in February 1784, leaving eight-year old Laura to help her father bring up the children just as the Revolutionary War in Massachusetts finally came to a conclusion.

Ingersoll House in Great Barrington, Massachusetts
Courtesy: Niagara Historical Society

The Ingersoll well-furnished and comfortable house stood on the crest of five acres of land that sloped gently to the Housatonic River. The Ingersolls had been on this land since Thomas' grandfather built a cottage there in 1724. Today there is a plaque to Laura Ingersoll Secord outside the Mason Library on this site.

Thomas Ingersoll was a reasonably prosperous businessman, owning several acres between his Main Street home and the Housatonic River in Great Barrington. Self-employed as a hatter, Ingersoll also had other business interests including a grist mill, partly owned with Moses Hopkins in 1792. He also served as town constable and tax collector. With the outbreak of the American Revolutionary War, Thomas had enlisted in the Massachusetts Militia as a second lieutenant. While British Loyalists ("Tories") fled to Canada and New York state, Thomas had served his country until the end of the War, rising to the rank of captain in 1781. He served actively at various times and was later commissioned as a Major in the Regiment commanded by Col. John Ashley. In 1785, Massachusetts instituted some fiscally harsh government policies to solve the state's post-war debt problems. When Shay's Rebellion broke out in 1786-7, Thomas again answered the call and helped suppress the rebellion. There was no doubt that the Ingersolls were patriots. Nevertheless Thomas's business interests had suffered during the War, and the weak post-war economy did not help.

Within fourteen months of his first wife, Betsy Dewey's passing, Thomas Ingersoll married Mrs. Mercy Smith, a delightful widow, who brought warmth of spirit and drawing and sewing skills to the home. Mercy's first husband, Josiah Smith, had been killed during the Revolutionary War. Unfortunately for Thomas and the children, Mercy died of tuberculosis just four years later in May 1789. The tragic experience of losing two mothers before the age of 14, seeing her father grieve twice, and later coping with a more head-strong third mother resulted in Laura becoming a quiet, gentle child with composure not normally found in teenagers. She had become the primary care-giver for two of her sisters at the ages of 8 and 13, and had developed a home management competence well beyond her years.

Just four months after Mercy Smith Ingersoll died, Thomas married Sarah (Sally) Whiting, in September 1789. Sally wanted children and Thomas needed more land to accommodate the family. His duties as a magistrate took him away from Great Barrington for long periods, and his local merchant's business suffered in the severe post-war depression. On a chance meeting around Albany, New York, with Captain Joseph Brant, the well-respected and loyalist Indian chief, he became aware of land which could be made available to him by petition to Lieutenant-Governor John Graves Simcoe, along the Thames River valley in the Burlington area of Upper Canada (later to be known as Ingersoll, Ontario, named after Thomas). In the intervening period after the Revolutionary War, Thomas Ingersoll's business still had not recovered, and so Thomas decided to benefit from the economic advantage offered him and his family in Canada. Although it took almost two years to sell his property in Great Barrington, he uprooted his family and migrated with all their possessions in 1795 a hundred miles along the Mohawk River from Albany, portaging to the Norner Creek, and then following the creek to Oneida Lake, crossing the lake and travelling down the Oswego River to the Town of Oswego on Lake Ontario.

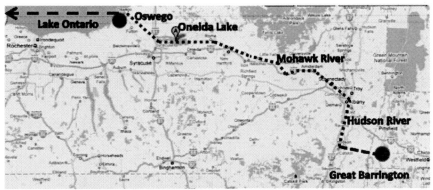

The Ingersoll Family Journey by waggon and boat to Canada.
230 miles (370 km) Great Barrington, MA to Oswego, N.Y.;
then 120 miles (190 km) Oswego to Queenston.

Once again, at age 19, Laura's skills and tenacity were needed to help her father move his growing family to a new country. While his land was being approved in the Thames River valley, Thomas lodged his family in Queenston, Ontario where he ran a tavern. The tavern, located at the south end of the Queenston Landing and close to the riverside warehouses owned by such traders as Robert Hamilton and Richard Cartwright, was the meeting place for an early Masonic Lodge that Thomas Ingersoll joined in 1796. During the days here, Laura worked with her father and met a local merchant, James Secord. James' family were well established as storekeepers just up the road in St. David's. Some of his merchandise came by ship that docked at Queenston, and he would occasionally come to collect and transport it back to St. David's.

Queenston Landing, as drawn by Elizabeth P. Simcoe in 1793.
Courtesy: Archives of Ontario

In the 'History of Freemasonry in Canada' it states:
"The first meeting was held at Fairbank's Tavern, Queen's Town on the 24th May, 1795, when Col. John Butler [was] Grand Master... It was decided to meet again on 1st Saturday in August at the house of Fairbanks but it was the 14th November 1795 before the lodge met in emergency at Ingersoll's Tavern, Queen's Town. The only business was a discussion respecting the present

regulations... Seventeen meetings were held during 1796, several different meeting places being used. For the first half of the year the lodge met at Thomas Ingersoll's Tavern, sometimes given as Queen's Town, again as Ingersoll's Landing, and at other times as Ingersoll's Queen's Town Landing... During 1797 thirteen meetings were held, degree work being the principal business transacted. The meeting places were divided between Bowman's (later Detton's, or Dayton's) Tavern, Stamford and Ingersoll's Tavern, Queenstown."

A map of Queenston in 1849 shows the wharves on the right (or north) end of the landing and other buildings (probably including the former Ingersoll's Tavern) on the left (or south) end of the same landing.

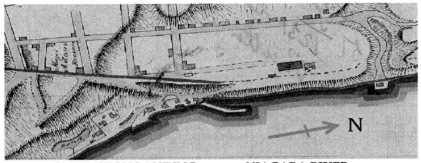

QUEENSTON LANDING   **NIAGARA RIVER**
Courtesy: Niagara Historical Society

James Secord had become a Freemason the previous year, when he was age 21. His father had been one of the earliest settlers in Niagara Township, and the younger Secord had been awarded 200 acres in Grantham Township as a United Empire Loyalist grant, but lost it through the foreclosure of a mortgage given to discharge debts incurred as a merchant in St. David's and Queenston. James met Thomas Ingersoll's eldest daughter during one of his numerous visits to the tavern. She was described by her daughter Harriet as "fair of skin, with abundant light brown hair, expressive dark eyes, with a slender figure. Of medium height, with a small frame and fair complexion, she looked delicate and fragile." However, as time would tell, her looks were to belie her character.

Thrown together by propinquity, Laura Ingersoll married James Secord sometime in 1797. As the eldest child of Betsy, Laura received her birth mother's fragile ornaments and silver spoons from her father. The marriage date and place are unknown, probably because they were married by an itinerant minister or local justice of the peace whose records were lost in the burning of St. David's in July 1814 or sometime thereafter. Laura came to live in St. David's in a house built for James. As was customary for merchants in small villages, the front ground floor of the house was used as a store; of necessity he displayed his wares in the front windows so that passers-by on the street could see them clearly. The rest of the house was their private residence. In addition to the store, James owned a lumber mill powered by the current of Four Mile Creek [much greater than today] in St. David's.

Within the first two years, Laura had established a network of good friends in St. David's, including her sister-in-law Annatie (or Hannah) DeFreest Secord, the wife of Stephen (or Etienne) Secord, and she had her first child, Mary who was born in 1799. Two years later, Laura delivered her second child, Charlotte, before the family's move to Queenston. Many of the Secords had children in the village of St. David's, and Laura had become one of several mothers in a growing Secord clan.

On the Niagara River, just four miles east of St. David's, the village of Queenston was rapidly developing into an important trading post. It had become the northern end of a portage run for commercial goods to and from Chippawa at the southern end, to bypass the Falls on the Niagara River. When the village was officially designated Port Queenston in 1801, James purchased some land on what was once the end of the village. He would later establish a general store at the southeast corner of the property on Queen Street. His original store was at the intersection of Partition, Front and Prince (now Princess) Streets, a short walk away from their later Queenston house. For almost two years, his investment and assurance of a sufficient return required James to commute to Queenston daily from St. David's.

Although a merchant of flour, potash and other products in 1795, James found difficulties making ends meet. His inventory management practices at the store did not endear him to his creditors, such as Richard Cartwright, Andrew & James McGill, Samuel Street and Robert Macaulay. As a young man, James' prudence and caution in business practices were put in question, and he fell badly into debt. He failed to pay down on his promissory notes in a timely manner at a time when money in Upper Canada was scarce. By 1801 James had mortgaged his Queenston property to Cartwright in payment of some of these debts and Laura appeared before a Niagara judge to sign away her "claim of Dower" for "granted Lands", which had probably come from her father. Within 10 years James would claim to be "in easy circumstances" as a merchant in Queenston. His cash position may have improved by then, but his business and inventory management skills never matched those of Richard Cartwright or Samuel Street.

Laura delivered another daughter, Harriet, on 10 February 1803. By the spring of 1803, James was confident that his business would soon be a profitable venture and that his family were fit enough to make a move to a new home in Queenston.

Laura Secord Homestead, Queenston, Upper Canada
Including the store and the stables.
Painted in 1913 by John Wesley Cotton (1869-1931).
Courtesy: Toronto Metropolitan Reference Library.

Queenston was to become Laura's residence from 1803 for over 30 years. The house, originally one and half stories (with two small rooms upstairs), is now at 29 Queenston Street. It was restored and furnished with period furniture in 1971, and gifted to The Niagara Parks Commission in 1998.

Mrs. James Secord now lived in a white frame house at the edge of the hill that sloped upwards to Queenston Heights. Women deferred to her opinion, sought her advice and were impressed by her dignity. She lost her quiet shyness and learned to communicate easily with acquaintances. She seemed, at last, to have become a person in her own right.

The winter of 1803-04 was long and cold, with heavy snowfalls and periods when the residents of Queenston were housebound for several days at a time. Winters were a period for James Secord to reflect upon the statements in his account books and to retain only that inventory which justified holding in storage. His business appeared to prosper, although balancing his accounts was complicated by the fact that some of his transactions were in trade or barter.

In the early years of the nineteenth century, shipping on the high seas was a tenuous business and James' income depended on imports from Britain. The ships themselves were not always sea-worthy in storms, and the political climate between England and France remained confrontational. However, on 21 October 1805 at the Battle of Trafalgar, Horatio Lord Nelson gave Britain a resounding naval victory over the combined French and Spanish Navies that ultimately guaranteed British control of the high seas for more than a hundred years. This outcome for North America was double-edged; it enabled the British to interfere with the growing American fleet of ships largely at will. James Secord continued to get most of his supplies from England, but the means by which Canadians received these trans-Atlantic goods infuriated the Americans because their own Atlantic sea trade was interfered with by the dominant British Navy.

In 1806 this interference was contentious for Britain, the USA and Canada. James Monroe, first the Ambassador to France and then

Minister to the Court of St. James in London, England, negotiated a treaty with Britain to replace the Jay Treaty of 1794, but President Jefferson rejected it in 1807 because the treaty contained no ban on the British practice of impressment of American sailors. As a result, the two nations moved closer toward the War of 1812. By April 1811, James Monroe had become Secretary of State and a confrontation with Britain in Canada was becoming more of a reality.

Nevertheless, despite the concerns, life on both sides of the Niagara River continued on much as it had done for the prior decade. The Lincoln Militia had been formed and some of the British Regulars were stationed on the Niagara frontier.

Early Land Deals across Ontario for the Secords and Ingersolls

Over the years James and Laura had been granted land from the Legislature for their loyalty, and had also inherited additional land from their fathers. To grow James' business, some of this property was sold to others and some was mortgaged.

Niagara Township Farmland Records:
"On 18 Jan 1799 (Reg 25 Nov 1799) James Secord et ux sold to Thomas Dickson 11585 in the Village of Queenston (146);
On 1 May 1801 (Reg 19 Jun 1801) David Secord sold to James Secord 189 acres along the Mountain (278);
On 20 Jun 1801 (Reg 20 Jun 1801) James Secord gave a mortgage to Richard Cartwright on the Secord Farm for 792.10.2 (279);
On 12 Jan 1803 (Reg 28 Jan 1803) Samuel Street sold to James Secord Lots 6 and 8 in the Village of Queenston (471);
On 4 Dec 1817 (Reg 1 Sep 1820) James Secord et ux sold to Samuel Street Lots 20, 21, 22, 23, 24 and 25 in the Village of Queenston for 625 (5843).

East Grantham Township Farmland Records:

On 2 Dec 1802 The Crown granted a patent to James Secord for all 100 acres in Lot 4 Con. 8;
On 27 Nov 1815 (Reg 9 Jun 1835) James Secord sold to Solomon E Secord 100 acres in Lot 1 Con. 8 (6031);
On 27 Nov 1815 (Reg 9 Jun 1835) James Secord sold to Solomon E Secord 100 acres in Lot 2 Con. 8 (6031).

The Town of Niagara-on-the-Lake Land Records:
On 28 May 1822 (Reg 26 Aug 1826) James Park sold to James Secord 1 acre in Lot 100 for £100 (6833). This lot is on Johnson Street, at the northwest corner with Victoria Street.
On 15 Aug 1823 (Reg 19 Sep 1826) James Secord sold to Robert Cannon ¾ acre in Lot 100 Town of Niagara for £125 (6902)"[1]

Over the first 15 years of married life, James' business affairs had had their difficulties. He had mortgaged his birth right of land and property injudiciously and had left hostage the finances of his family to the uncertainties of his short-term mercantile successes. In 1809, Laura Ingersoll Secord received 228 acres of land in Nelson (now Burlington, Ontario), given by her father; a year later Laura sold the property in pursuit of the cash needed to run James' business. [The property then changed hands several times and was used as a working farm until 1929, and was then replaced with the Palette Mansion and Lakefront Park which is still in Burlington today.] In the meanwhile, Laura had delivered two additional children – Charles Badeau in 1809 and Appolonia (known as 'Appy') in 1810.

On 31 March 1807 Laura Secord had also received a Crown Grant of 172 acres in Uxbridge, York County, Ontario; this property was located on Lot 37, Concession 7. Laura and James sold this land to George Moffatt on 16 August 1819. There is some evidence that Laura may also have owned land in the U.S.A., possibly some residue of her father's estate; however, being a resident of Canada created an encumbrance for Laura to sell this

[1] Niagara Settlers Land Records in this book come from Abstracts of Deeds Registers (1796-1865) in a new website established by R. Robert Mutrie: https://sites.google.com/site/niagarasettlers2/

land during James' lifetime and she may have signed a power of attorney to enable her sister Myra to sell it on her behalf.

Enlarged

Laura Secord's land in NELSON TOWNSHIP (now Burlington) in 1806

LAKE ONTARIO

228 acres

Laura Secord's inherited land in Nelson Township

In 1793 Laura's father, Thomas Ingersoll with four others had obtained a land grant of 66,000 acres (267 km²) in Oxford County from Governor John Graves Simcoe. He had named the new settlement Oxford-on-the-Thames, and was made a justice of the peace for the county. Despite his meeting the promissory condition that he bring 40 settlers to the area so that each of them had 200 acres to develop, Thomas Ingersoll failed to secure the resources for additional roads and other improvements in Oxford-on-the-Thames (now Ingersoll, Ontario). During the years around 1805 government land policy changed dramatically in Upper Canada. Thomas Ingersoll's entire land claim was taken away from him, even though he had built the first roads there and brought the requisite number of families to his settlement of Oxford-on-the-Thames. This decision by the Legislature was at a time when too much land had been obtained by Americans who had no intention of swearing allegiance to Canada but were simply investing on foreign soil for economic reasons. Whatever the political issue was with Thomas and the proof of his loyalty, he became discouraged and disillusioned.

Ingersoll	Thomas	1 1 Broken Front	N part 20 N part 21-25 20	West Oxford	17/05/1802	part of 600 total
Ingersoll	Charles	2	19	West Oxford	31/07/1804	200
Ingersoll	James Hamilton	Broken Front	SW part 22	West Oxford	17/07/1847	150
Ingersoll	James	2	25	West Oxford	28/12/1839	62
Ingersoll	James	1 [on Dundas Street]	NW part 13	North Oxford	19/09/1843	50

| Secord | James | 10 | 21 | East Nissouri | 19/09/1823 | 200 |
| Secord | James | 7 | 4 | West Nissouri | 15/03/1822 | 200 |

Oxford County Land Patents (1798-1852)
[L->R: Surname; First name; Con.; Lot; Township; Date of Patent; Acres]

By 1806, therefore, he had left the settlement and moved to the Credit River near Port Credit (close to Fort York, later Toronto). He opened the first hotel there. However, early in 1812 Thomas Ingersoll had a stroke and called for his eldest daughter to be close to him. Laura arrived in far-away Port Credit the day before her father died. In July 1812, the records of Sessions stated:
"Jan. 16th, 1813, Charles Ingersoll, son of the late Thomas Ingersoll of the River Credit, applied to the Court to be allowed, jointly with his Mother, a Tavern License for the Government House at the River Credit, stating that his father had kept said house for some years. Granted."

By the time Sally Whiting Ingersoll, his third wife, died in the summer of 1833, his son Charles had re-possessed the land in Oxford-on-the-Thames and renamed it 'Ingersoll' in his honour.

James Secord also accumulated land. In March 1807, as the son of a serving Loyalist, James was granted 400 acres on Lots 5 and 6, Con. 9 in distant Walpole, Norfolk County. In March 1811, James and his brother David received Lots 5, 6, 7, 8 and 10, Con. 7 in Walpole from the division of the Will of their father Lieut. James Secord, amounting to 1,000 acres.

At the age of 36, Laura had seen the death of both her parents, but her family was moderately prosperous and her children were growing and in good health. In her own lively house, Laura was enjoying her family and friends. However, the clouds of war were forming, and prospects were uncertain.

The village of Queenston had grown rapidly and many more properties had been developed there. The portage trade had remained strong, and local warehouses were well stocked. By the summer of 1811, the impressment of American sailors and confiscation of ships' cargos by the British, which was greatly injurious to the United States, reached a crisis point in Congress. James Madison had succeeded Thomas Jefferson as President and citizens of the United States were starting to talk openly about the prospect of American annexation of Upper Canada. This loose talk had reached the ears of British and Canadian subjects in London, York (Toronto) and the Niagara Peninsula. Loyalist Militias in the peninsula had already been drilling for some time, but no concrete plan of operations had been initiated. As concerns rose in the vulnerable Niagara region, supervised training of local Militia started in the late summer of 1811. James Secord rose in the Militia ranks to Captain, a position he relinquished about a year before the War because of pressing business affairs.

With a house of five children for Laura and a more stable business for James, life at the Secords was active. James continued to operate his store and warehouse in Queenston and collect rents from tenant farmers on his lands further afield. At the Secord Homestead, Laura took charge of the growing family, her vegetable garden, dressmaking and participation in the social calendar of events in the village and surrounding farmland.

Laura Ingersoll m. James Secord

Mary Lawrence Secord m. Dr. William Trumble
  Children: Elizabeth
              Mary
Charlotte Secord (unmarried)
Harriet Hopkins Secord m. David William Smith
  Children: Laura Louisa
              Mary Augusta
              William James
Charles Badeau Secord m. Margaret Ann Robins
  Children: Charles Forsyth
              James Badeau
              Alicia
Appolonia Secord (unmarried)
Laura Ann Secord m. (1) Capt. John Poore
  Children: John
              Albert James de Lisle
                m. (2) Dr. William Clarke
  Children: William
              Laura Secord
              Millicent
Hannah Cartwright Secord m. (1) Howley Williams
  Children: Katherine Emma
              Caroline
                m. (2) Edward Pyke Carthew
  Children: Hannah
              James Morden
              Caroline
              Charles Edward
              William

Laura Ingersoll Secord had 7 children and 20 grandchildren.

The War Years: 1812-1815

1812 The War of 1812 is formally declared by U.S. President James Madison and the Americans invade the Niagara Peninsula.

The United States of America declared war on Great Britain on 24 June 1812, but did not invade Canada at Queenston on the eastern end of the Niagara Peninsula until 13 October of that year. It was the capture of Mackinac Island in northern Michigan on 17 July 1812 that transformed the situation in Upper Canada. The Americans had been trying to defeat the British, who retained control of the area around Sault Ste. Marie and made great use of their Indian allies in the fighting to the east. The news of this early American defeat at Mackinac Island played a significant part for Major-General Isaac Brock in the subsequent British capture of Detroit on 16 August 1812.

From 1803 to 1805 Isaac Brock was based at York. In 1805-1806, while on home leave, he was promoted to Colonel and returned from England to Canada in 1806 when the first threat of war with the United States developed. In 1810 he was appointed to command all troops in Upper Canada, including the Niagara peninsula, which was the area seen as most vulnerable to American attack. On 4 June 1811 he was promoted to Major General. By the start of the War of 1812 he was also the Lieutenant Governor of the province, which by then was under military law. Brock had made his main contribution to the British war effort before the outbreak of the fighting, gaining the confidence of Tecumseh and thus ensuring that the British would fight with Indian allies. He also played a part in retaining the British 41st and 49th regiments in Canada at a time when the British were battling Napoleon's forces in Western Europe.

Business in Queenston carried on as usual, especially the portaging of goods to and from Chippawa. But on 13 October 1812 cannon and musket fire awoke the village early in the morning. It was obvious that the Americans were invading and the village was in an uproar. Laura and her eldest daughter, 13-year old Mary, dressed the children and left the house for shelter in a loyalist farmhouse inland, away from the shells falling on Queenston. There they awaited news from James Secord and the outcome of the invasion.

Not all the incoming news was good for Laura. Queenston Heights were taken by the Americans, the village was in turmoil, and Brock had been killed. However, over 600 British Army regular reinforcements from Fort George under Major-General Roger Sheaffe were on the way, supported by local Militia and Indians. By taking a circuitous route through the countryside and up the escarpment to St. David's, then turning east up the trails onto Queenston Heights, and deploying the Indians and local Militia in the woods encircling the western perimeter of the American forces' advance, they forced the Americans to retreat over precipitous terrain on the eastern edge of the Heights.

As rumours of war increased in 1812, James Secord had re-enlisted as a Sergeant of the local 1st Lincoln Militia in Captain Isaac Swayze's unit of Provincial Royal Artillery Drivers, the Car Brigade, who moved a militia battery of field guns drawn by farm horses during a battle. His company was part of Colonel William Claus' 1st Lincoln Militia Regiment, which included Captains James Crooks and John McEwan, and a Coloured Company under Robert Runchey. No news came from James, although news of the rout and capture of the Americans provided some comfort for a period of time. Finally, late in the day, word came that James was badly wounded and needed Laura's help.

Laura's life experiences had taught her to handle such news with courage, energy and determination. She made arrangements for the care of her children and set out for the Heights and the aftermath of the battle to find her husband. Finally she heard a call and came upon James on the north-eastern slope of the Heights. When found, James was on the ground and bleeding, weak and in great pain, wounded in the shoulder and knee during the engagement with the enemy on the Heights. With no medical supplies at hand, Laura did the best she could and obtained the assistance of a gentleman to carry James back to their house.

Unfortunately, while the family sought shelter and James was fighting, the house had been ransacked by invading American soldiers as they searched the abandoned homes in the village for loot. So now Laura had a wounded husband, a pillaged house with shattered effects, and everything of value taken from James' store. Her first task was to stabilize James's wounds, removing the musket ball from the shoulder and providing a splint for his smashed knee. Upon relief from some of the pain and after partial convalescence, James and the family moved more comfortably to St. David's – probably to Hannah Secord's gristmill on Four Mile Creek – to spend the winter among their relatives and friends. Stephen Secord, one of James' elder brothers, had died in 1808, leaving his widow Hannah in charge of his mill and nearby farm.

From the scant information available in war reparations claims made by Queenston residents, it is evident that James Secord and his neighbouring merchants in Queenston – John and Joseph Brown, and George Hamilton – all sustained substantial damage and loss to their homes and businesses. As the Upper Canada Gazette of 24 October 1812 cited in *Poulson's American Daily Advertiser of Philadelphia*, 24 November 1812 (DHC, 4:126) and Combe in *'The War of 1812 Losses Claims'* stated: "Inadequately restrained by their commanders and allured by the hopes of plunder, the Americans had plundered the houses of everything they could conveniently carry away". Confirming this, American Captain Wool wrote to Sally Wool, 17 October 1812 (John Ellis Wool papers): "considerable property taken by the

Soldiers". This was a democratic war for political purposes, in which the U.S. Militia, many of them drafted, did not have much interest and sought only personal gain.

The winter of 1812-13 was grim and bitterly cold, but everyone managed to share what they had. More Lincoln Militia died of disease and lack of shelter during this winter than were wounded in battle throughout the entire war. The Natives brought meat to Queenston and St. David's, and the British Army spared what they could. The Niagara Township villages and Laura Secord's family survived. After the miseries of the winter passed, the people of Queenston planted their fields and gardens, and James Secord grew a little stronger back home at his house in Queenston. Hopes for peace were dashed in May 1813, however, when the Americans landed again under the command of Colonel Winfield Scott, this time occupying a demolished Fort George in Niagara/Newark downstream at the mouth of the Niagara River opposite Fort Niagara, New York.

With the British forces withdrawn from Niagara Township to 40-mile Creek (now Grimsby), the Americans rapidly took control of both sides of the Niagara River, including Queenston. One of their first actions was to arrest all Canadian males between 16 and 60 years of age, and march them to an internment camp in Greenbush, near Albany, New York, close by the headquarters of the American Northern Army. The American General Orders were: "Every man of serviceable military age should be considered and treated as a prisoner of war." However, one glance at James Secord was enough to demonstrate that he could not be a threat to the Americans since he was still unable to walk without assistance.

Although not making James a prisoner of war, the Americans billeted three of their officers in Laura's home. These officers took the two upstairs rooms and had dinner at the house every day. Fortunately this arrangement enabled the Secords to get more supplies that helped feed their five children.

1813 James and Laura Secord listen to American plans for the Battle of Beaver Dams on the evening of 21 June, and Laura then walks to DeCew House to inform Lt. James Fitzgibbon.

For about a month during late May and June of 1813, the American officers used the Secord dining room for their conversation and planning during the evening hours. They were abusive to Bob and Fanny (or Fan), the Secords' two black servants (probably escaped slaves), and so Laura Secord had to wait on them herself. Occasionally an additional officer would also join the dinner group, and one penetrating army voice was enough to be overheard by others in the house. There was no more important evening for private discussion among three or four American officers than that of 21 June 1813 when one or both of Laura and James overheard the American officers discussing the message from Lt.-Col. Charles Boerstler of the 14th U.S. Infantry about overwhelming British Lieut. James Fitzgibbon and his force of 50 selected Irishmen, the 'Green Tigers', at Beaver Dams. It is possible that Capt. Cyrenius Chapin, a Buffalo doctor, was a guest of his fellow officers at dinner in the Secord house that evening. Being the protagonist – it was he who gained Brig. Gen. John Boyd's approval for attack - and self-proclaimed guide of Lt.-Col. Boerstler's subsequent march on Beaver Dams, he would have had prior knowledge of the intended action. His known bluster and infamy would certainly suggest that Capt. Chapin was capable of having the penetrating voice that the Secords heard.

Unlike British spies and Indians who could only report on observations of the American forces and their status quo to Lieut. FitzGibbon, Laura and James had the sort of information that could only be obtained directly from a knowledgeable American officer. They had unintentionally become a primary source of intelligence which Lieut. FitzGibbon needed to confirm his suspicions and Indian espionage on current American troop movements.

In 1913, Elizabeth J. Thompson added another dimension to the urgency of warning this outpost. "Most of the ammunition and supplies for the Army were at DeCew's, near the Beaver Dam, under the charge of Lieut. Fitzgibbon, and if the Americans had destroyed these supplies, they would have cut off Upper Canada from the base of supplies in Lower Canada, and the Country would then have very easily been taken by the invaders."

Clearly James Secord could not deliver this information, and so Laura accepted the challenge. They planned that Laura would leave their Queenston house before dawn on the morning of 22 June 1813 and go first to St. David's. Various scenarios and ruses were likely discussed by Laura and James before she left – such as milking her cow, visiting her sick half-brother Charles or perhaps James' family in St. David's or a family in the farmland, etc. One of the ruses to get out of Queenston and across to her Secord family in St. David's was her dress. If she had left the house dressed formally at about 5:00am, any one of the three Americans staying in her house or any American sentry in the village or along the road nearby could have suspected a motive beyond doing some local chores. It is clear from all accounts that she did not.

Mrs. Agnes Chamberlin of Ottawa, whose first husband was Col. James Fitzgibbon, writes: "I had heard so often from Col. Fitzgibbon all about Mrs. Secord. In my eyes she was more of a heroine than is generally known, for, like the Lady Godiva, her journey was performed, not exactly without any clothing, but next to nothing, being only a flannel petticoat, and what old-fashioned people call a bed-gown; in fact, a short night-dress worn over the petticoat. I am not positive about this last, but I rather think she had neither stockings nor shoes on. If fully and properly dressed, she never could have passed the sentries, and really appeared, as she likely did every morning, in search of her cow." Mrs. Harriet Secord Smith, aged 10 in June 1813 and the third child of Laura Secord, was still living in July 1891 when she said to Sarah Ann Curzon: "I remember seeing my mother leave the house on that fateful morning, but neither I nor my sisters knew exactly on what errand she was bent. She had on house slippers and a flowered print gown; I think it was brown, with orange flowers; at least a yellow tint is connected in my mind with that particular morning."

Once past any possible American sentry in Queenston, she moved quickly along a "circuitous" route to St. David's, normally an easy four-mile walk. She probably climbed to the top of the escarpment on Queenston Heights and kept to edge of the woods along her route; by that route she would have come down off the escarpment at the south end of St. David's, and forded the Four Mile Creek by a log behind the grist mill in that area. Laura visited her sister-in-law Annatie (Hannah) DeFreest Secord, Stephen's widow, in the early morning at about 7:00 am, probably for some sustenance, rest and comfort. In 1806 Stephen Secord had purchased the Grist Mill in St. David's from Peter Secord (now at 137 Four Mile Creek Road, having survived the burning of the village in July 1814). When he died in 1808, Hannah became the miller, continuing their family business and Stephen's farm. She had 10 children ranging in age from 3 to 23, to help her. It is probable that this was the house Laura Secord visited during her walk early on 22 June 1813.

The Old Grist Mill, St. David's, Ontario, abt 1900
Courtesy Bill & Carol Bannister

There is some likelihood that Laura had hoped to persuade her half-brother Charles Ingersoll, also living in St. David's, to walk or ride the rest of the route to FitzGibbon's headquarters for her. However, Hannah confirmed that Charles was too ill in bed and offered Laura her daughter Elizabeth, who was Charles' fiancée, as a companion to assist her along the way. They both knew that the next leg of the journey was complicated by the uncertain prospect of American sentries on the road to Homer, requiring a circuitous route to the Homer bridge.

Between St. David's and Homer lay the Black Swamp. As John Ross Robertson surmised, Laura and Elizabeth probably took the First Nation's trail through the Black Swamp and some dense underbrush. They then continued to avoid the road to arrive undetected at 10-mile Creek by Homer.

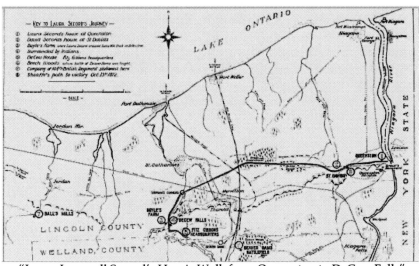

"Laura Ingersoll Secord's Heroic Walk from Queenston to DeCew Falls"
Courtesy: Toronto Metropolitan Reference Library

"This map or plan of Laura Secord's journey is absolutely accurate, and shows the exact path she travelled in 1813 from Queenston to Beaver Dams. The artist walked over the route and verified by the aid of notes and interviews with old inhabitants every mile of the route."

    A.   Laura Secord's house in Queenston
    B.   David Secord's house at St. David's
    C.   Boyle's Farm where Laura Secord crossed 12-Mile Creek on fallen tree
    D.   Surrounded by Indians
    E.   DeCew House

At the appropriate moment they crossed Homer bridge and moved more rapidly along or in parallel to Queenston Road. This was a somewhat more populated area and away from the volatile frontier zone in Niagara Township. Travel towards Shipman's Corners (at the corner of St. Paul and Ontario Streets in St. Catharines) was now easier. Unfortunately, Elizabeth, exhausted and needing to retire to a local friend's house, could not go any further. So Laura continued on alone south on Pelham Road on the west side of 12-Mile Creek towards the village of Power Glen. There she reached the Turney house; the Turneys were good family friends and probably assisted her in the route to take through the fields of Boyle's Farm. After a short respite Laura crossed 12-Mile Creek again, using a fallen tree as a bridge before climbing the Niagara Escarpment through a wooded area.

At various places along the route, especially between St. David's and Homer and between Shipman's Corners and the DeCew house, Laura had made diversions to avoid possible American sentries or Indian scouts, and to re-orient her bearings to get to a house she had not visited before. Her route, though perhaps 15 miles, had extended to about 19 miles with these diversions and had taken about 17 hours. Laura finally finished her walk, starting at about 5:00 am and arriving well after 9:30 pm when it was dark. In St. Catharines on 22 June, the sun rises just after 5:30 am and sets just after 9:00 pm; dawn and dusk are each about one half hour.

As Laura's oldest child left in Queenston to look after her father and her four younger siblings, Mary used to reminisce when her own grand-daughter visited her at the farm in County Sligo, Ireland. In 1928 Laura Mary Davis Mack wrote in her family history, 'To My Children', about her grandmother:
"She used to say she remembered well the day her mother set off to warn the troops under Capt. Fitzgibbon and her father's anxiety while she was away. The Americans invaded Queenstown, plundered and stole, even ripping the bedding to look for money. Three or more of them came to her house (Secord) where James lay ill of his wounds, and demanded food and money. The latter she had not but prepared some food for

23

them. While eating, they discussed several plans their leaders had of cutting off and destroying the British troops. She determined to try to frustrate one at any rate. She set off making the excuse that she was going to visit her son, living at the mill a little beyond the village. Her daughter, Mary, was to look after house and husband (father), though she was not much more than fourteen years old at the time. Laura had to walk through nearly impenetrable forests full of tribes of Indians and infested with snakes and insects of all kinds. It was June and fearfully hot under the trees and although summer, nearly dark, the growth was so thick. She was in time to warn him. In Coffin's chronicles of the war we read: 'Whether for advance or retreat the bypaths of the forest were such as the imagination of the present day cannot compass. A backwoodsman, laden with his axe wading here floundering there, stumbling over rotten trees, protruding stumps, a bit of half submerged road for a short space, then an adhesive clay bank, then a mile or two of black muck swamp – may possibly clay clogged and footsore find himself at sundown at the foot of a hemlock or cedar with a fire at his feet, having done manfully about ten miles for his day's work. The deep woods were Mrs. Secord's only security. There she must keep to as even a blazed path was not safe.' One great difficulty too, was getting through the American lines. They were ten miles out in the country, that is at any point commanding a possible line of communication within a radius of ten miles from Fort George."

Arriving after dark in John DeCew's field and exhausted by her climb, she encountered the First Nations (probably Kahnawake) who, after some persuasion, lead her to the DeCew house. With the help of Indians over the last mile, she arrived at Lieut. James FitzGibbon's headquarters in DeCew house, very weary, barefoot and dishevelled. As Laura Secord's own account stated: "I found great difficulty in getting through the American guards, which were ten miles out in the morning, walked nineteen miles over a rough and difficult part of the country where I came to a field belonging to Mr. DeCew. Here I found all the Indians encamped; by moonlight the scene was terrifying. They all rose and yelled 'Woman' which made me tremble."

DeCew stone house – Beaverdams (c. 1925)
Courtesy: Francis J. Petrie Collection, Niagara Falls Library

Laura Secord tells her story to Lieutenant James FitzGibbon, 1813.
W.C. Jefferys, Picture Gallery of Canadian History, 1945.

Cross-questioned by Lieut. FitzGibbon, Laura identified her
source and the circumstances of her information disclosure. Her
persuasion was not inconsequential since she had to demonstrate
that she was not an American spy and had positive intentions to

assist the British outpost and their allied Indians. She stated clearly what she and James had heard from the American officers the prior evening. FitzGibbon had already received some information from his scouts, but this detailed news of American forces' intent directly from a Loyalist family in Queenston provided important confirmation of his suspicions. Based on Laura's evidence, FitzGibbon deployed his Indian force of Kahnawake (Caughnawagas and Mohawks) in the woods and positioned his selected Irish detachment of the British Army to skirmish with the advancing Americans and to entrap their commander into believing that the opposing force was larger than it really was. The Indians poured heavy musket fire into the confused American ranks.

The following is what Ruth McKenzie wrote in the biography of FitzGibbon and his Indian detachment:
"During the war FitzGibbon demonstrated personal initiative. ... In June 1813, after the battle of Stoney Creek in which he participated as a company commander, FitzGibbon obtained permission to select '50 chosen men to be employed in advance of the Army, and with authority to act against the Enemy as he pleased and on his own responsibility solely.' Operating from John DeCou's stone house near Beaver Dams, FitzGibbon's men with loyal Indians harassed enemy troops and observed their movements. Based at Fort George (near the town of Niagara), the Americans resolved to send an expedition to dislodge FitzGibbon's force. Some 500 American troops, led by Lieutenant-Colonel Charles Boerstler, marched from Fort George to Queenston, encamped there for the night, and proceeded next morning, 24 June, towards Beaver Dams. On entering a beech wood they were ambushed by 400 Indians commanded by Captain William J. Kerr and Captain Dominique Ducharme."

The battle had been raging for three hours when FitzGibbon hoisted a white handkerchief and brazenly rode up to the Americans. He bluffed them into believing that they were greatly outnumbered and that more Indians were expected, and Boerstler surrendered. Lieut. FitzGibbon implied that his Indians would be hard to control if the fighting went on; he suggested that a bloody, scalp-taking massacre by the Indians

26

might result if the Americans held out any longer. Lt. Col. Boerstler himself had been wounded shortly after the battle started, and was in considerable pain. On the other hand, the boastful Captain Chapin was nowhere to be seen; he was later found hiding in a ditch some distance from the action.

Battle of Beaver Dams Park, Thorold
Courtesy: Author's Collection

FitzGibbon was widely praised for achieving the surrender of 462 American officers and men to his '46 rank and file'. General Edward Baynes commended him for his 'most judicious & spirited exploit,' and the *Montreal Gazette* spoke of 'the cool determination and the hardy presence of mind evinced by this highly meritorious officer'. FitzGibbon's fellow officers presented him with a gold medal. The coveted promotion came in October 1813 when FitzGibbon was appointed captain in the Glengarry Light Infantry Fencibles. FitzGibbon later acknowledged that his First Nations allies had fought and won the battle for the British. As John Norton wrote in his journal: 'the Caughnawaga fought the battle, the Mohawks got the plunder and Fitzgibbon got the credit.'

The Indians felt cheated of the military credit due them. In 1818 Captain Kerr obtained a letter from FitzGibbon in which he acknowledged that at Beaver Dams the Indians 'beat the American detachment into a state of terror, and the only share I claim is the taking advantage of a favourable moment to offer them protection from the Tomahawk and the Scalping Knife.' It also became known later that FitzGibbon had received advance warning of the American attack from Laura Secord [Ingersoll], who had walked from Queenston by a circuitous route of 20 miles to bring him the warning. FitzGibbon certified this fact for Mrs Secord in 1820, 1827, and 1837. In the 1827 certificate he stated that because of the information she had brought to him he had 'placed the Indians ... together with my own Detachment in a Situation to intercept the American Detachment'.

This defeat at the Battle of Beaver Dams, coming in the same month as the fiasco at Stoney Creek, blunted the American drive into Canada for the year 1813 and once again put them on the defensive along the Niagara frontier. The Americans retreated for the rest of 1813 to Niagara-on-the-Lake and Fort George.

After his coup at Beaver Dams, FitzGibbon served mainly in reconnaissance, observing the movements of American troops. The Glengarry Light Infantry Fencibles were disbanded in 1816 and FitzGibbon went on half-pay until 1825 when he sold his commission. He became a militia colonel in 1826." He died in London, England in 1863, age 83.

Analysis of the events shows that American forces had from time to time been deployed along primary roads and villages in the area before Lt. Col. Boerstler came down from Fort George with his force of over 500. British Major Peter W. De Haren and Canadian Fencibles' Captain John Hall (later Inspector of Cavalry), with his men, were not in place during the days of 22 & 23 June 1813; only at the express request of FitzGibbon did they arrive at a faster pace, and then not until the final actions at Beaver Dams battle were being resolved on the morning of 24 June 1813. On her 19-mile walk Laura Secord had some long-standing knowledge of much of the journey – at least to Shipman's Corners (where St. Paul Street meets Ontario Street in St. Catharines today). Because De Haren and other British forces were not in place along 12-Mile Creek on the schedule previously set by British Brigadier-General John Vincent (and certainly not close to where Laura Secord crossed that creek during her walk),

Laura did not have to pass through British lines until she was close to the DeCew house. Walking alone to St. David's (with the excuse of seeing her sick brother and her Secord in-laws there), and then with her niece Elizabeth Secord to Shipman's Corners (with the ensuing excuse of visiting acquaintances in St. Catharines), the most important concern for Laura Secord was to avoid confrontation with American sentries on the primary roads before reaching Homer bridge over 10-mile Creek.

If known, this act of espionage would have put Laura Secord, her immediate family and knowledgeable friends in jeopardy of reprisal or retribution. Being away from home for three days required Laura to be circumspect about the motives for her westward journey, especially with her young children. Few references are made to her return journey. Laura's first requirement was a good night's rest, probably after being assisted back across the creek to the Turney house. The DeCew house was too busy, with its ground floor being used as FitzGibbon's outpost headquarters from 12 June 1813.

Turney Property – surveyor, Augustus Jones, 25 October 1791

The Turneys were friends of the Secord family and would have invited Laura Secord for the night. Their house was an easy walk from the DeCew house and located on a 600 acre parcel of land on lots 227-8, 237-8 and 247-8 in Grantham Township, just west of 12-mile Creek on the border with Louth Township. It stood on an Indian trail that later became Pelham Stone Road.

Laura Secord was escorted by a British officer back to St. David's or Queenston after the battle. By then the Americans were in disarray and retreating fast to Fort George, leaving the way clear of enemy soldiers for Laura to make her way home without confrontation. With Americans gone from Queenston, her spy mission was complete without immediate retribution, provided her family and friends remained silent. At the time of her walk on 22 June the Americans had failed to intercept both her and her message to FitzGibbon. With such a one-sided action at Beaver Dams delivered in favour of the British and Canadians, Queenston residents were left for the remainder of 1813 to harvest their limited fruit and vegetables without hindrance. Weaving and quilting could resume and shattered lives could start to be rebuilt, at least until the Americans returned to the region in mid 1814. Many of the houses in the central part of Queenston had been destroyed, but those on the periphery survived

For a week after Lt.-Col. Boerstler's surrender there were no movements of any significance in Niagara Township, and as all the American forces rapidly withdrew to Fort George, the British Army and Canadian Militias closed ranks in an arc around the fort. There were few battles so decisively won. However beneficial this may have been militarily, the Secords and all the residents of the Township now had to feed themselves and two thousand military mouths from disturbed fields and vegetable patches in what had become no-man's land between the American forces clinging to their control of Fort George and Niagara-on-the-Lake and the British forces protecting their advanced position behind 12-mile Creek. Yet another lean year had developed in 1813 as local loyalist families shared what little they had.

As Ruth McKenzie wrote in 1971 about the state of the farmland back in 1813:
"The countryside was ravaged by marching troops. Where they encamped they dug field entrenchments and refuse pits. They burned rail fences for fuel, destroyed bridges, and ruined the rough pioneer roads with the transport of their heavy guns and ammunition." And the Canadian militia, many from the local

farmland, "were constantly worried about their crops and livestock. While they were away the women stayed home to manage on their own. They had to cope not only with farm operations but with marauding troops and visits from Indians who demanded food and accommodation for the night, and other unexpected hazards such as fires."

Then came the burnings. At the end of the 1813 fighting season, as winter took its firm grip on the countryside, the Americans decided to leave Niagara – but not before some renegade troops had gained tacit approval to burn the town. On 10 December 1813 the residents of Niagara were given fifteen minutes to leave their houses and watch as firebrands rode along every street setting fire to their properties. Shocked, cold, hungry and destitute, many of the residents fled to their friends in the farmland and smaller villages. This action made the British so irate that they planned and executed the immediate capture of Fort Niagara and the burnings of all the towns and villages down the eastern shore of the Niagara River – Youngstown, Lewiston, Buffalo and Black Creek.

In July 1814, when the Americans invaded the Niagara Peninsula once more, St. David's was burned and Laura and James Secord gave shelter to their Secord relations in their Queenston home. In all these burnings, some of the remoter houses survived intact and some were not totally burned to the ground. The futile war continued through 1814, primarily down at Fort Erie. By the early winter, both sides were seeking peace. Signed by the British on 24 December 1814 and ratified by the Americans on 16 February 1815, the Treaty of Ghent brought peace to the Niagara frontier – leaving in place the country boundary we know today. However, picking up the pieces and re-establishing trade was a more difficult endeavour that took many years to accomplish.

1815-1820 Laura and James Secord have two more children in difficult times

When veterans returned to their homes and their peacetime work, life in Niagara Township had changed. Commercial trade had diminished as the American side limited its access. Harvests had not yielded a return for three years, and many houses were shattered or needed reconstruction. James Secord had 200 acres of land on lots 37 and 38 in Grantham Township, just west of 8-mile Creek, but it took years for tenants to be able to pay their rents. War claims and other petitions were long in being processed by the Upper Canada administration.

James Secord Property – surveyor, Augustus Jones, 25 October 1791

Slowly but surely over the years, fruit, vegetables, milk and beer returned to the tables. Meat and eggs remained scarce. Women restarted their looms to weave, and quilting sessions began again, but commerce took many years to be re-established. During these times, storekeeping was an uncertain business as supplies and people's requirements started to change.

After the War, the heads of most local families submitted claims for possessions and materials lost to the British and American forces during the War. James Secord submitted Claim No. 235 [transcribed near the end in this book] to the Upper Canada administration for loss of 20'x16' room furnishings, a porch, stable, store house and shelves, chimneys, two horse wagons and other materials. Although not all his claim was approved, as was typical of most claims of that time, James collected about 485 pounds to assist him in rebuilding his family's livelihood.

Laura delivered her sixth child, Laura Ann on 20 October 1815 at home in Queenston. Her seventh and youngest child, Hannah Cartwright was born in 1817, also at Queenston. Family life for the Secords was a most happy one. Harriet, at age 86, remembered her parents being very devoted to each other.

In the meanwhile, Laura's oldest child, Mary had married Dr. William Trumble in Niagara Falls on 18 April 1816 and immediately went to Ireland to visit his parents, Harloe and Elizabeth. Dr. Trumble had courted Mary while he helped her father with his wounds. More about the Trumbles later in the book...

Reminiscences of Laura's Walk and Personality

In 1913, on the first centennial anniversary of Laura Ingersoll Secord's walk to warn the British at Beaver Dams, Mrs Elizabeth J. Thompson, wrote in a Niagara Historical Society publication:
"It may be interesting to know what Mrs. Secord wore on this occasion. From various sources, I have had descriptions given me, and they all agree on the main points, and she herself used to show her grandchildren pieces of a brown cotton or print with a little pink polka dot, and she said these were pieces of the dress she wore when she walked from Queenston to De Cew's.

Laura Secord's later Spoon Bonnet
Courtesy: Niagara Falls History Museum

She wore a cottage bonnet tied under her chin. She had balbriggan stockings, with red silk clocks on the side, and low shoes with buckles." Later in the 19th century Laura Secord wore this spoon bonnet of horsehair braid.

Mrs. Thompson continued:
"She was always very kind and thoughtful to children, giving them many little gifts, cakes and bread and butter, and a great many of the old soldiers, who had served with her husband, used to visit her in Chippawa. She always helped them -- not so much by what she gave as by her kind sympathy and thoughtfulness for them. She was very fond of gardening and had beautiful flowers, many of which are still growing... "

In a letter to Mrs. Thompson, dated about 1900, the Guelph schoolteacher who had lived with her grandmother for many years, Laura Louise Smith wrote of Laura Secord:
"I have a small photograph of her taken a short time before her death, but those taken from it have not been satisfactory; probably it might be useful to Miss [Mildred] Peel [painter, sculptor, wife of Ontario premier]. None of her granddaughters resemble her at all. There are few living now who knew my dear grandmother personally."

The Middle Years, 1816-1840

1820 Laura Secord's heroic deed is included in her husband, James Secord's petition for a "licence of occupation".

For fear of reprisal, Laura and James kept the Walk in 1813 a secret from most of their family and friends, requesting those who already knew to maintain silence. They could simply state that Laura had been to see her sick half-brother in St. David's for three days.

Life in Upper Canada after the War of 1812 required rebuilding with the assistance of the British Crown. This often involved petitioning the provincial Lieutenant Governor for the basic needs to make a living. Such petitions were opportunistic, but James had to provide for his family by whatever means he could. With the appropriate justification, it was commonplace to receive the favour of the Lieutenant Governor by the Legislature's issuance of a property, position or pension through the vehicle of petitioning, and any claim of injury in battle or a deed of heroism was useful supporting evidence for a request. In the case of the Secords, war claims were certainly in order, but would take years to materialize. The transcriptions of their petitions are at the end of this book.

One of James Secord's early petitions was for a Stone Quarry on military land near Queenston in 1820. It was unusual for a woman to submit a petition in the early 1800s, unless she was a widow of an esteemed or military gentleman of rank. It was very rare for a woman to be mentioned in a petition for heroism in a British battle victory. However, five years of painful recuperation from his debilitating wounds and dealing with his financial interests forced James to cite Laura's heroic contribution to the 1813 campaign in the Niagara Peninsula. This petition also provided proof of the honesty and trustworthiness of James' claims, with his family and Richard Cartwright as guarantors of social and political respectability. Laura Secord had also requested Captain James FitzGibbon to provide her with a Certificate to support this petition. It was the first time that Lieutenant Governor Maitland had received written and open evidence of Laura's successful secret service for her country and the British crown.

Taken from Benson Lossing's
"The pictorial field-book of the War of 1812",
New York, 1869

It was also the first time that the Legislature became aware of this deed being performed two days prior to the Battle of Beaver

Dams, even before the main body of American troops had left their encampment along the Niagara River.

Unfortunately, although James was successful in obtaining the rights to this stone quarry, it did not yield real wealth for the family. The market for stone was limited in the years following the war because funds were tight.

The same Queenston quarry 100 years later
Courtesy: Niagara Falls Library

As a historical note, FitzGibbon's 1820 certificate was rediscovered by Henry Cartwright Secord in 1934, although it had been referred to in a Niagara Historical Society publication a decade before. This rediscovery refuted earlier detractors who had minimized Laura Secord's role due to lack of more complete source materials.

Until Laura Secord's request in 1820, FitzGibbon had been reticent to publicize her contribution to the 1813 campaign for two reasons:

1. It was highly dangerous to the Secord family to divulge Laura's espionage and communication for fear of retribution.
2. It could have detracted from his own reward of promotion to Captain, which he had received by 1814.

However, with the promotion received, FitzGibbon was able to support the Secords' cause, which he did on three occasions – in 1820, 1827 and 1837. The third of these came when FitzGibbon had been promoted to Colonel and was doing extraordinary work for the Upper Canada administration against the Mackenzie-led uprising.

Up to the mid-1800s it was most unusual for a woman, except as a widow, to submit a petition. However, Laura Secord presented a petition to the government in 1820, asking either for money or a government position in return for her services to the country. This was also supported by FitzGibbon's Certificate. Sadly for the Secords, this petition was unsuccessful.

Laura continued to press her claims to the Legislature for family remuneration. Her writing style was subjective and action-oriented. She hinted of tribulations of war, particularly Queenston Heights and her courageous but crippled husband, to sway colonial government decision-making in her favour. She was not averse to accepting some employment for herself, and she reflected on her strong commitment to Upper Canada and Britain. Although she was not well recognized until the 1880s and 1890s when the local women's suffrage movement and Women's Literary Club created public awareness of her heroism, she continued to press for significant compensation for her family – rarely seen from a married woman of that time.

At one time she had hopes of being in charge of the Brock Monument, completed on 13 October 1824 but destroyed by Benjamin Lett, a rebellious anti-British agitator, on 17 April 1840. In a note, Chief Justice John Beverley Robinson said that Lieutenant-Governor Sir Peregrine Maitland "had a favourable opinion of the character and claims of Mr. Secord and his wife." Maitland had also promised Laura the position of caretaker of the Brock Monument. There was, however, an unfortunate series of changes of Lieutenant Governorship and the sudden death of Lt.-Col. Robert Nichol, a judge in the matter, that resulted in the position being given to Nichol's wife whose family of four children were undergoing greater hardship.

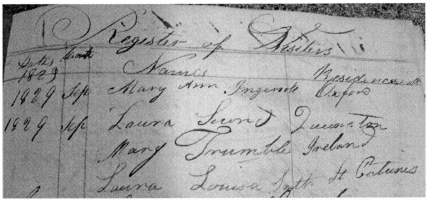

Register of Visitors at 1st Brock Monument, September 1829
Courtesy: Miss Kate Symons of Toronto, the Homestead in Queenston, and the Niagara Historical Society

Despite her courageous and resilient style, Laura could not contain her disappointment this time. With the FitzGibbon certificate of 11 March 1827 attached, on 17 July 1831 she penned a stinging letter to Edward McMahon, the secretary of the new Lieutenant-Governor Sir John Colborne, reminding him that Maitland had "positively offered her the position." It was also somewhat embarrassing for Laura because she had taken the family – including Mrs. Ingersoll (her step-mother); Mary Ann Ingersoll, of Oxford County (her niece); Mary Trumble, of Ireland (her daughter); and Laura Louisa Smith, of St. Catharines (her grand-daughter) – on a trip to the Monument in September 1829 with the assumption that she would have the position.

1820-1830 Continuing financial difficulties due to James Secord's inability to handle physically demanding work

By 1820 James Secord was walking with the aid of a stick. His knee never healed sufficiently for him to walk easily or to pick up goods. He needed help to stock the store and bring in new goods for sale. To add to family difficulties, rent collection from his tenants was complicated by his inability to visit them regularly. To assist his father, Charles took over the rent collection for the land tenants and started to make small but beneficial financial contributions for the family. As the 1820s decade closed, Charles Badeau Secord, Laura's 21-year old son was becoming an attorney-at-law. He married Margaret Ann Robins on 26 November 1830 in Kingston, Ontario, and it is probable that as many of the family as possible, including James and Laura, attended the marriage of their only son.

As Charles pursued his life as a lawyer and farmer, he started to build his wealth. He married and had two sons and a daughter; the sons, at least, were well educated – his elder son became a professor in Drummondville and later in Nebraska, USA, and the younger son was for many years Division Court Clerk and Notary Public, as well as being the Superintendent of St. Mark's Sunday School. As a successful lawyer, Charles built his property holdings as time passed:

"On 14 Jul 1832 (Reg 16 Aug 1832) William Graham oldest son and heir at law of Richard Graham deceased sold to Charles B Secord 100 acres in Lot 8 Concession 3 from Lake Erie, Bertie Township for $300 (A547 #3733);
On 29 Oct 1834 (Reg 6 Jul 1853) the Executors and Executrix of Samuel Street sold to Charles B Secord 23,200 square feet in Lots 4 and 5 Queen Street in the Village of Queenston for £150 (4822);
On 18 May 1843 (Reg 6 Nov 1846) Joseph Hamilton sold to Charles B Secord 1 acre in Lot 4 Niagara Township for £12.10 (1948);

On 22 Jul 1856 (Reg 9 Sep 1856) Charles B Secord et ux sold to Charles Sunter 1 acre part of Lot 4 Niagara Township (7536);
On 26 Oct 1860 (Reg 27 Oct 1860) F M Whitelaw and R Warren sold to Charles B Secord 8736 square feet in the southwest part of Lot 153 Town of Niagara for $400 (11188). This lot is on the southwest corner of Gage and Victoria Streets;
On 26 Oct 1860 (Reg 27 Oct 1860) Charles B Secord et ux gave a mortgage to Mr Whitelaw and R Warren on 32200 square feet in Lots 4 and 5 Queen Street in the Village of Queenston, Niagara Township for $400 (11189);
On 15 Apr 1864 (Reg 21 Jun 1864) Samuel L St. John et ux sold to Charles B Secord 8736 square feet in the southwest part of Lot 153 Town of Niagara for $200 (14579);
On 15 Apr 1864 (Reg 21 Jun 1864) Charles B Secord et ux gave a mortgage to Samuel L St. John on 8736 square feet in the southwest part of Lot 153 Town of Niagara for $200 (14580)."[2]

Charles Badeau Secord, attorney, was the Registrar to the Surrogate Court of the District of Niagara from about March 1853 (when his signature appears first) to after 1872. The large and ever-growing family of Secords around Ontario offered him a clientele base best served by a family member. His business, not just for his father, extended to Walpole, Norfolk County, and beyond. Family members such as Elijah G. Secord in Houghton, Clear Creek became clients.

Early in this decade, Laura had lost her sister Abigail Ingersoll Woodworth on 27 February 1821; her frail sister Elizabeth Franks Ingersoll Pickett had already passed away on 15 August 1811. Laura's only surviving sister in these years was Myra Ingersoll Hitchcock. As James' local Secord relatives went their separate ways, in some cases exchanging expensive land in Niagara Township for much cheaper land in the western parts of Upper Canada, and Laura's own family dwindled in size and her married daughters lived some distances away from Niagara

---

[2] Niagara Settlers Land Records in this book come from Abstracts of Deeds Registers (1796-1865) in a new website established by R. Robert Mutrie: https://sites.google.com/site/niagarasettlers2/

Township, Laura and James could rely only on their son Charles for continuing assistance in immediate family business matters.

During the 1820s, in addition to petitions for the quarry and disability compensation, James Secord wrote at least two petitions for gainful employment. His mercantile and land income had been only just sufficient to raise their family and continue to maintain their position in local society. Fortunately, Laura appears to have been resourceful, and frugal with what funds they had.

To enhance his family's income, James Secord's pursued a military compensation petition to the Lieutenant Governor Sir Peregrine Maitland in 1823. Maitland affirmed that James Secord was a Captain in the 1st Lincoln Militia, and, in connection with this affirmation from the Lieutenant Governor, M. Coffin of the Adjutant General's office for Militia Services acknowledged that James Secord was wounded in action with the enemy on 13 October 1812. These affirmations gave James Secord greater standing in his quest for financially rewarding positions.

In 1823 James Secord was granted a government pension from the Medical Board, which declared that he was "incapable of earning his livelihood in consequence of wounds received in action with the Enemy" at the Battle of Queenston Heights. Lord Palmerston, the British Secretary of War at that time had personally approved this compensation award to James Secord on 21 August 1822 in a letter to Maitland. Military Secretary Colonel H.C. Darling in Quebec passed notification of the award to Maitland on 30 December 1822.

However, this pension was very small -- £18 per year – and it took another six years before Lieutenant-Governor Sir Peregrine Maitland gave James the position of Registrar of the Niagara District Surrogate Court. James had previously written two urgent letters stressing his precarious financial position with the statement: "There is now no remedy for me but to be thrown upon the world penniless, lame and in ill health." However "the emoluments were very small" which drove James to write to his sister-in-law, Myra Hitchcock: "With respect to our worldly affairs, I am sorry to have to say we are not very prosperous. We make out to live and have clothing and food, but riches, my dear woman, it seems to me, is not for James Secord..."

Capt. James FitzGibbon penned another original certificate on 11 May 1827 to confirm that Laura Secord had walked all day and communicated with FitzGibbon on the evening of 22 June 1813, which was the day before the main contingent of Americans troops had left Fort George. It also stated that, in consequence of Laura Secord's information, FitzGibbon was able to place his forces strategically before the American forces arrived. On 23 June 1813, FitzGibbon's loyal Indians were able to confirm the veracity of Laura Secord's information as the American forces advanced on the Beaver Dams area, and to be fully prepared for the skirmishes and battle on 24 June 1813.

As a historical note, FitzGibbon's 1827 certificate was discovered by John Moir in 1959 and communicated publicly in the Ontario History journal. This discovery removed all doubt that earlier detractors had failed to understand the full impact of Laura Secord's heroic act on the campaign of 1813. This certificate, with the others, is in the Public Archives of Canada in Ottawa and transcribed at the end of this book.

Several of the Secord petitions were unsuccessful, although they ultimately had a different effect for James FitzGibbon who received a sum of one thousand pounds. The rewarding of a woman, a civilian and a spy in such a public manner for a military operation was not considered appropriate in the early nineteenth century. Sufficient time had not passed for her deed to be fully and officially recognized. But such recognition was to come in her lifetime.

1827-1835   The final years in Queenston

Queenston held many memories for the Secords who had struggled through the long post-war period in difficult circumstances with unsuccessful petitions for assistance. However, the village had become an important commercial destination during these days.

By 1828, James Secord's standing with the Lieutenant Governor of the province and with the local community had become well established. The second certificate from FitzGibbon had provided the Legislature with assurances of the circumstances of Laura's heroism, and other communications had established the physical condition that James was enduring. So in 1828, he was made the Registrar of the local District Surrogate Court; and from 1833 to 1835 he was a surrogate court judge.

In 1829 James wrote to his sister-in-law, Myra Hitchcock: "Your sister Laura never had health better. She bears her age (54) most remarkably considering her former delicate state of body. We are however, Mira, getting old and grey heads, and now and then a tremor of the body..."

Sadly for Laura and James, their fourth daughter, 18 year old Appolonia, died on 20 December 1828 in Queenston, probably of consumption (tuberculosis). In November 1829, one of the Secords' servants, Fanny died of cholera.

When the Niagara Peninsula – including St. David's – suffered from a more widespread cholera epidemic, Laura's half-brother Charles died of the disease on 18 August 1832, leaving his widow Anna Maria Merritt Ingersoll and eight children. On 8 August 1833 Laura's 71-year old stepmother, Sally Whiting Ingersoll, who had been infirm for a few years, died in Port Credit and was buried nine days later – the delay probably due to waiting for the attendance of family members.

There was, however, better news to come. Charles and Margaret gave Laura and James their first Secord grandson, Charles Forsyth who was born on 9 May 1833. His is the only surviving line of Secords alive today. Charles' birth was followed by a brother, James Badeau, born in 1836, and a sister Alicia, born in 1838; although both married, neither of these two siblings had children.

More exciting news was to follow. Hannah Cartwright Secord, Laura and James' youngest child, married Howley Williams on 22 August 1833 in Queenston; he was an attorney in Guelph and a friend (and now brother-in-law) of David William Smith, Harriet's husband. Howley purchased land in Guelph Township in 1833, and two town lots in 1834 and 1835. Her elder sister, Laura Ann Secord's marriage to Captain John Poore on 17 October 1833 in Queenston, shortly followed Hannah's wedding. Laura Ann and John had two children; John raised a Company of the 1st Incorporated Battalion of Militia based at Hamilton Barracks, Ontario, for service during the uprising of 1837-8, known as the Mackenzie Rebellion. He had also been the first cousin of Maj. Gen. Sir Isaac Brock.

In 1832 James Secord realized, rather belatedly, that he could potentially use his Captaincy of the Militia to seek further remuneration from the Government. He wrote a petition to Lieutenant Governor Sir John Colborne on 18 July 1832. By September the Presiding Councillor of Council, J. Baby, had acknowledged a recommendation in James Secord's favour. Although details of the remuneration are scarce for the three intervening years, by July 1835 James had secured the Collector of Customs position in the Chippawa Port of Customs. This was to be the best-paying job of his life.

Laura Secord Homestead, Queenston, Upper Canada
Courtesy: Author's Collection

1835-1841   Fitzgibbon's third Certificate, the Ferry Petition and Chippawa Days

In 1835, Laura and James took lodgings at the Customs House in Chippawa to accommodate the new Collector of Customs position that James had secured at the age of 62. Shortly thereafter, their only son Charles took over their Queenston house for his growing family, and he retained responsibility for rent collection from land tenants for James. This relaxed former monetary tensions in the Secord house, and allowed James to assume his new duties in Chippawa with vigour.

James' income from the Collector position, however, was based upon the customs he collected. With the uprising in 1837-8, Chippawa became susceptible to rebel activity from the Mackenzie-inspired supporters on the American side of the Niagara River. Smugglers and marauders were a constant hindrance to the customs collector. James' income suffered and his hopes for the new position were not fully realized.

The Collector's position appeared to have had the potential for more than £150 per year, although he only exceeded this amount in 1838, when James collected more than £157, surpassed only by the ports of Toronto, Kingston and Oakville. His income from customs fees generally ranged from £100 to £150 per annum. Unfortunately, although the first Welland Canal in 1829 continued to route traffic flow via the Chippawa Creek (Welland River), the second Welland Canal in 1839 started to route traffic through to Port Colborne for places west. By 1841 the Port of Customs at Chippawa – only 35 years after it had opened – was being sustained mostly by local primary industries, such as ship building, warehousing, foundries, tanneries, breweries, distilleries and saw mills. Over time, and especially with a suspension bridge opened to the USA in 1848, road traffic started to replace river and lake traffic, and eventually Niagara Falls was to become the Port of Customs for the region. Before his death, James Secord could envisage the demise of Chippawa to a backwater village and the loss of its status as a primary Port of

Customs. In 1840, customs fees and his health both went into decline. To complicate matters, Chippawa residents continued to be alarmed by Mackenzie "patriots" who caused commando-style raids on the village.

However, as the threat of war declined, James and Laura had established their social position in the Chippawa community, and their married life continued to be most pleasant. Their ability to earn more income in the late 1830s coincided with continuing family responsibilities to accommodate their widowed daughters and their children.

Amos Sangster sketch, 1887, no. XXXVIII. Chippawa Docks after fire.
Courtesy: RiverBrink Art Museum, Queenston

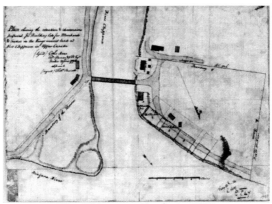

The Chippawa Docks in 1798
Courtesy: Brock University Map Room

The Customs House in Chippawa, where the Secords lived between 1835 and 1841, is no longer standing – probably pulled down after a fire in 1887 that gutted most of the docklands buildings. It was believed to have been on the north side of Chippawa Creek (Welland River), where Kings Bridge Park is today, and close to the terminus for river traffic that flowed between the many warehouses and dockland wharves in Chippawa to places west.

Although relatively comfortable, Laura continued to petition the Upper Canada government. Because of her early inexperience in dealing with legislative officials, Laura had sent the originals of the 1820 and 1827 certificates from FitzGibbon to the government attached to earlier petitions. She had obviously not kept copies of them for herself, since they were buried in government files – to be found much later by archive researchers.

In February 1837, at Laura Secord's request, Col. James FitzGibbon again provided his reminiscences of her heroic act in June 1813. This certificate largely confirmed the impact of Laura's communication on the extraordinary success of the Battle of Beaver Dams.

In late 1839, Laura sent a petition seeking the Queenston Ferry concession, which had become vacant. She may have seen the management of this concession as a less physically demanding position for James than the Collector of Customs job in Chippawa. His limited agility did not help in carrying out his job effectively, and he wrote in a letter in the late 1830s that he was "broken down". As was common practice of the day, Laura embellished this petition to Lieutenant Governor Sir George Arthur, in an attempt to increase the potential for a positive outcome. A copy of Colonel FitzGibbon's 1837 Certificate was also attached to the petition. It is possible that, in 1839, Laura would have gratefully accepted a return to her friends in Queenston. However, the petition was unsuccessful and the Secords continued at the Customs House in Chippawa.

This petition was again sent to Governor Lord Sydenham in 1840, when he took office, because the ferry concession had still not been awarded. Further petitions and letters to Governor Lord Sydenham were sent during this period. However, because of the nearly biannual turn of provincial governorship after Sir Peregrine Maitland left for New Brunswick in 1828, later administrations either lost touch with the understanding of the Secords' particular circumstances, or simply believed that the Collector of Customs position was sufficient recompense for the Secord family. Sadly for Laura Secord, the Ferry petition was again denied.

The Ferry Petition would also suggest that, even after James Secord had taken up his position as Collector of Customs in Chippawa in 1835, the income from this position had not achieved its potential and the Secords were seeking additional income to live in modest comfort. Clearly, they would have returned to Queenston to achieve a better position for themselves. It is likely that James was frustrated by his inability to walk easily with his knee wound. The extra burden of widowed daughters and fatherless grandchildren must also have stressful, even though they were sustained by their faith (being parishioners of the local Anglican church) and the efforts of their close family to make the years go by more pleasantly.

Since the time that the Secords' supporter Sir Peregrine Maitland left office after ten years in Upper Canada in 1828, Laura Secord lived to see nine more Governors of Canada, most of whom stayed in their position for only two or three years. It therefore became more difficult for 1812 War veterans, such as the Secords, to get any continuing knowledgeable attention from the provincial administration, which was by then more concerned about the 1837-38 uprising against the Family Compact in Upper Canada government. This became particularly significant to Laura after her husband died in 1841 – in the same year as Lord Sydenham.

Six years before James had taken up his position in Chippawa, the first ship had passed through the first Welland Canal, thus introducing some reduction in portage traffic between Queenston and Chippawa. By 1839 plans for the second Welland Canal were submitted to the government and it was obvious to

49

all that the old portage route's days were numbered. These plans included reducing the number of locks from 40 to 27, deepening the canal's minimum depth from 8 foot to 9 foot, and increasing the size of the locks from 110 ft. x 22 ft. to 150 ft. x 26.5 ft., thus accommodating much larger ships. Such plans for modernization must also have contributed to James' demise, as portage traffic dwindled and illegal trafficking of goods from the American side of the river continued to be an important issue.

James died of a series of strokes (formerly known as apoplexy) at the age of 67 on 22 February 1841, probably upstairs in the Customs House, after some of the most financially rewarding years of his life. He chose to be buried with his militia companions on the north side of the cemetery at Lundy's Lane (today the Drummond Hill Cemetery in Niagara Falls, Ontario).

From the death announcements in The Christian Guardian, March 3, 1841
"In Chippawa on the 23rd ult. James Secord Esq. Collector of Customs at that place – sincerely regretted by a large circle of connections, friends, and acquaintances for his frank, conciliating, and Christian-like manners both in public and private life."

The Commercial Herald of Toronto, in a March issue, 1841, contains the following notice:
"At Chippawa, on the 22nd instant, James Secord, Senior Collector of Her Majesty's Customs, long known as an old and much respected inhabitant of the Niagara District, universally and deservedly regretted, both in public and in private life. Mr. Secord came into this country at a very early age [actually born in St. David's] and has always sustained the character of a good and loyal subject of his country, which was evidenced in the eagerness with which he flew to the British Standard in the late war with the United States of America. He was severely wounded in the memorable battle of Queenston, the 13th of October, under Sir Isaac Brock. Mr. Secord was wounded in the final attack in the afternoon, when General Sheaffe was victorious. The story of the rescue of Mr. Secord is given in

another place by his son. Mr. Secord died on the 22nd of
February, 1841."

The Reverend William Leeming of the Church of the Holy
Trinity in Chippawa performed the funeral. A passage from the
pastor's funeral sermon states:
"And here I think you will agree with me when I say or our
departed friend that no one has passed through life and
descended to the grave with an unblemished reputation. That he
was a conscientious and upright man, amiable in all the relations
of life, a kind husband, an indulgent parent, a sincere friend and
an obliging neighbour. And in the discharge of the duties of his
public trust as the Collector of Customs at this place I have
repeatedly heard him spoken of in terms of high commendation.
Of a considerate and benevolent disposition he performed those
duties with such moderation as to gain the good will of the
community with whom he had to do, with credit to himself and
with greater advantage to the Government than a more severe
and exacting course has been known to produce. Nor should we
omit to notice, whilst paying this last tribute of respect to the
memory of a departed friend and respectable man the need of
praise which was due to him for his loyal and patriotic
principles. Those principles which under all circumstances he
maintained steadily to the last, had been evinced in an honorable
defence of his country's dearest rights throughout the last
American war. For those rights he fought, and to his dying day I
believe suffered from the wounds which he received whilst
engaged in maintaining a cause which reflected honor upon
himself and his fellow soldiers in arms and loss and disgrace
upon an unnatural foe."

Laura, at 65, became a widow without a husband's pension. As
she wrote to her sister, Myra Ingersoll Hitchcock later in 1841:
"You cannot think what grief we are in."

A few days after James' burial, Laura penned a petition to
Lieutenant-Governor Sydenham requesting that her son, Charles
be appointed Collector of Customs in Chippawa to succeed her
husband. The petition was supported by John Mewburn, the
Coroner from Danby House, Stamford who stated that James'

"gunshot wound... had material effect on hastening the fatal result" – a report prepared during the probate proceedings. Married and living in the Secord homestead in Queenston, Charles had already succeeded his father as Registrar of the Niagara Surrogate Court in 1835. He was also a practicing attorney by this time, and wrote a covering note to his mother's petition on his behalf. Sydenham again showed no signs of understanding his predecessors' awareness of the Secords' contribution to Upper Canada, and the petition was denied.

So on 10 May 1841, Laura wrote a second petition to Sydenham asking this time for a pension. However, just two months before his own death on 19 September 1841, Sydenham denied the request, stating that: "The Petitioner's late Husband enjoyed up to his death a pension of £20 (actually £18) for his wound, besides holding the Situation of Collector of Customs at Chippawa."

The Quiet Years, 1841-1868, etc.

1841 Laura Secord moves to Water Street in Chippawa

At the time of James' death, Laura's family was scattered. By the early 1820s, Laura and James Secord had welcomed their daughter Harriet's suitor, David William Smith, a capable barrister from St. Catharines into their family. David Smith had been born in Fort Erie to wealthy farming parents, William and Mary, who had moved there to a riverside tract from Quebec; his parents sold some of their land to St. Paul's Church in Fort Erie in 1821. Harriet and David had married in Queenston on 23 November 1824. Over the next eight years they had three children, Laura Louisa (born September 1826), Mary Augusta (born November 1828) and William James (born October 1829). Living in St. Catharines, Laura and James saw Harriet's children often. Capable though he was, David was an alcoholic; a year after James Secord died in 1841, David Smith passed away from alcohol poisoning. He was buried at his father's church, St. Paul's in Fort Erie, where his parents are also buried close to the church.

The 1840s had started for Laura Ingersoll Secord with a series of tragedies. Her own husband had died in February 1841, with no enduring pension for his widow. Then Laura Ann, her fourth daughter's husband, Captain John Poore, died at Hamilton Barracks in February 1842. Then Harriet, her third daughter's husband, David William Smith, died in St. Catharines in May 1842. That same year Laura wrote to her sister Myra: "My dear

Sister, how often I wish I could be near you to tell you my griefs. I feel so lonely; all will soon be in the grave." [Laura's letters to her sister in this period are reproduced at the end in this book.] Then to add to her grief, Hannah, her sixth daughter's husband, Howley Williams, died in Guelph in 1844. By the mid-1840s all five of Laura's surviving daughters had experienced widowhood. Fortunately her son Charles and his wife Margaret lived on happily together in Queenston until they both died in 1872, whereupon they were buried together in St. Mark's Cemetery in Niagara-on-the-Lake.

In late 1841 Laura acquired a house and two lots on Water Street, Chippawa, a short walking distance from the stores, the church and the docks. Her friends, such as Rebecca Green Biggar, were close by.
The land records state:
"On 1 Nov 1841 (Reg 4 Jul 1842) James Cummings & Sophia Cummings his wife sold to Laura Secord Village Lots 108 & 109 on Water & Adelaide Street and Lot 13 South on Water Street in the Village of Chippawa (A510 #881)."

The House on Water Street (3800 Bridgewater St. today)
Courtesy: Author's Collection

Just eight months after James' death, Laura Ingersoll Secord's purchase of a cottage and its extensions on the banks of Chippawa Creek was probably completed with some modest

54

private financial assistance from her family. The 1837 Regency-style cottage was originally built for and owned by James Cummings, a merchant and landowner, who was the first reeve of Chippawa and whose father, Thomas was the first settler in 1783.

Within fifteen months Harriet had lost her father and husband. So she and her two daughters went to live with Laura in Chippawa. Charlotte, who would remain Laura's unmarried daughter, travelled between her home base with Laura in Chippawa, her younger sisters in Guelph, Ontario and her eldest sister Mary's home in Ireland. As fate would have it, the five ladies lived together in Queenston until Laura's death in 1868. Harriet's son, William James Smith went to live with his Smith grandparents on their farm in Fort Erie.

Harriet Hopkins Secord Smith
(1803-1892)
Courtesy: St. Catharines Library

Although Laura Ann, now a widow, sought a brief solace from her mother in Chippawa in 1842, and perhaps some assistance in the care for her son John Jr., she quickly returned to Guelph where the following year she married William Clarke, a wealthy doctor, and had three more children of whom only one survived infancy. Sadly, Laura Ann died in August 1852.

Dr. Clarke's home was "Rosehurst" in an upscale neighbourhood of Guelph. It would later become the Homewood Sanitorium, and was torn down in about 1927.

'Rosehurst', Guelph
Courtesy: Goldie Family Collection

Laura had been left small land inheritances by her husband (rent from land) and her father. This money enabled her to live her remaining years without depending on charity, although she never had much. She wrote in a letter to her sister Myra again after James' death: "the lands are mostly sold to the Canada Company. I have given up the idea of trying to do anything about mine." Some of her family may have assisted her financially from time to time.

Widowed, Laura had been left at the age of 65 without any pension to defray basic everyday expenses, and so she and her daughters ran a school in this cottage for a number of years to support themselves and their closest family. From the time their grandmother first set up a small school in their house at Water Street in Chippawa after 1841, both of Harriet's daughters were able to teach other children there. Trained by this experience, Laura Louisa and Mary Augusta, who remained spinsters, taught drawing, watercolours and leatherwork in select schools for girls. After Laura's death they moved to Guelph and Toronto; her granddaughter, Laura Louisa had a private school that is still standing at 110 Waterloo Avenue on the corner of Yorkshire Street in Guelph.

Laura's house on Water Street, on the corner of Adelaide Street (now 3800 Bridgewater Street, on the corner of Laura Secord Place), represented a modest Upper Canada style cottage of the mid 19th century. Most of its current decoration is concentrated on the entranceway, which features two flanking Doric columns supporting an entablature, sidelights and a transom now enclosed by a modern porch. The roof and interior were rebuilt after a fire in November 1931. The house was designated as a heritage site in 1983.

Across the street, Chippawa Creek had been the up-river terminus for Portage Road for commercial portages to and from Queenston (the down-river terminus) in the days before the opening of the Welland Canal. Laura Secord crossed this creek every Sunday to go to services at the Church of the Holy Trinity about ½ mile up the Portage Road.

Laura's elegant youngest daughter Hannah Cartwright Secord Williams was widowed in 1844, and left to raise two young daughters, one of whom died at age five. The other daughter, Katherine would later marry John A. Lamprey, the Mayor of Guelph in 1895-96. Hannah remarried well to Edward Pyke Carthew, the Collector of Customs in Guelph, in March 1847. Edward purchased lots in Guelph and owned a farm on the corner of Edinburgh and Woodlawn Road. In May 1858 their home was destroyed by fire; there was no insurance, but most of the furniture was saved.

Mayor John A. Lamprey
Courtesy: City of Guelph

Hannah Cartwright Secord Howley Carthew (1817-1877) and her second husband, Edward Pyke Carthew (1808-1879).
Courtesy: Barbara Innis March

Charles visited his mother regularly and urged her to dispose of her house and return to Queenston to be part of their family, but she refused. Laura enjoyed her independence, her new-found friends in Chippawa and was resigned to living independently but frugally. She suffered from rheumatism in later life, but it did not stop her meeting her friends, reading and going to church. She also took pride in the dresses she made for her daughters and granddaughters, and her cooking for which she is still famous. In fact, her fine needlework probably brought her some money, and her large family would contribute more. Fortunately for Laura, or perhaps in large measure because of her character and personality, the family remained a closely knit, happy group.

Laura Ingersoll Secord, by Mildred Peel.
Courtesy of Public Archives of Ontario
This comes from the painting in Parliament Building in Toronto.

As the years passed, Laura's loneliness and sorrow turned to a dependence on her faith, resoluteness and family. Harriet and her two daughters kept her from declining too rapidly into old age. Her grand-daughter, Laura Louisa Smith, described her as "ever sensible and courageous." Another grand-daughter, Alicia Cockburn, stated:

"Laura Secord was of fair complexion, with kind, brown eyes, a sweet and loving smile hovering about the mouth. This did not denote weakness. She was five feet four inches tall and slight in form." Laura Secord's skills in home education, needlework, cooking and dress-making were well known in Chippawa. And Laura became deeply religious in her older age, frequently using the expression "If God so decrees..." in her letters.

Alicia Secord & Isaac Cockburn
Courtesy: Barbara Innis March

The residents in the village of Chippawa saw many changes during the 33 years that Laura Secord lived there, primarily due to the building of a railroad and the development of local industry. Four years before Laura and James arrived in 1835, a group of businessmen including Samuel Street and James Cummings had formed a company to build a railroad between Chippawa and Queenston. In 1835, a charter was granted and construction on their railroad began. It was to be the first railroad in Canada.

By 1845 the railroad, known as the Erie and Ontario Railroad Coach, was in operation. Cars, carrying about 20 passengers with luggage on top, were being wheeled around by a team of three horses along a wooden roadway at 5 miles per hour. The summer-only railroad ran from a station at the foot of Queenston Heights just above the wharf. The line followed a general north-south direction along a route that is today Stanley Avenue. Approximately ¼ mile north of the current Ferry Street, the railroad turned to a south-easterly direction and followed the path of the moraine at Falls View. The railroad then travelled along the high bank past Clark Hill and into Chippawa where the terminus was located at a steamboat wharf on the current intersection of Front Street and Norton Street.

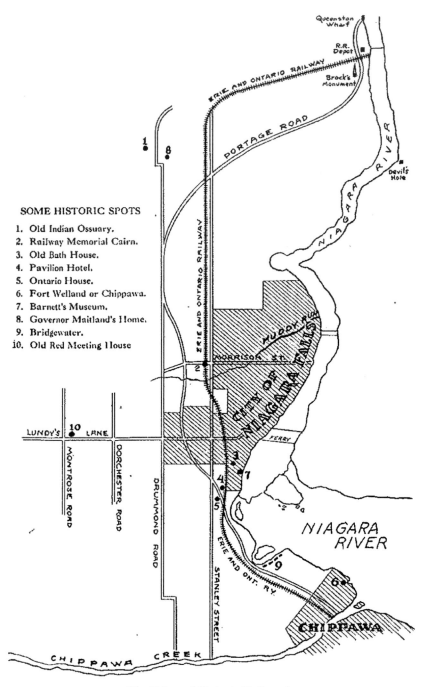

SOME HISTORIC SPOTS

1. Old Indian Ossuary.
2. Railway Memorial Cairn.
3. Old Bath House.
4. Pavilion Hotel.
5. Ontario House.
6. Fort Welland or Chippawa.
7. Barnett's Museum.
8. Governor Maitland's Home.
9. Bridgewater.
10. Old Red Meeting House

The Erie and Ontario Railroad
Courtesy: Lundy's Lane Historical Society

In 1854, the original railroad was rebuilt for steam operation. The route was changed to provide for a gentler grade at Queenston and to be closer to the Railway Suspension Bridge in Niagara Falls. The railroad was extended from Queenston to Niagara on the Lake, and then extended again in 1860 from Chippawa to Fort Erie. It was operated by the Erie and Niagara Railroad before becoming part of the Michigan Central Railroad.

Several other industrial activities occurred during this time. In 1832, the first shipyard was built along the banks of Chippawa Creek by Mr. William Lovering. Ship engines and boilers were built at James Macklem's Foundry, which burned to the ground in 1842 but was rebuilt. All were located on River Street (now Macklem Street). The Village of Chippawa was incorporated on 6 October 1849. A distillery was built in 1852 on Main Street in Chippawa, producing 1,200 gallons of whiskey per day.

By 1850, King's Bridge was gone as were the fortifications of Fort Chippawa. A new road was built from Bridgewater to Chippawa and became known as Bridgewater Street. By 1850, Main Street had John Bartley's Tannery and Mr. Thomas Davidson's planing mill as well as a sash, blind and door factory. In 1853, Chippawa had two common schools, a dozen inns and taverns, a Post Office, a dry goods store, a tailor's shop, a steam cabinet and chair factory, and John Thomas' grist mill.

Health care had also started to improve in the early 1800s. For example, people were starting to be given vaccinations against smallpox, a disease that often reoccurred in the first half of the nineteenth century. Chippawa's first Doctor was Dr. Robert Aberdein. By 1864 the population of Chippawa had grown to 1,450 people.

1841-45   Letters from Charles Badeau Secord

Early in this period of expansion in Chippawa, and within a month after his father's death in 1841, Charles B. Secord had sent the petition to Lord Sydenham, Governor of British North America, requesting the position of Collector of Customs at the Chippawa Port of Customs. This position remained open for more than a year, and Charles wrote again to the new Governor General, Sir Charles Bagot. Unfortunately for the Secord family, the Governor General rejected this petition, which does not appear to have been well argued nor supported by excellent references either for his father or for himself. Both references, from Macaulay and Cartwright, were circumspect and not overly supportive. It appears as if Charles had realized that his mother's own petition should be followed up, but he had little expectation or interest in it gaining approval. The passage of time and change in Upper Canada administrations had also clouded awareness of the Secords' circumstances.

Seven years after FitzGibbon's last of three certificates was penned on behalf of the Secords, a proposal was made to grant Colonel FitzGibbon, then Chief Clerk of the Legislative Council, the sum of £1000 in lieu of a former grant for five thousand acres of crown lands. This recorded proposal was strongly opposed in the Legislative Assembly by Mr. Thomas C. Aylwin of Quebec, and was subsequently disallowed as illegal. It was now the Secords' turn to support FitzGibbon, one of their most respected supporters and the extraordinary victor at the Battle of Beaver Dams. Charles B. Secord addressed a letter of support for FitzGibbon to a religious periodical, called "The Church," published at Cobourg, Ontario, which was printed in April, 1845. FitzGibbon's grant was approved.

1840s – 1860s   Laura's family grows, as Canada moves to become a nation

This period saw significant events in the growing Secord family. Shortly after James died, Laura got word that her youngest daughter, Hannah, had given birth to Katherine Emma Williams in 1841 and later to Caroline Williams on 24 July 1843. Hannah and her husband, Howley Williams, had waited eight years for their first child; however, Howley died at age 34, in 1844, at their home in Guelph, Ontario, and within four years their youngest daughter Caroline had also died. Fortunately for Hannah, her acquaintance with Edward Pyke Carthew flourished and they were married on 17 March 1847 in Guelph. Edward, born in England, had been the local Deputy Sheriff and then Collector of Customs; he was a gentleman who managed his affairs carefully. Their five children born between 1848 and 1856 ultimately produced a large descendancy of Carthews in Laura Secord's family. Hannah and Edward lived happily together in Guelph for another thirty years.

When David William Smith had died on 23 May 1842 from the excessive alcohol consumption, Harriet was left with three children without a father. William James went to his grandparents in Fort Erie and, after his grandfather died eighteen months later at age 75, he was raised by his grandmother who remained on the Fort Erie farm until she died in 1866 at the age of 88. The Smith grandparents and their son, David William, were all buried in the St. Paul's churchyard. Harriet and her two daughters, Laura Louisa and

Mary Augusta Smith (1828-1911)
Courtesy: Don Ede's Collection

Mary Augusta, became the constant companions of Laura Secord in her latter days in the cottage on Water Street in Chippawa. In the years after Laura Secord's death in 1868, they all relocated to Guelph to be with Charlotte. Harriet remained a living witness of her mother's accomplishments until she died in 1892, giving the new breed of female biographers, such as Sarah Ann Curzon, a real link to some of the details of Laura Secord's life.

William James Smith's Volunteer Enlistment paper

By 1856 Harriet's only son William James Smith had immigrated to the United States from Windsor, Ontario with his sweetheart, Elizabeth Bresnahan, who had been raised in western Ontario. William (27 years old) and Elizabeth (17 years old, orphaned at 13) moved to Chicago, Cook County, Illinois and were apparently married there in 1856 – the Chicago fire in 1875 is believed to have consumed their marriage record. They set up a grocery store business from 1857 to 1863 on West Fulton, just east of Halsted; this site was later lost in the building of the I-94 Interstate highway. By 1864 William and Elizabeth had moved their family to Ellsworth, Wisconsin; and William worked as an accounting clerk in Prescott, about 20 miles away. On 24 September 1964, William volunteered to serve for one year as a volunteer soldier in the American Civil War.

They later moved to Browns Valley, Minnesota. The Smith farm, located in sections 29 and 32 of Windsor Township, MN, had its beginnings in 1876 when William James settled in that area and ploughed the first land the following year. In 1878 he moved his wife Elizabeth and family from Prescott, Wisconsin. Following William's death in 1901, one of his sons, Frank D. Smith succeeded in the ownership of the farm. He had married Serena Fossen of Big Stone County, MN, and to their union were born ten children, including Arthur W. Smith, the next owner. Emily

Moland, a Browns Valley teacher, became his bride and their children were William Moland and James Secord Smith. Secord and Catherine Bourland Smith were the recent owners, and the farm is now worked by their sons Larry and Gary. The township of Windsor was organized in the Smith kitchen and was named in memory of the town where William and Elizabeth left Canada and immigrated to the USA. Four generations of Smiths are now buried in the Valley View Cemetery near Browns Valley, Minnesota.

William James Smith Sr.
Courtesy: Sandra DiNanni

Laura Ann, Laura and James Secord's fifth daughter and a widow by about 1841 with one surviving son, remarried in Guelph. Her second husband was Dr. William Clarke, an Irish physician. He held several positions of public service, including Commissioner of the Court of Requests in 1833, Warden of Wellington County 1852, M.P. 1853 to 1863 and Mayor of Guelph

1864/65. He also took a leading part in procuring the formation of the College of Physicians and Surgeons of Ontario and served as its president for six years.

Sadly, after delivering a son William and two daughters, Laura Secord and Millicent in the mid-late 1840s, Laura Ann died in Guelph on 18 August 1852, leaving William Sr. a widower who remarried and had three more children. None of her children had children of their own, and William Jr. and Millicent had died in infancy. Only John Poore, from Laura Ann's first marriage, and Laura Secord Clarke, from her second marriage, lived into the twentieth century.

Laura Secord Clarke (1846-1936)
Courtesy: Don Ede's Collection

Laura Ingersoll Secord lived within visiting range of many Secord in-laws, mostly in St. David's. Her scattered direct line consisted of 7 children, 20 grandchildren (of whom only 10 married and had children of their own) and 59 great-grandchildren. Laura Secord's grandson, and eldest son of Charles Badeau Secord, became Professor Charles Forsyth Secord and had 14 children by two wives. The Carthew-Secord family connection yielded 31 of the 59 great-grandchildren of Laura Secord. As of the publication of this book, there are over 700 descendants of Laura Ingersoll Secord and her husband, James. There are over 130 surnames in this family today.

1860 The Prince of Wales arrives in Niagara Falls, Ontario and receives a memorandum. Laura Secord is finally rewarded

1859: His Royal Highness Prince Albert Edward (1841-1910)
Taken from the Prince's Tour of British America report, 1860

In September 1860, the 19-year old Prince of Wales, Queen Victoria's eldest son and the future King Edward VII, visited the Niagara Peninsula. Although advanced in years at 85, and still living in her home at 3800 Bridgewater Street, Chippawa, Laura Secord had gone to the office of the Clerk of the Peace at Niagara-on-the-Lake a month before the prince's arrival, where she insisted on signing the 'address' over the objections of the clerk. She was supported by the Niagara Mail who printed this about Laura Secord:
"She had done her country more signal service than half the soldiers and militiamen engaged in the war. We say the brave, loyal old lady not only be allowed to sign the address but she deserves a special introduction to the Prince as a worthy example

of the fire of 1812 when both men and women vied alike in the resolution to defend their country."

As noted earlier, it has been said of the Battle of Beaver Dams that "The Caughnawagas did the fighting, the Mohawks got the plunder and FitzGibbon got the praise." And Laura Secord got nothing.

Courtesy: Niagara Falls Public Library

Prince Edward learned of Laura's twenty mile walk from the petition describing her war-time service. Of all who presented an address for the Prince' attention, her name was the only woman's among the veterans of War of 1812.

As Professor Alan Hughes stated in his article 'Laura Secord and the Prince of Wales':

"The Niagara Mail on April 3, 1861 reported that the memorial was delivered to the Governor General, who at first seems to have ignored it. Only through the intercession of one Sir William Fenwick Williams was it presented to the Prince. Laura subsequently met the Prince in person (this is confirmed in her obituary), probably on the Sunday during his stay at the Falls. He was due to attend church in Drummondville, but at the last minute it was switched to Chippawa where Laura was living at the time, and to the very church, Holy Trinity, that she attended. One can't help wondering how the meeting of the elderly Laura and the teenage Albert went, but there are no eye-witness accounts." [Lieutenant General Sir William Fenwick Williams of Kars played a key role in Laura's later life. He had been a hero of the Crimean War, and at the time of the Prince's visit was Commander-in-Chief of British forces in North America.]

Although she was never given the formal platform to present her achievement, Laura probably saw the Prince briefly at Holy Trinity church on the morning of 16 September 1860 or on his carriage ride through Chippawa. She had provided the Prince with her own words on the elements of the War of 1812 in which she and her husband, James, had participated with courage and bravery "in the hour of trial and danger" and that they both had "stood ready and willing to defend this Country against every invasions come what might". She described her heroic act and supported it with a copy of FitzGibbon's 1837 Certificate.

Uncertain of Queen Victoria's and the British Government's position on female civilian heroines in financial distress, the Prince returned to England and sought counsel from his mother. The young Prince would not forget the frail Canadian grandmother who had so heroically altered the course of an important action of the War in 1813. A few months later, forty-eight years after her deed, he sent Laura Secord a hundred pounds in gold, the only financial reward she was ever to get for her service to her country and Great Britain.

Laura's petition, the Prince's reward and the local press reports that followed, all galvanized wide public acclaim for her efforts.

Fitzgibbon had certified Laura's contribution to the victory at Beaver Dams, in his own words:
"Laura Secord informed me that the enemy intended to attempt by surprise to capture a detachment of the 49th Regiment then under my command she having obtained such knowledge from good authority as the event proved. She made the effort in weather excessively warm and I dreaded at the time she must suffer in health in consequence of fatigue and anxiety, she having been exposed to danger from the enemy through whose lines of communication she had to pass."

It was not until 1861 that the £100 gift from the Prince of Wales was finally received by Laura Secord at her home in Chippawa. As the Niagara Mail stated it: "The Prince of Wales is a true, gallant Prince, with a warn regard for the old ladies as well as for the young ones." With this gift, Laura had become famous, but the fame came slowly. The Niagara Mail continued to cover the story: "Her patriotic services during the War of 1812, which are well known, were brought under the notice of the Prince during his visit last summer, have thus been handsomely acknowledged." Upon review, the Niagara Mail reporter realized that time had passed and a reprint of an article from the Welland Reporter would be helpful to the public:
"During the war of 1812-13, Mrs. Secord who was quite a young woman at the time, was living on a farm about mid-way between Queenston and St. David's, both of which places were at that period occupied by American troops. During their frequent visits at their house she overheard them planning a surprise and night attack upon a detachment of British soldiers stationed near the Beaverdams, under the command of Lieut. Fitzgibbon. Without betraying any knowledge of the affair, this brave woman set off by night through the woods, a distance of thirteen miles to the British camp notwithstanding the imminent peril of falling into the hands of the American scouts or hostile Indians, and gave the British commander such information as enabled him to successfully repel the attack and defeat the Americans with great slaughter... Mrs. S. is now over eighty years of age, in possession of all her faculties and she yet takes much pleasure in recounting her adventures upon the occasion above alluded to. The gift of the Prince will doubtless afford much satisfaction, as

70

well to the members of her family and other relatives as to her many friends by whom she is held in much esteem. We trust the old lady may long be spared to the unimpaired enjoyment of all the comforts of this life."

Despite the numerous journalistic errors in the early part of this text, particularly as they relate to the endeavour itself, this newspaper article and others helped to acquaint the Canadian general public of the significance of her walk to warn a British outpost.

The early 1860s witnessed the first stirrings of Canadian nationalism, and in 1861–62 an Ontario historian, William Canniff even participated in attempts with George Coventry and others to set up an Upper Canadian historical society. In 1869 he completed the research and writing of his '*History of the settlement of Upper Canada (Ontario)*', a project he claimed to have undertaken in 1862 at the instigation of the short-lived society. In this monumental study, Canniff's developing interests in loyalist history and "the future prospects of the Dominion" fused, producing a distinctly British Canadian sense of nationality.

1853-70   Publicity surrounding Laura Secord's Heroic Act after the Prince's recognition

A '*History of the War of 1812*' was printed in November 1853 as a serial in the Anglo-American Magazine, and afterwards appeared in a book, authored by Gilbert Auchinleck. In a note on the Battle of Beaver Dams of June 1813, Auchinleck introduced Laura Secord in her own words, and followed it with FitzGibbon's 1837 Certificate, the originals of which Laura had kept at least through December 1863.

In the summer of 1860, the American artist and writer, Benson J. Lossing, visited Canada to collect material for his '*Pictorial*

Fieldbook of the War of 1812', which was not published until 1869 – the year after Laura Secord died. Although they did not meet, he corresponded with her, and on page 621 of his book in a footnote he related the communication of the Americans' secret plan by Laura Secord to FitzGibbon.

In 1864 the former sheriff of the Montreal district and staff officer in the militia, William F. Coffin wrote his book, *'1812: The War, And Its Moral, A Canadian Chronicle'*, providing reference on page 146 to Auchinleck's account, and introducing the first major opportunity for male historians to establish a myth about Laura Secord – the cow. And so, even in Laura's lifetime, the seeds of discontent were being sown in the next generation of male historians that female historians were establishing their own heroines. The issue of the cow, and the pail, have now been sufficiently embedded in the mind of the general public that the source of this myth is worth some scrutiny.

As Coffin actually and credibly wrote:
"Her first difficulty was the American advanced sentry. He was hard to deal with, but she pointed to her own farm buildings a little in advance of his post, insisted that she was going for milk; told him he could watch her, and was allowed to pass on. She did milk a cow, which was very contrary, and would persist in moving onwards to the edge of the opposite bushes, into which she and the cow disappeared. Once out of sight, she pushed on rapidly. She knew the way for miles... At length she reached a brook. It was very hot, and the water refreshed her, but she had some difficulty in crossing. At last she found a log, and shortly after got to the mill [Hannah Secord's grist mill which is today at 237 Four Mile Creek Road]."

Coffin described several important facts and, although taking the cow along the path that she took on her Walk may have been a fable, his description of the action with the cow is plausible – unlike accounts of subsequent writers who inappropriately ascribed her leading a cow in front of her during her Walk to William Coffin. According to Coffin, she left at the crack of dawn, crossed 4 Mile Creek, visited Hannah DeFreest Secord (her sister-in-law, the miller) in St. David's and met both American and British sentries.

Sometime in the early 1860s, following the reward and in view of her growing fame, Mr. Joel Lyons of Chippawa took a daguerreotype photograph of Laura Secord, and another of the house on Water Street. A copy of this photograph may be seen in the Niagara Historical Society Museum in Niagara-on-the-Lake.

While Laura received some public attention during her lifetime, more was to come after her death and is described later in this book.

LAURA INGERSOLL SECORD
This is believed to be the only picture of the heroine

HOME OF LAURA SECORD AT CHIPPAWA

Courtesy: Niagara Historical Society Museum
Publication No. 25

1863 Fitzgibbon dies a poor man in Windsor, England but is buried, a hero, in St. George's Chapel

Laura Secord was likely saddened at the news of the death of her ardent supporter, James FitzGibbon who played a significant role in the Secords' lives. He was born 16 November 1780 in Glin, Co. Limerick, Ireland, and died 10 December 1863 in Windsor, Berkshire, England. Fitzgibbon gained fame as a British Army hero of the War of 1812. At the age of 15 he joined the Knight of Glin's Yeomanry Corps, and at the age of 18, the Tarbert Infantry Fencibles. In 1799 he fought in the Battle of Egmond aan Zee, Holland, and the Battle of Copenhagen, Denmark, for which he won the distinguished Naval General Service Medal for bravery. In 1802 he was made a marine, in 1806 a Sergeant, and finally in 1809 a Lieutenant. In 1802, he had been ordered to Canada and began serving under Lieut.-Colonel (later Major General Sir) Isaac Brock, another Canadian war hero. Fitzgibbon also fought in the Battle of Fort George, the Battle of Stony Creek, the Battle of Lundy's Lane, and of course, the Battle of Beaver Dams, for which he is best remembered. Supported by Laura Secord's confirming information, he became a national hero and was promoted to Captain in the Glengarry Light Infantry Fencibles. After the war he became a public servant, Colonel, and Acting Adjutant-General of the Militia for Upper Canada. He had been promoted to a Militia Colonel in 1826.

FitzGibbon was indebted mainly to lieutenant governors Sir Peregrine Maitland and Sir John Colborne for his appointments, though they carried little power or prestige. He was a prominent Mason, and from 1822 to 1826 he held the highest office in Upper Canada as Deputy Provincial Grand Master (the Provincial Grand Mastership was retained in England). He was Secretary of the Society for the Relief of Strangers in Distress, and was a founding member, in 1831, of the York Mechanics' Institute. His later work as peacemaker during the 1837-38 riots was an important contribution to the stability of Upper Canada. It was Lieutenant Governor Sir Francis Bond Head who made

FitzGibbon acting adjutant-general of militia at the peak of the latter's career.

Taken from "A Veteran of 1812",
Toronto, Briggs, 1894

In May 1838 the citizens of Toronto held a public meeting and expressed gratitude to FitzGibbon for "rescuing them from the horrors of a civil war," but the financial gift they proposed to raise by subscription never materialized. Only in 1845 did the legislature reward him with the sum of £1,000, which was half the total of FitzGibbon's debts and less than half the estimated value of the land grant originally proposed. FitzGibbon tried in vain to persuade the British government to supplement his reward, arguing that he had saved Upper Canada for the empire. In 1847 he assembled all his documentation in a pamphlet entitled "An appeal to the people of the late province of Upper Canada", but this achieved nothing.

So, in 1847 he moved to England, where he became a Military Knight of Windsor. He died there in December 1863 at the age of 83, a poor but proud servant of the Crown, and was buried in St. George's Chapel of Windsor Castle. In 2003 some of his personal belongings, including a ceremonial sword and signet ring, were donated to the Canadian Military Museum in Ottawa, Ontario.

1868 Laura Secord dies at home in Chippawa, aged 93, and is buried in Drummond Hill

Laura Secord died quietly at home in 1868. Her obituary in the Niagara Mail stated:
"DIED
At Chippawa on the 17th Oct. Inst. aged 91 [actually 93] – Mrs. Secord, relict of the late James Secord Esq. Mrs. Secord was one the Canadian women of the war of 1812, whose spirit and devotion to their country contributed so much to its defence. Having ascertained during the night that a large American force under Colonel Boerstler was proceeding in the direction of the Beaver dams, in the Niagara district, Mrs. Secord hastened on foot through the dense forest, and in the night – a distance of twenty miles – to inform Colonel [then Lieutenant] FitzGibbon – then in command of a small force of British troops and Indians – of the movement of the enemy. Acting on this information, Colonel FitzGibbon marched at once to intercept the enemy, and at daylight next morning encountered, defeated and captured the whole force of Colonel Boerstler, in the battle known as that of the Beech Woods. At the visit of the Prince of Wales to Canada in 1860, Mrs. Secord was introduced to him, and received from him a substantial token of his respect for her patriotism and intrepidity."

Her funeral was held in the Church of the Holy Trinity in Chippawa, Ontario. The Rev. D.I.F. McLeod, the vicar in residence from 1863 to 1879, had succeeded the founder of the

Parish, Rev. William Leeming, who predeceased Laura Secord by five years.

Holy Trinity Church, Chippawa
Courtesy: Author's Collection

This church, originally built in 1820 as a frame wooden structure, was burned during the anti-Family Compact movement in 1839, six years after Laura Secord had joined it as a parishioner. It was rebuilt in 1841, as a brick structure. The Prince of Wales visited the church during his visit in 1860. The church still stands on Portage Road ½ mile north of the centre of Chippawa.

Laura Ingersoll Secord was buried beside her husband in the high north-eastern section (#1) of Drummond Hill Cemetery, Lundy's Lane, Niagara Falls, Ontario – subsequently close by the memorial to those who fought at the Battle of Lundy's Lane on 25 July 1814, at which the British and Canadian forces were also successful.

The original gravestones for Laura and James Secord at Drummond Hill Cemetery were moved when the second memorial to them was built there in 1901. These gravestones are now on the wall of the Church of the Holy Trinity in Chippawa. They read:
"Here rests LAURA. Beloved wife
of JAMES SECORD. Died Oct. 17th, 1868. Aged 93 years."

"In Memory of JAMES SECORD Senr., Collector of Customs, who departed this Life on the 22nd day of Feb. 1841, in the 68 year of his age. Universally & deservedly lamented as a sincere Friend a kind and indulgent Parent & an affectionate Husband."

Grave markers in situ.
Taken from Emma Currie's book.

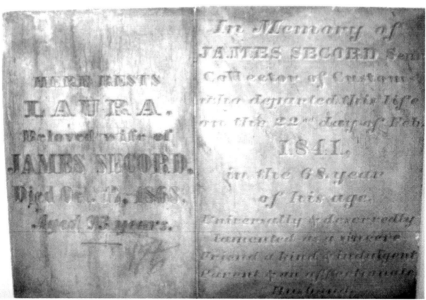

Original Grave Markers of Laura and James Secord
Courtesy: Church of the Holy Trinity, Chippawa

In Memoriam

LAURA SECORD, 1813.

In Drumond's Lane Cemetery is the following inscription on a marble head-stone

HERE RESTS
LAURA,
BELOVED WIFE OF JAMES SECORD,
Died Oct. 17, 1868,
Aged 93 Years.

Laura Secord's Death Announcement or Funeral Card
Courtesy: Niagara Falls Public Library

As a part of Laura Secord's will, her daughter Hannah and her husband Edward Carthew were forgiven their mortgage loan by the Estate. Carthew provided a written confirmation of the mortgage discharge to Charlotte Secord:
"Registered 3rd October 1871.
To the Registrar of the County of Welland.
I Edward Carthew of the Town of Guelph... do Certify that Charlotte Secord of the Village of Chippawa in the County of Welland administratrix of the Estate and effects of Laura Secord deceased late of the same place hath satisfied all money due on or to grow due on a certain mortgage made by the said Laura Secord deceased to me [bearing date 1856]... and that the said Mortgage has never been assigned and that I am the person

entitled by Law to receive the Money and that such Mortgage is therefore discharged, witness my hand this Twelfth day of June... [1871]
Sgd. Edward Carthew"

After bequests, the balance of her will was in favour of her only other two living daughters, Charlotte and Harriet. Laura and James Secord had already given the Queenston house to their only son, Charles B. Secord.

In 1871, the cottage of Laura Secord located on Water Street, Chippawa, was purchased by Ernest Peters, the undertaker for Laura's funeral. In 1841 the cottage had been sold to Laura Secord for the sum of 155 pounds; it sold on 14 June 1871 for 450 pounds. The house passed to widow Peters and then to her niece Cathereen McKenzie; the latter then passed it to her son, Grant. It has had numerous owners since that time.

Lot 108 on the west side of Adelaide Street (Laura Secord Place), Twp. Lot 22, Con. 2, Willoughby						
Instrument	Instrument Date	Registry Date	Grantor	Grantee	Quantity	Amount
Buy & Sell	1 Nov 1841	4 Jul 1842	James Cummings et ux.	Laura Secord	inter-alia Lot 108 (109)	£150
Mortgage	28 Nov 1856	10 Dec 1856	Laura Secord	Edward Carthew		£28
Probate of Will	26 Nov 1857	23 Jan 1869	Laura Secord	Charlotte Secord and Harriet Smith, her 2 daughters, as Tenants in common all lands in Village of Chippawa		
Discharge of Mortgage	12 Jun 1871	3 Oct 1871	Edward Carthew	Charlotte Secord	inter-alia Lot 108	
Buy & Sell	14 Jun 1871	3 Oct 1871	Charlotte Secord, spinster, & Harriet Smith, widow, as devised by Laura Secord's will	Ernest Peters	inter-alia Lot 108 (109)	£450

Earlier Land Records for Laura Secord's House in Chippawa

Captain James Cummings of Chippawa always honoured Laura Secord's birthday, September 13th, by hoisting the flag. He had received Captain Chapin's sword when he surrendered at Beaver Dams. (See Vol. 7, page 179, Ontario Historical Society Papers and Records)."

1887 The "mythification" begins as the women's movement, drama, poems and ballads extol the virtues of their Canadian heroine, Laura Secord

Prior to her death and following the visit of the Prince of Wales, there was some publicity surrounding Laura Secord and her feat. She appears to have contributed directly to this publicity and saw it in her own lifetime. Following her death, much was made of Laura's life and exploits. In 1887 Sarah Anne Curzon published her new drama: '*Laura Secord: the Heroine of 1812*' which was well received. She also wrote Laura Secord's biography in the same year. A year later, in 1888, Charles Mair published '*A Ballad for Brave Women*' in the Toronto Week. Then, in 1894, Mary A. FitzGibbon published the life story of her father, James FitzGibbon which included his 1837 Certificate for Laura Secord and added comments about Laura arriving at DeCew House barefoot (quite likely, if a shoe was lost in marshy ground or at the crossing across 12-mile Creek) and with a milking stool (most unlikely, unless she picked it up near the DeCew House). As a part of this mythification came the story of Laura Secord's cow and the milk-pail as an excuse to leave the house in the early morning of 22 June 1813. As Laura's granddaughter, Mrs. Elizabeth Ann Gregory recalled: "The cow and the milk-pail are fable", invented by William F. Coffin in his 1864 book. Other myths were also added to make the reading of historical novels about Laura Secord more interesting and exciting. Passing through enemy (American) lines or, for that matter, British lines were blown out of proportion to the endeavour. Although she had to prepare herself for such possibilities, in fact she fortuitously encountered neither American nor British troops on her walk – and as it turned out no Indian supporters of the Americans. The story of her being seen 'barefoot' when she arrived at the DeCew house was not surprising because her slippers (or moccasins) could well have been lost in soft ground, especially on the steep slope up the escarpment.

In speaking of his grandmother as a humble heroine, James Badeau Secord of Niagara wrote in his letter of 1887 to Sarah

Ann Curzon how Laura addressed her courageous deed within the inner circle of her family: "My grandmother was of a modest disposition, and did not care to have her exploit mentioned, as she did not think she had done anything extraordinary. She was the very last one to mention the affair, and unless asked would never say anything about it." As we recall from her earlier situation, it was only because of the family's economy and a war-crippled husband that Laura Secord made her petitions, along with those from James, to secure sufficient recognition at a time when petitions, patronage and claims were commonplace to an ever-changing leadership of government in Upper Canada.

From 1887 to the turn of the century, the legend of Laura Secord grew in the minds of the general public. Her legend's advocates – women, poets, playwrights (such as Mrs. Currie, Mrs. Curzon, Mrs. Thompson, Ms. FitzGibbon and Mrs. Carnochan), old acquaintances (such as Mrs. Munro), her family and finally the provincial government – could provide plausible information about the real character and personality of Laura Secord, being within one generation of this period and having access to her immediate family. Publications were now extolling the virtues of a secret mission that could not come to light until the American offensives (primarily the War of 1812) and internal strife (largely the 1837-38 rebellion, led by William Lyon Mackenzie) had settled and the emerging Canadian nation demonstrated stability and unity. Just as with espionage endeavours in twentieth century wars, it was to take a generation for Laura Secord's contribution to Canadian sovereignty to reach the general public's full awareness.

Ernest Cruikshank, who compiled much of the data about Laura Secord and the War of 1812, claimed that: "the Battle of Beaver Dams was indissolubly linked with the memory of one of the most patriotic and courageous women of any age and country."

The legend of Laura Secord was not without its detractors. Educated at Toronto and Oxford, and a major in the Canadian Expeditionary Force during World War One, the University of Toronto's librarian, William Stewart Wallace (1884-1970) was tasked with determining what topics should be in the history books for school children in Ontario. In 1932, predated by a stream of newspaper stories in the Mail & Empire in December 1931, Wallace used earlier storytellers' views of Laura Secord's exploits to chip away at the value of her deed and its subsequent contribution to the overall defence of Upper Canada. However, he had failed to do his research diligently, which he later recognized. Although published by the Niagara Historical Society a decade before, the 1820 FitzGibbon certificate had not received widespread publicity until Henry Cartwright Secord found it (again) in 1934, and Fred Williams of the Mail &

Laura Secord, the woman who made Confederation possible
Charles Fraser Comfort (1900-1994, Canadian artist)
[The scourge of William S. Wallace, 1932:
This image is reminiscent of the Jeanne d'Arc trial by the English
after being captured at Compiègne in 1430 and burned at the stake
– Laura Secord on trial by male historians and ready
to be burned at the stake, led by the infamous cow.]

Empire publicized the new find. Combined with the discovery of the 1827 FitzGibbon certificate in 1959, published by the Ontario Historical Society in an article prepared by John S. Moir, it became clear over time that these detractors had erroneously assumed that Laura Secord made her Walk on 23 June 1813. The reality is, that based on all the evidence available to us today, she made the Walk on 22 June 1813 before the American forces had left along the Niagara River near Queenston, allowing FitzGibbon and his Indian supporters a whole day to watch the enemy advances towards the Beaver Dams and to position themselves for the final entrapment of all these American forces. Visual confirmation of the American advance on the FitzGibbon outpost came from loyal Indians at about 7:00 am on the morning of the battle, 24 June 1813. The finding and publication of these documents provided vindication of the Laura Secord legacy.

Moving rapidly forward in time, the most balanced view of this heroine in the twentieth century was written by Ruth McKenzie in her 'Laura Secord, the legend and the lady' in 1971, which properly reassesses the evidence and Laura Secord's place in history. This rendition of her life continues to be the generally-accepted view of Laura Secord today, a balanced portrayal supported by the federal and provincial governments of Canada and espoused by the Laura Secord Homestead museum in Queenston, Ontario. This work successfully countered those who would minimize her role in the defence of Canadian soil in 1813.

1887-1910 Monuments and histories to Laura Secord's heroism

As these legends grew up around the name of Laura Secord, an officially recognized early Canadian heroine was created. She became celebrated in song and story, by the efforts of liberated women. To support these women, in 1887 W. Fenwick, principal of the Grammar School at Drummondville and then Niagara

Falls South, wrote a letter to the Toronto World and Mail, published on 6 June 1887, in which he called attention to the neglected state of the graveyard and the need for a national memorial to those who fell at Lundy's Lane in defence of their country, and urged that a monument be erected in memory of Laura Secord. In 1892 Rev. Canon Bull, Rector of All Saints Church, Drummondville, asked for monument contributions by Public & High School students and women in the Counties of Lincoln and Welland. The two plain marble slabs in Drummond Hill had been surrounded by a wooden fence, but weeds and tall grass hid the fence and the stones until the end of the century. The matter was then taken up by the Ontario Historical Society. The work started by Sarah Ann Curzon in 1895 and accomplished by Mrs. Elizabeth Jane Thompson, the Convenor of the monument committee in 1899, was significant, as shown in her scrap book which is now the property of the Ontario Historical Society.

By 1901 local funds had been raised for the new monument at Drummond Hill Cemetery to replace the common grave markers of Laura and her husband James Secord. These grave markers were acquired by the Church of the Holy Trinity in Chippawa, Ontario.

The day fixed for the unveiling was 22 June 1901, and Mrs. G.W. Ross (Mildred Peel, wife of the Ontario Premier) was asked to perform this office. A large concourse of 2000 people indicated the interest taken in the proceedings. In the programme there was first an address of welcome by Rev. Canon Bull, addresses by Dr. James H. Coyne, Dr. Bryce, Hon. J. G. Currie, Hon. P. Porter, and many others, among them the Mayor, Warden and Reeve of the municipality.

The words on primary face of this memorial grave marker, with bust, at the Drummond Hill Cemetery in Niagara Falls, Ontario, read:
"To perpetuate the name and fame of LAURA SECORD, who walked alone nearly 20 miles by a circuitous, difficult and perilous route, through woods and swamps and over miry roads to warn a British outpost at DeCew's Falls of an intended attack

and thereby enabled Lieut. FitzGibbon on the 24th June 1813, with less than 50 men of H.M. 49th Regt., about 15 militiamen and a small force of Six Nations and other Indians under Capt. William Johnson Kerr and Dominique Ducharme to surprise and attack the enemy at Beechwood (or Beaver Dams) and after a short engagement, to capture Col. Boerstler of the U.S. Army and his entire force of 542 men with two field pieces."

Laura and James Secord's graves in Drummondhill Cemetery
Courtesy: Author's Collection

The other three faces of this grave marker read:
"Here rests LAURA INGERSOLL, beloved wife of James Secord, born Sept. 13, 1775, died Oct. 17, 1868, aged 93 years."

"In Memory of JAMES SECORD, Collector of Customs, who departed this life on 22nd of February, 1841, the 68th year of his life."

"This Monument erected by Ontario Historical Society from contributions of schools, societies, the 49th Regt., other military organizations and private individuals. Was unveiled 22nd June 1900."

Loyal Indian veterans at Laura's grave, 1914
Courtesy: St. Catharines Standard

The Acton Free Press on 27 Jun 1901 stated on page 3, column 2: "'Monument to Memory of Laura Secord'. Mr. and Mrs. Alex. Secord and Mr. and Mrs. T. E. M. Secord, and Miss Rachel, went to Lundy's Lane on Saturday to participate in the unveiling of a monument erected there as a tribute to the memory of Canada's heroine, Laura Secord. The monument consists of a shapely shaft of granite, rectangular in shape, some seven feet in height, resting upon a base of the same material. Upon three sides are polished shields bearing suitable inscriptions cut into the stone. Surmounting the shaft is a life-size bust in bronze of the heroine. Among the friends and descendants of the woman whose memory all honour present were Mrs. C. W. Young, wife of Mr. C. W. Young of the Cornwall Freeholder, who is the daughter of Mrs. Secord's youngest daughter; Messrs. T. E. Secord and Alex. Secord, Acton; Mr. W. F. Secord, Thorold, grand-nephew; Miss Laura Clarke, Toronto, and Miss Augusta Smith, Guelph, granddaughters, and Mr. Andrew Carnochan, who for many years was a next-door neighbour of the Secord family at Chippawa. These were all introduced to the thousands who thronged the historical spot by Rev. Canon Bell, President Lundy's Lane Historical Society. The unveiling was performed by Mrs. Geo. W. Ross, wife of the Premier. The event was one of very great interest."

Emma Currie had written in 1900:
"Laura Secord was of a kindly disposition, always doing something to help others, and while I was collecting for the Monument, which we erected at Lundy's Lane, an old man came to see me one day at Canon Bull's house, and told me he had walked twenty-two miles to bring me a dollar towards the Monument. He said that when he was a boy at Chippawa, and very poor, he used to shovel snow for Mrs. Secord, and that she always had a hot breakfast for him, and that she knit the first pair of mitts he ever owned, so he always wanted to do something for her memory, and when he heard I was at Niagara Falls, he walked there. He would not tell me what his name was.
One day when I was collecting for the monument at Lundy's Lane. Mrs McLeod, wife of the late rector of Chippawa, who had known Mrs. Secord very well, came to see Canon Bull; and we asked her how it was that James and Laura Secord were buried at Lundy's Lane instead of at Chippawa, and she said she remembered very well her husband coming home shortly before James Secord's death and saying that "Secord wanted to be buried on the Battle field where all the good men who had fought in the War of 1812 "had left their bones," and that after his death, Mrs. Laura Secord made Dr. McLeod promise that when she died, she should be laid beside her husband."

In 1910, the Government of Canada erected another monument to their heroine in Queenston Heights Park just south of

Queenston on the northeast edge of the escarpment. At the unveiling ceremony on 5 July 1911, the Toronto Globe stated:

Memorial to Laura Secord on Queenston Heights
Courtesy: Niagara Falls Public Library

"Three thousand Canadians, in the presence of not a few United States visitors from Buffalo, Lewiston, and other centres, to-day honoured perhaps their greatest heroine, Laura Secord, to whose memory the Dominion Government has erected a monument on a superb site at Queenston Heights."
The government had denied her the position of caretaker of the Brock Monument but had finally acknowledged Laura Secord as a heroine of significant distinction.

In 2003, the Minister of Canadian Heritage designated Laura Secord a 'Person of National Historic Significance' for her heroic actions during the War of 1812. A life-sized statue of Laura Secord also stands at the Valients Memorial, located by Confederation Square near the National War Memorial in Ottawa, Ontario. One of five full-length statues at this memorial site, it was dedicated by Governor General Michaëlle Jean on 5 November 2006.

Memorial to Laura Secord at Valients Square, Ottawa
Courtesy: Author's Collection

Laura Secord has also been honoured by other means. In 1905, the Ontario Government paid tribute to their heroine with the unprecedented honour of commissioning a painting of Laura Secord and hanging it in the Parliament Building in Toronto (currently on the third floor). The commission went to Mildred Peel, who portrayed her as an elderly woman in a bonnet with lace mitts on her hands. The painting was reported on by the Christian Guardian. Although the resemblance to the only known photograph is considered poor, the honour is extraordinary for a woman of the period, and ensures that official Canadian recognition of her courageous deed will remain high. It is somewhat amusing that Laura Secord's portrait was painted over on an unsold canvas depicting Sir George W. Ross, the Ontario Premier of his day (1899-1905).

Portrait and Bust of Laura Secord in
Provincial Government Buildings in Toronto
Courtesy: Author's Collection

There have also been schools named after our heroine: among
them are *Laura Secord Elementary School* in Queenston, *Laura
Secord Secondary School* in St. Catharines, and a memorial hall
established in her honour. Other monuments tell of the tale of
Laura's illustrious place in the history of Canada.

Laura Secord Stamp
Courtesy: Canada Post

In addition to official Canadian Government recognition, Laura Secord's walk over 19 miles of swampy land, through woods and across creeks on fallen timbers to reach Lieutenant FitzGibbon at the DeCew (or DeCou) House, was honoured in 1992 by the Canadian Post Office. The stamp includes members of Iroquois, Caughnawaga and Six Nations tribes in the lower right corner of the stamp.

And in Massachusetts, USA, in 18 October 1997 the Historic District Commission dedicated a marker to the town-born woman to be featured on a postage stamp. The Great Barrington Board of Selectmen proclaimed this date as Laura Ingersoll Secord Day in recognition of her role in history. The bronze dedication marker is located on the front lawn of the town's Mason Public Library on Main Street, Great Barrington – on the site of her father's house, since demolished. The text of this marker yields the ultimate recognition of a heroine – the praise of her enemy.

Through the generous gift of Laura Secord Candy Shops Ltd., the Laura Secord Homestead became part of the public trust in 1998, enabling The Niagara Parks Commission to ensure the Homestead's preservation and safekeeping for future generations.

Emma Currie eloquently summarized Laura Secord's later life and her character:
"She was always very kind and thoughtful to children, giving them many little gifts, cakes and bread and butter, and a great many of the old soldiers, who had served with her husband, used to visit her in Chippawa. She always helped them -- not so much by what she gave as by her kind sympathy and thoughtfulness for them.
Many questions have been asked as to why this daring deed of Mrs. Secord's was not recognized before 1860; but one must remember that after the war a great deal of bitter feeling prevailed along the border, and there were many cases of insult and injury to those who had taken any prominent part in the struggle. One can understand a timid woman like Mrs. Secord dreading the insults of such people, and her anxiety to keep the

92

part that she had taken to herself -- although she always recognized that her walk had meant a great deal to the British officers, who were striving to protect such a large tract of country from the invading army, and with a very small force at their command."

As a woman and a civilian, engaging in wartime espionage, it took decades for Laura's exploits to achieve public recognition. Laura Secord was not only a heroine in the War of 1812, but is deserving of the recognition that she has in Canada.

"Ah! Faithful to death were our women of yore!
Have they fled with the past to be heard of no more?
No. No! Though this laurelled one sleeps in the grave,
We have maidens as true, we have matrons as brave;
And should Canada ever be forced to the test –
To spend for our country the blood of the best –
When our sons lift the linstock and brandish the sword,
Her daughters will think of brave Laura Secord."

By Charles Mair (1838-1927)

Laura Ingersoll Secord m. James Secord

Mary Lawrence Secord Trumble m. Dr. William Trumble

Elizabeth Trumble m. William Henry Davis
Children: William Henry Rowland m. Amelia Elizabeth Protzman
      Children:
          Elizabeth (Bessie) m. Guy Tresingleon George
          Frank Stewart
          Eric F. m. Susie F. Uriens
          Rollo William
    Laura Mary m. Henrik Martin Fredrik Mack
      Children:
          Harald m. Ragnhild Petersen
          Edith m. Nils Astrup
          Nanna Elisabeth m. Fin Meier
          Dermot m. Effie Anne Reiber
          Fredrik Wilhelm Stuart (Freddy) m. Olga Sørsdal
          Gerda
    Edith
    Gertrude
    Robert Evans Stuart (Lt.Col., Dr.)
    Frederick
Mary Trumble
[Others were unmarried.]

Notes:
Mary Lawrence Secord Trumble was Laura Ingersoll Secord's eldest child. She died in Dublin, Ireland in 1876.
Laura Mary Davis Mack was Mark Lawrence Secord Trumble's eldest granddaughter. She died in Norway in 1932.

A New World for Mary, 1816-1928

Since the first edition of this book was published in 2010, the author has continued to research and collect material relating to Laura Ingersoll Secord. Several family members have graciously shared the contents of their shoeboxes; three of Laura's daughters can now be recognized through the photographs in this 2nd edition, as can many other family members. Unsolicited emails have also played their part in connecting the more remote family members with the author, hopefully making this edition the more interesting for the reader.

This new material has added substantially to our general knowledge of the circumstances of Laura's direct descendants. This edition specifically sheds light on two illustrious great-grandchildren of Laura Ingersoll Secord - Laura Mary Davis Mack in Norway and Dr. Clayton (Carlos) Forsythe Secord in Guatemala. In DNA terms, Laura Mack represented one of the few surviving female direct descendants of her generation carrying the mtDNA of Laura Ingersoll Secord; since others had no issue, her line became most significant. And Dr. Secord represented one of the few remaining male direct descendants of his generation with the same Y chromosome as James Secord, Laura's husband; since others had no children, his line became most significant. But more of him in the next section of this book...

The material that follows in this section is based on a family history written in 1928 by Laura Mary Davis Mack, Laura Ingersoll Secord's great-granddaughter through her eldest daughter Mary's line – as shown in the tree opposite. For those in the Americas, this history first came to light 18 months ago when Eldrid Ingebjørg Mageli contacted the author and graciously sent the written record and associated photographs upon which this section of the book is based, and allowed excerpts to be included.

A little more than a year after the end of the War of 1812, so devastating to the Niagara Frontier, Mary Lawrence Secord, age 17, and Dr. William Trumble, age 22, were married in Niagara Falls on 18 April 1816. They had immediately sailed to Ireland on their honeymoon to visit his parents, Harloe and Elizabeth. They then returned to the Caribbean where Dr. Trumble had been posted in late 1816. Within five years Mary's husband was dead and she was left to raise two young daughters.

By 1830, after a sojourn in Niagara-on-the-Lake, Mary was back in Ireland, having inherited the Trumble estate. At time passed, Mary's eldest daughter, Elizabeth, married William Henry Davis in Ireland and they had a family of six children. Their eldest daughter was Laura Mary Davis.

Henrik Martin Fredrik Mack   Laura Mary Davis Mack (Berlin, 1866)
(1843-1914)   (1847-1932)
Courtesy: Eldrid Ingebjørg Mageli

Laura Mary Davis Mack had a long and interesting life, with three sons and three daughters. Born in Armagh, Northern Ireland in October 1847, she had met and married Fredrik Mack, a Norwegian lieutenant, in September 1872. As she left Ireland and embarked for Tromsø, Norway with her new husband, her life was to change forever. Later, after a lifetime of pleasure from her children and grandchildren, she was ready to ensure that her descendants did not forget their extraordinary roots. Carrying the name 'Laura' had its own responsibility for this great-granddaughter of Laura Ingersoll Secord.

The family had moved in about 1880 to the capital of Norway, Kristiania (known as Óslo from 1925), where her husband was a City Assessor. Now aged 81 in 1928, she sat at her desk and started to write her family history: "*To My Children*". She had promised her children she would do this, and remain as faithful as possible to the detail she had been told and could remember.

Laura Mack wrote:
"My mother's father was, as I said before, a Trumble. I do not know much about them. [The Trumbles were descendants of a Cromwellian soldier who settled in County Sligo in the mid 1600s.] They lived at a place called Kilmorgan not far from Sligo. I do not know how long they lived there, but I read in an old book that Mary Harloe, daughter of William Harloe of Willowbank, Co. Sligo, married a Trumble of Kilmorgan in 1723 or 5. Her son Harloe Trumble, was my great grandfather. He had two sons, Thomas and William. His wife was Elisabeth Sodan. His four daughters all married, Mary Knott, Catherine Phibbs, Elizabeth Gethin and Eleanor Powel. Their crest was a bull's head and motto "courage". Some ancestor had saved a king's life, said to be King James the first of Scotland, by coming between him and a wild bull. The result [was a grant of] these lands in Ireland, Kilmorgan, Lughany Dove and Knockmunnagh. I remember the house at Kilmorgan as a long low building covered with ivy. It was of course said to be haunted, but only by a little friendly old woman dressed in old-fashioned green kirtle and red petticoat. Behind the house was what I remember as a big wood in which there lived many crows. One of my

pleasures was to sit on the doorstep and watch for the crows returning to their nests in the evening."

1816-1830   The Caribbean and Niagara

During the latter stages of the War of 1812, Dr. William Trumble (or Trumbull in British documents) had been employed in Canada as an assistant surgeon, and had given Mary's father some medical advice about healing his knee wound. Dr. Trumble was with the British 37th Regiment of Foot (North Hampshire regiment).

The next posting for Dr. William Trumble in the late summer of 1816 was to Kingston, Jamaica, where their elder daughter, Elizabeth, was born on 27 March 1817. Within another couple of years the family had moved to British Honduras (Belize) where Mary delivered a second daughter, also called Mary. Sadly, Dr. Trumble died of sunstroke there in early 1822.

As Laura Mack described it:
"Mrs. Trumble returned to Canada and had a fearful experience on the way, their ship being pursued by pirates. She told me she sat with a revolver in her hand, determined to sell her life dearly. She was a courageous woman and accustomed to danger. The pirates were quite close when a thick fog came on, when it cleared again there was no sign of the other boat. She was in Jamaica when the great negro insurrection took place, when many planters' houses were burned, themselves and their people killed, but I do not remember enough to tell any story. She and her daughters lived some years in Canada..."

Mary returned to Queenston in the late spring of 1822, a widow with her two small girls. Queenston was home for Mary, but not a place to live; they visited the family for a while, as she looked for accommodation.

Mary Secord Trumble's house (1822) in Niagara-on-the-Lake
Courtesy: Author's Collection

As part of the destruction of Niagara-on-the-Lake on the night of 10 December 1813, many dwellings were burned to the ground by enemy troops. One such building was a frame house on a ½ acre property on Lot 13 (today at the southwest corner of Front and Gate Streets); this property had originally been granted to Joseph Clement by the Crown in 1796. On 10 August 1822 the property was sold to Mary Secord Trumble, the widow of an Irish surgeon in the employ of the British Army in the Caribbean. At £56.5.0, this was a good price for Mary, who was the eldest daughter of James Secord and the now-famous Laura Ingersoll of Queenston. She rebuilt a dwelling house on the property in late 1822; this house still exists, with an 1860s extension, at 168 Front Street. To reimburse some of her house-building costs, Mary then sold the ¼ acre of garden on the corner of Gate Street to Charles Rowe [and today the Oban Inn stands on his property]. She and her two daughters, Elizabeth and Mary lived in the house for the next five years until 26 May 1830 when she sold the house with its ¼ acre to James C. Crysler, of the now-well-known automobile maker's family, for £150. The house overlooked Lake

Ontario and the military land that ultimately became the oldest golf course in Canada.

Oban Inn (left) and Mary Trumble's house (right) in earlier architecture
Courtesy: Oban Inn

The land records for Mary Trumble's home in Niagara-on-the-Lake are as follows:
"On 10 Aug 1822 (Reg 10 Jun 1830) John B Church et ux sold to Mary Trumble all ½ acre in Lot 13 for £56.5 (7953);
On 5 Apr 1825 (Reg 8 Feb 1833) Mary Trumble sold to Charles Rowe the southwest ¼ acre in Lot 13 for £28.2.6 (9010);
On 26 May 1830 (Reg 16 Jul 1830) Mary Trumble sold to James C Crysler ¼ acre with dwelling house in the north part of Lot 13, for £150 (7989)."[3]

During her sojourn in Niagara-on-the-Lake, Mary Secord Trumble would have been acquainted with many of leading residents of the town and other dignitaries – Sir Peregrine Maitland (Lieut. Governor of Upper Canada 1818-1828, and friend to her father), Rev. Robert and Rebecca Addison, Dr. James and Deborah Muirhead, William and Catherine Claus,

---

[3] Niagara Settlers Land Records in this book come from Abstracts of Deeds Registers (1796-1865) in a new website established by R. Robert Mutrie: https://sites.google.com/site/niagarasettlers2/

Ralfe and Elizabeth Clench, Andrew and Elizabeth Heron, and the various merchants along Queen Street.

1830-1876   Life in Ireland

Early in 1830 Mary Secord Trumble, her two children and her sister Charlotte left Niagara to take ownership of her in-laws' estate in County Sligo, Ireland.

Kilmorgan, County Sligo
Courtesy: Google Maps

The Trumbles were still on their farm in Kilmorgan during the 1820s. Harloe and Elisabeth had had two sons and four daughters; the sisters were all well married and their second son Thomas had apparently died young. So the widow of their son Dr. William Trumble was the heir to this farm 3,200 miles away to the east across the Atlantic. When the news came in 1829 that her father-in-law, Harloe Trumble, was failing in health and the farm needed another firm hand, Mary decided to sell her house in Niagara-on-the-Lake and prepare for her move to Ireland. She had not found another husband during her eight-year sojourn in Niagara and her in-laws probably made the offer of an interesting life in County Sligo. Dr. Trumble had had welcoming and generous Irish parents who had decided to leave their estate to his widow Mary after their days. Mary's husband had also left her with a good pension from his medical services to the British Army, so she was able to take on this responsibility.

Picking up Laura Mack's description of her family:
"Then came the news of Harloe Trumble's death, and she went over to Ireland, to look after her inheritance there. That voyage was not to pass without its troubles too. The captain of the vessel

was a cruel, bad man. My grandmother is said to have been a fine looking woman, and he made love to her, which she resented. This boat was a slave trader; they were to carry slaves back to America. He locked my Grannie up in her room, and her two children he shut up in one of the slave cells. They were boarded with openings between as to be able to put in water and food without opening the door. There these two children had to stay without food or water according to his decree, but the sailors thought a pity of them, and when they had an opportunity they gave them what they could. My mother has told me that she remembers quite well getting ships biscuits so hard that they had to tramp on them to break them, and they were full of worms so bad they were, but all the same the children were so hungry they ate them and thought them very good. Grannie was brought up or down, I do not know which, to see her children, but she would not yield to him. At last the sailors mutinied, he was cruel to them too of course. They put the captain in irons and freed my Grannie and the children. But the law was so strict those days, gave captains of vessels such absolute power that although she told the court all that had happened, she could only get the sailors pardoned, they would not punish the captain."

After her ordeal on the trans-Atlantic voyage and facing the significant challenge of running a farm in a foreign country, Mary sought assistance from Charlotte to look after the teenage children and help with the farm in Ireland. Charlotte's availability, and her lifelong unmarried status, may possibly have stemmed from her love for another officer who died in the Caribbean. And so Charlotte visited her elder sister for an extended period of time on the Trumble farm in County Sligo. Although she returned after a few years, Laura and James never saw their eldest daughter again.

Mary and her two daughters arrived in Ireland at a time when there was a great flood of emigration that was permanently altering the character of Ireland. Over the two generations before Mary arrived in the late summer of 1830, the population of the country almost quadrupled. Since the vast majority was already living in the most abject poverty even before this increase, a disaster was clearly in the making. This population increase had been overwhelmingly the poorest labouring classes, and it was these Irish labourers and their families who saw the most value in emigration. Although many other factors contributed to the reasons for such emigration, the fundamental cause was population growth.

The relative prosperity brought about by rising prices during Napoleonic wars from 1790 to 1814 had encouraged early marriage, lowered infant mortality and made it possible for more people to exist off smaller holdings. In the aftermath of the Napoleonic wars there was an immediate and dramatic economic slump: prices fell precipitously, major industries collapsed, investment and growth stagnated, and unemployment and destitution became widespread. The resulting depression was accompanied by a series of natural catastrophes.

After crop failures in 1825-30, famine was averted only by the import of large amounts of Indian meal from America. Throughout the early 1830s, cholera repeatedly ravaged the poorest classes, and, in the decade as a whole, the potato crop failed on a local level in eight out of the ten years. 1838 saw a savage winter, and "on the night of the big wind", snow buried on the cottages and cattle froze to death in the fields. Finally, in 1840-1844, the potato crops partly failed three more times. Small wonder that the Irish should feel God had abandoned them. By 1800, despite poverty and disease, emigrants to North America and Australia had reached 4,500,000; by 1841 it was 8,100,000.

During Mary and her daughters' time on the Trumble farm life was difficult for the owners, but totally intolerable for the poor Irish farm labourers and locals in the area around Kilmorgan. If labourers were lucky, they immigrated to Canada; if they were too poor or sick, they just died of starvation. Some simply stayed on the land and became disenchanted by English legal and political oppression. Maintaining the farm and finding loyal workers was difficult.

As Laura Mack continued:

"My grandmother [Mary Lawrence Secord Trumble] was a widow when she came to Ireland. She had a great deal of trouble with the people round about. I have heard my father say that her relations tried to get all they could from her; she knew nothing of Ireland or perhaps of business either. The peasants refused to pay rent, and sometimes tried to kill her. She has told us many a story of that time which unfortunately I have quite forgotten. Those years from 1840 nearly to 1850 were bad years for Ireland. There was the great famine and the plague during those years. So she sold Kilmorgan [in 1855]. I was there twice, and I suppose I was five or six at the time. I remember going with my mother to visit her. We went by coach, no railways in Ireland those days. We stayed the night at Enniskillen and on the next day to Sligo, then longcar to Ballymote, jaunting car to Kilmorgan, a long journey.

The Trumbles had of course a banshee who wailed over the house whenever any misfortune was impending; and I must not forget, if any member was about to die, a huge black carriage, four horses equally black and a headless driver, galloped up to the hall door and then disappeared. I was there when she moved from the house and remember sleeping the last night on the floor with a big, old-fashioned coat with many capes and collars over me. Also when we drove off on the car all the peasants [were] following after us crying and wailing.

Another incident I remember. I and my grandmother were standing in the hall door when I saw a man with a wooden leg coming up the drive, he had a gun over his shoulder. I do not know what he wanted. Whatever it was, she would not give in to him, and he raised the gun and fired. The bullet went into the door. What more happened is rather shadowy. I have an idea she stood there and scolded him; I crept in behind her skirts. She was a very courageous woman."

In June 1855 Mary Trumble, a widow and Mary Trumble, spinster [her daughter], offered for sale their property at Kilmorgan, barony of Corran, county Sligo. Their property was purchased by members of the Duke family. It had been 25 years of hard work and close scrutiny of the local Irish farm labourers for Mary on her farm during the period of the Great Famine and the worst days in Irish history for the poor Irish folk of the Kilmorgan, County Sligo area. Mary was now 56 years old and ready for retirement.

Her elder daughter Elizabeth had been courted by a banker, William Henry Davis. He was born in June 1815 at Belturbet, County Cavan. As Laura Mack recollected:
"[His] father was born in Tipperary, and his mother was a Southerner, lived in a place called Gorey in Wexford near the coast. He lived in the South till 1830 at least, perhaps longer. Gerty has an old prayerbook printed 1790 in Dublin that his mother got in 1800 as some sort of a prize when she lived in Gorey."

William and Elizabeth married in June 1844 at Lisnagore church, just 8 miles east of Trumble farm, on the other side of Ballymote in County Sligo. Mary's younger daughter, Mary remained unmarried.

Elizabeth Trumble   William Henry Davis
Courtesy: Eldrid Ingebjørg Mageli

105

Charlotte, who had supported her elder sister in the early days on the farm in County Sligo, lived most of her life in Chippawa and Guelph, Ontario until late in her mother's life. After the administration of Laura Secord's will in the early 1870s, Charlotte visited Ireland once more before she retired to Guelph where she died in Mayor Lamprey's house on Waterloo Avenue in October 1880, aged 72.

Mary Lawrence Secord Trumble, now a wealthy widow with investments and a good pension, could live comfortably for the rest of her life in Dublin, Ireland, where she died in 1876 at age 79.

In Mount Jerome Cemetery in Dublin, an extant grave marker No. 4313 states:

"Sacred To the Memory of MARY TRUMBLE, widow of the late WILLIAM TRUMBLE Esq., M.D., Staff Surgeon, who died March 11th 1876 aged 73. Yea though I walk through the valley of the shadow of death I will fear no evil for thou art with me. Psalm 23.
Thanks be to God which giveth us the victory through Our Lord Jesus Christ. 1 Cor. XV. 57."

Mary Lawrence Secord Trumble
Courtesy: Eldrid Ingebjørg Mageli

1860-1922   Early Strife in Northern Ireland

Laura Mack added a brief description of her father's family:
"My father [William H. Davis] told me about his family as
follows: The two brothers of the name Davis joined the Duke of
Monmouth's troops [in 1685 against catholic King James II of
England]. After his defeat [at the Battle of Sedgemoor on 6 July
1685] they fled to Ireland. Richard went North, Thomas south.
The latter became a priest. The people were very fond of him
and looked up to him as to a saint. After his death, while lying in
state, an old woman, who had been lame for many years,
touched his hand and was able to walk without her crutches. He
was proclaimed a saint at once, and my father told me that when
he was in Tipperary as a young man, people still made
pilgrimages to his grave."

Laura Mack continues:
"Richard settled in the North was, or turned protestant. When
his brother the priest died, all his books and other possessions
were sent up to Richard, who made a grand bonfire of them, he
would have nothing belonging to a "papist". His son, Richard
too, married 1733 Mary Ann Patterson, daughter of George
Patterson of Tyrgormerly. His son or grandson married Jane
Beck 1813. Her mother was Margaret Newland, daughter of
Henry Newland, Tutor of Trinity College and Dean of
Rath[breasail, Ferns, Wexford], I forget the name. My father's
grandfather took an active part in the rebellion of 1795 against
the catholics. He rode round the country with important
messages and to warn people of intended attacks on the part of
the rebels. There were no telegrams or telephones those days,
hardly any post, communication and roads were bad. It was
dangerous to have any written matter if one were caught and
searched, so they had an ingenious device, filled their pockets
with straw cut in a peculiar manner or bits of wood, each of
which had a meaning. People rode around the lanes calling here
and there, leaving behind them dumb messages. My father's two
sisters, Mary Ann and Fanny, and also his brother Richard, died
unmarried at Prospect Hill, Cavan."

"We were 6 children: William Henry Newland went to America married there, one girl three boys, died when 72 years old. Never seen either wife or children. I myself married 1872 Fredrik Mack, Lieutenant Norwegian army, afterwards Byretsassessor [City Assessor] and Krigsdommer [Military Judge] in Norway. My sister Edith, not married, died of cancer in 1919, 21 Malone Park, Belfast, Ireland. 2nd sister Gertrude living now same place, also my brothers Stuart (Col IMS.) and Fred. Stuart lived for many years in Rangoon [Burma], was what they call a "big Bug" out there, now retired. My mother died 1893 of heart disease, my father the year following in April. He was bank manager first Armagh [Northern Ireland], where we three eldest children were born, then Dungannon and lastly Belfast, where he died. The house in which I was born, "Avon Lodge" was said to be haunted. Many strange noises were heard there, such as of a big bundle of pots and pans were being thrown down the stairs, or that thieves were breaking down the shutters, washstands and basins dancing with jungling things in them. Also a ghost, a major, who was said to have hanged himself there. My father said he often sat up at night with a gun, he was so sure somebody was trying to break in. "

"My father and I travelled a good deal through Europe. Our last journey together was to Norway. There in 1871 I met my husband at Gudvangen. We slept at a little inn there. My sister Edith and I were awakened during the night by men marching and commands. We got up to see what was going on. There were soldiers leaving small steamers, and an officer commanding them. It was summer and daylight. We met the officer at breakfast next morning and joined company with him first to Bergen then up to Molde. We met again next year and were married in September 1872."

Before Laura Mack finished the message to her children, she wrote some experiences of her life in Northern Ireland:
 "At the time of the riots we lived in the country a little outside Belfast. My mother and I took train in to do some shopping. She left me in a shop, while she went to do some further business, as the streets were full of crowds of excited men and women, police riding, marching here and there... My mother returned, and we

had some difficulty in getting through the town and in starting, as they were afraid the rails had been tamped with. She of course, had no idea when we started that the town was in such a state. We could not see the actual fighting, but heard the guns and saw the men trying to escape… Our train was going slowly for fear of accidents. I remember well the long stretch of mud and the struggling figures on it. Close to the train I saw three men up to their necks in a drain. They were hiding there for fear of the bullets, which were sweeping across the mud every now and then… At one time we had two regiments camped in fields behind our house, and at either end of the next avenue soldiers had built up little shelters of sandbags and controlled all people going into and out of town. We could not use the car very much, only for very short distances, and the curfew must have been very disagreeable for many."

1831-1928   Fjords and Family

Within nine months of their marriage on 25 September 1872 and leaving Ireland, Laura Mary Davis Mack and her husband Fredrik had their first son, Harald, followed shortly by daughter, Edith and Nanna Elizabeth. Caring for young children and learning Norwegian in Tromsø kept Laura Mack busy. However, with three children under the age of seven, the family moved to Oslo to accommodate Fredrik's job. Over the next 15 years, Fredrik and Laura Mack had three more children - Dermot, Freddy and Gerda (she died as a small child). The five surviving

Laura Mary Davis Mack
early in her marriage.
Courtesy: Eldrid Ingebjørg Mageli

children all married and produced 16 grandchildren over the years up to 1922.

And so it was at age 81, with her eldest granddaughter Henriette Laura (Etti) Astrup being in her late twenties and about to get married, that Laura Mary Davis Mack took up her pen and started to piece together the family history in 1928, as her legacy *'To My Children'*. Eighty-five years later Eldrid Ingebjørg Mageli, Freddy Mack's granddaughter, donated this exciting evidence about Laura Secord's eldest daughter Mary for the author's transcription into this book.

Laura Ingersoll Secord m. James Secord

Charles Badeau Secord m. Margaret Ann Robins

Charles Forsyth (Prof.) Secord m.(1) Elizabeth Ellis
    Children (1): Charles Frederick Secord
        Agnes Elizabeth Secord
        Appalonia (Lona) Joseph Secord
        William Henry Secord
        Frank Alexander Secord
        Anna Secord
        Claude Secord
        Jesse Secord
        Margaret (Ella) Secord
                m.(2) Elizabeth Nancy Neff
    Children (2): **Clayton (Carlos) Forsythe (Dr.) Secord**
        Harold R. Secord
        Ross H. Secord
        Cyril Paul Secord
        Geraldine A. Secord

James Badeau Secord m. Clara Flint
Alicia Secord m.(1) Joseph Clayton; (2) Isaac Cockburn

A Mission in Guatemala, 1900-1928

Laura Secord's only son, Charles Badeau Secord (1809-1872), became an attorney and married Margaret Ann Robins (1813-1872) in 1830. Of their three children, only their elder son, Professor Charles Forsyth Secord (1833-1899) had issue. In 1851 Charles Forsyth Secord taught school in Niagara Falls, but he moved his family to DeWitt, Nebraska in 1862. By his first wife Elizabeth Ellis (1835-1871), who moved with him to the U.S.A., he had nine children; his second wife, Elizabeth (Liza) Nancy Neff (1844-1931) gave him five more children, the eldest of whom was Dr. Clayton (Carlos) Forsythe Secord (1874-1955).

Dr. C. F. Secord was born in Blair, Nebraska in 1874 and in his teenage years worked part-time in a print shop. He attended medical school in Ohio; after graduating he went to medical school in France to specialize in poisons. Upon returning to the USA he married and went into the missionary field for the Primitive Methodist Evangelical Church. He began his independent medical missionary work in Guatemala in 1900, built his church, Santo Tomas di Chichicastenango. Dr. Secord was the first North American missionary to dedicate his work exclusively to the Indians. His unique work as a medical doctor and evangelist of that day, based in the highland town of Chichicastenango, was noted by the Central American Mission (U.S.-based Indian mission development organization working in Guatemala, etc.) and many others. Although he largely shunned denominational affiliations, Dr. Secord held a loose association with the Plymouth Brethren, a conservative and militantly anti-Catholic strain of Protestantism. He was also a supporter of the establishment of conservative churches known as Salas Evangelicas that became important in the 1920s. Dr.

Secord published a Spanish magazine called *El Protestante* at least from 1910-1912; some copies may be found in the Archivo General de Centroamerica (Seccion Hemeroteca). His address before the Medical Missionary Conference, "The Indians of Central America" was published in The Medical Missionary, International Health & Temperance Association in 1912. He was a prominent missionary voice at the 1916 Panama Conference; the proceedings (and his involvement) may be found in Christian Work in Latin America, published in 1917 and in the archives of Union Theological Seminary in New York.

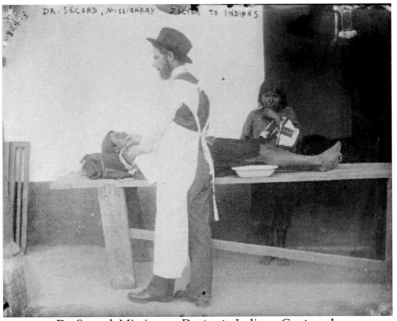

Dr. Secord, Missionary Doctor to Indians, Guatemala
Courtesy: Amazon, Newswire Photo (XL)

In his paper of 1912 to the Medical Missionary Conference, Dr. Secord wrote:
"There are about one million Indians in the republic of Guatemala, which is the largest republic of Central America, ruled today by a very brilliant lawyer, Mr. Cabrera, a man of progress and of civilized ideas, who struggles for the good of his people. I have had several private interviews with President Cabrera, and he understands just what the Gospel is and what is its purpose.

Until the year 1900, absolutely no efforts had been made to evangelize the Indians of Guatemala, called the Quiche Indians. At that time, feeling the need of these people, I left the United States, accompanied by my wife, and located in the center of the Quiche nation in the mountains of Guatemala. The most violent opposition was at once raised against us, and for several years we were in hourly danger of death, so much so that when the clouds blew away I was a little bit surprised; I had really expected them to do something. I was taken once to be hanged, and they said they intended afterward to burn me. They were going to do that because I had advised one of our first Indian brethren to burn his idol and throw the ashes in the river right below his house. They were going to apply the same treatment to me. I have been shot at several times, and once poisoned. On that occasion I was delirious for twelve hours, and I was so sick for three days I could not think of what medicine to take...

Dr. C. F. Secord
Taken from Medical Missionary
Conference record, 1912.

I do not believe that the Gospel would ever have entered the Quiche land except through the medicine case and the instrument case. I have literally cut my way through the palace of the governor to the cornstalk hovel of the poorest Indian. I have entered their houses and treated them successfully from one extreme to the other of the country... Today, thanks to our medical work, we have a large following of true believers in Jesus Christ."

Dr. Secord was well known in Guatemala and gained the recognition of President Cabrera when the President decided to find a long-buried treasure as part of his plan to make five Central American republics into one. The President had approached Dr. Secord for assistance in persuading the natives he knew so well. On 25 August 1913, The Toronto World published:

"Omaha, Neb. Aug. 23 - The treasure of the Toltec kings of Central America, worth hundreds of millions of dollars, hidden by the Indians upon the approach of the Spanish expedition after Cortez's conquest, will be used by President Cabrera of Guatemala to cement the five Central American States into one republic - provided he can find the treasure, says Dr. Charles F. Secord, long a medical missionary in Guatemala.

Dr. Secord is now in the United States on a scientific mission for President Cabrera, and is visiting his mother in Omaha. The secret of the treasure's hiding place has been held by the "witch doctor" caste of natives, and the whites have never been successful in learning the secret.

'I know that the treasure exists,' says Dr. Secord. 'I have seen and handled small images of gold, and once I was shown a great disk of gold that must have been worth a small fortune. I was informed that the images were from the secret hoard of the Indians, but no white man who values his life will attempt to discover that secret unless he be backed by a good sized army.'

D. Secord left a lucrative practice in Omaha and with his wife fifteen years ago went into the wilds of Guatemala. He was not attached to nor accredited by any church or missionary society. He did his work without pay and had to earn his living. He obtained the consent of the government to devote his services to the Indians.

Chichicastenango, Guatemala
Background image from Google Maps

'At first,' says Dr. Secord, 'the Indians were opposed to my coming among them. My life was attempted several times. I had to guard against poison in everything I ate. One somebody threw half a dozen venomous snakes into my room.'

114

'The witch doctors use snake venom as a cure for tuberculosis, and I have seen some remarkable cures by them. When I had been in Guatemala about a year the son of the chief witch doctor had an accident and I saved the boy's life. That made the witch doctor my friend, and I have had a comparatively easy time since.'

'It was from this old witch doctor chief that I learned the story of the great treasure, and from the government authorities that they intended making an effort at locating it. The Indians expect, some time, to use it to place their king on his throne, and for this reason they guard it jealously. It would be death to any man not of the witch clan to learn its hiding place.'

'The government has attempted to locate the treasure three times. The last attempt was made forty or fifty years ago. The means used were just what might have been expected at that time. Members of the witch clan were arrested and thrown into prison. Then, one by one, they were tortured.'

'Every means of torture known to the Central American Spaniard of fifty years ago, with the training of a thousand years back, were used against the witch doctors. I am told not a man whimpered. Not a clue of the treasure was obtained.'

'I have the confidence of the witch doctors, but they will not tell me the hiding place. And I would not have them do so. If I knew where the treasure cave is my life would be worthless. I could never get out of the country alive.' "

Dr. Secord also had a close relationship with local and national governments in Central America. He was regularly mentioned by the town council of Chichicastenango for his medical advice, and he had a close relationship with church-educated Guatemalan President Manuel Estrada Cabrera, who ruled from 1898-1920. He was Cabrera's personal doctor, and later for Guatemala President Juan Jose Arebalo Bermejo. Dr. Secord was also the personal medical advisor for the Nicaraguan President, Anastasio Somoza. For a short period after Cabrera's political demise in April 1920, the new administration expelled Dr. Secord from the country based on accusations of espionage. Sadly, his first wife, Susan Hazel James of Searsboro, Iowa (1874-c.1920), and daughter, Rachael, were kidnapped and disappeared on a trip to Mexico during this same period. Under these strange circumstances, Dr. Secord had to wait seven years and was then free to remarry. However, through years of personal turmoil he continued to maintain focus on his work.

Starting in the early 1920s the mission began to look for missionaries who would live among the Indian populations, learn their languages, and teach them the Bible. By the mid-1920s he had returned to Guatemala and merged his ministry and church with the Primitive Methodist Church ("PMC"); and he continued his ministry under PMC auspices. Although Dr. Secord's work was independent, the PMC absorbed most of his converts. Dr. Secord retired from missionary work in 1928, and the following year, at the age of 55, he married Cristina Alvarado-Mota (1909-1967), a local teacher from Guatemala City. He continued his medical work at the hospital that he had built with a US$85,000 family inheritance. Starting in 1931 they had five children in the aboriginal Mayan town of Chichicastenango.

At age 63, Dr. Secord and his family turned over the hospital in Chichicastenango to other missionaries and moved to Guatemala City on 7 August 1937. He purchased a property there and continued practicing medicine. The last child, Milton Paul Secord, was born in Guatemala City in 1943. By this time, these children represented the only direct descendants of Laura and James Secord carrying the Secord surname - all born in Guatemala.

In Guatemala City, Dr. Secord became a writer for a local magazine and had a radio program in 'La Voz de las Americas' called "the Hour of Philosophy from Dr. C. F. Secord". During a lifetime of service to the local community in Guatemala, he continued to provide for his family until January 1955 when he had a heart attack and passed away at age 81. Dr. Clayton (Jose) F. Secord had been an extraordinary evangelist and doctor to the Indians, a trusted medical advisor to Central American country Presidents, the founder of a local hospital in Chichicastenango, Guatemala and cherished father in his family, some of whom have now returned to the United States and continue to provide support for his legacy.

Clayton Forsythe Secord   Cristina Alvarado-Mota
Courtesy: Milton Paul Secord

These children of Clayton F. and Cristina Secord, born in Guatemala, are the only known all-male descendant line of James Secord, the husband of Laura Ingersoll Secord:

L->R: Robert Edward Secord (dec.), Clayton Charles Secord,
Frederick Albert Secord, Arnold Franklin Secord, Milton Paul Secord
Courtesy: Milton Paul Secord

Research into the lives of Laura Ingersoll Secord and her family remains active. The author continues to seek new letters, artefacts and photographs.

If you have any new material, the publisher would be interested: bygonespublishing @ gmail.com .

Petitions, Letters, Publicity, and Plaques, War Claim

This section provides the complete texts for the primary petitions, letters, publicity and plaques that relate to Laura Secord, her husband James, and her only son, Charles. These are generally in chronological order of Laura Ingersoll Secord's life.

Petitions

Petition, James and David Secord – 1795
Petition, James Secord – 1797
Petition, James Secord, Stone Quarry – 1820
Petition, FitzGibbon Certificate – 1820
Petition, James Secord, Military Pension – 1823
Petition, FitzGibbon Certificate – 1827
Petition, James Secord, Militia Pension – 1832
Award, Collector Customs for Chippawa, James Secord – 1835
Petition, FitzGibbon Certificate – 1837
Petition, Laura Secord, Queenston Ferry – 1839
Petition, Laura Secord, in support of her son Charles - 1841
Petition, Laura Secord, Pension – 1841
Petition, Charles Secord, Collector Customs, Chippawa – 1841
Petition, Charles Secord, Collector Customs, Chippawa – 1842
Petition, Charles Secord, in support of FitzGibbon – 1845
Petition, Laura Secord, Prince of Wales – 1860

Letters

Letter of James Secord to Mrs. Hitchcock (Laura's sister) – 1829
Letters (3) from Laura Secord to her sister – 1841, 1843, 1844
Last Will and Testament, Laura Secord – 1857
Letter from Elizabeth Ann Stewart Secord Gregory – 1884
Recollections of Miss Augusta Smith, of Guelph – abt 1900
Recollections of Miss Laura Secord Clarke – 1928
Tributes to the Memory of Laura Secord – 1890s
Laura's Legacy rises later in the Berkshires, Massachusetts

Publicity in the early years

Auchinleck – 1853
Lossing – 1861
Coffin – 1864
FitzGibbon – 1894
Curzon and Currie – 1883-1913

Plaques about Laura Secord's heroic act

Plaque, House at Great Barrington, Massachusetts
Plaque, Queenston Village, Ontario
Plaque, House at Queenston, Ontario
Plaque, Homestead at Queenston, Ontario
Plaque, Beaver Dams Battlefield park, Ontario
Plaque, Beaver Dams Battlefield park, Ontario
Plaque, House at Chippawa, Ontario
Plaque, Church at Chippawa, Ontario

War Claim

War Claim of James Secord of Queenston – after 1815

Petitions

These first two petitions are from the youngest son of a United Empire Loyalist, who with his elder sons served their new country in the American Revolutionary War. In those days, the sons of U.E.L. settlers were empowered to petition for land in their own names.

Petition, James and David Secord - 1795
To His Excellency John Graves Simcoe Esq., Lieut. Governor and Commander in Chief of Upper Canada, etc., etc., etc., in Council. The Petition of James & David Secord.
Humbly sheweth
That your Petitioners' father James Secord deceased having Joined his Majesty's as early as the year 1777 and brought to his Post forty six Loyal subjects all which joined his Majesty's Standard, and in the year following he also brought to his Post his family consisting of a Wife and Seven Children, three of which Joined Col. Butler's Rangers and served during the War – Your Petitioners' father likewise served as a Lieut. In the Six Nation Indian Department and having received five Hundred Acres Land hopes your Excellency will assign your Petitioners such further quantity of Land as they may be entitled to – And your Petitioners as in duty bound shall ever Pray.
(signed) James & David Secord
Endorsed –   rec'd Augt. 3rd 1795
               1500 Acres to make up the quantity to two
               thousand Acres to be granted to the Heirs of
               James Secord. Read in Council Augt. 3rd 1795

Petition, James Secord - 1797
"Respectfully Sheweth: That your Petitioner gave in some time past a Petition stating the services of his Father [Lieut. James Secord] during the late War between Great Britain and America and of his having Brothers in Col. Butler's Rangers, one of whom held the Rank of Lieutenant (Solomon Secord). The others were Stephen and David.

That your Petitioner's Father brought in to this Province, about forty men who all joined Col. Butler's late Corps of Rangers and for which he was promised a Company of said Corps, but was afterwards withheld from him.

That your Petitioner is the brother-in-law to the Honorable Richard Cartwright and having only received two hundred acres, prays your Honor would be pleased to reconsider him, and grant him such an addition of Lands as your Honor may think proper, and your Petitioner as in duty bound will ever pray.

Niagara, Jan. 12, 1797   James Secord, Jr.

Endorsed & Read Feb. 25, 1797.

Recommended for 600 acres, including what he has already received. See a former petition."

Petition, James Secord, Stone Quarry - 1820

One of James Secord's opportunistic petitions was for ownership of a Stone Quarry on military land near Queenston during this post-War period. It reads:

"To His Excellency Sir Peregrine Maitland, K. C. B., Lieutenant Governor of the Province of Upper Canada and Major General Commanding His Majesty's Forces in Upper and Lower Canadian, &c., &c., &c.

The Petition of James Secord, Senior, of the Village of Queenston, Esquire.

Humbly Sheweth

That your Petitioner is one of the Oldest inhabitants of this Province, has had numerous Relatives in the British Army, is Brother-in-Law to the late Honourable Richard Cartwright, is Captain in the 2nd Regiment of Lincoln Militia, was wounded in the battle of Queenston, and twice plundered of all his Moveable property. That his Wife embraced an opportunity of rendering some service at the risk of her life, in going thro' the Enemies' Lines to communicate information to a Detachment of His Majesty's Troops at the Beaver Dams in the month of June 1813. That Your Excellency's Petitioner is desirous of obtain license of Occupation of so much of the Military Reserve at Queenston as is described by Captain Vavasour of the Royal Engineers now stationed at Fort George, including a Stone Quarry, a sketch which is transmitted by Capt. Vavasour.

122

Wherefore your Petitioner prays that Your Excellency may be pleased to grant him a license of occupation of that part of the Military reserve described by Captain Vavasour, subject to such conditions, restrictions and limitations as Your Excellency may be pleased to impose.

And Your petitioner will ever pray.

J. Secord, Senr.

"York   25th February, 1820."

Petition, FitzGibbon Certificate – 1820

Laura Secord had requested Captain James FitzGibbon to provide her with a Certificate to support James' petition (above). This certificate, the original of which was sent to the Lieutenant-Governor's office (in error) by Laura Secord without making a copy, was found in 1959, long after the early detractors had been defused. It clearly stated that Laura Secord had informed FitzGibbon on 22 June 1813, before the main contingent of American troops had left Fort George:

"I certify that Mrs. Secord, Wife of James Secord of Queenston, Esquire, did in the Month of June, 1813, come to the Beaver Dam and communicate to me information of an intended attack to be made by the Enemy upon the Detachment then under my command there, which occasionally occupied a large Stone House at the place. The information was substantially correct, and a detachment did march for the Beaver Dam, (on the morning of the second day after the information was given) under the command of Lieut. Colonel Boerstler, which detachment was captured. Mrs. Secord arrived at my station about sunset of an excessively warm day, after having walked twelve miles, which I at the time thought was an exertion which a person of her slender frame and delicate appearance was unequal to make.

"James FitzGibbon"

Captn. Half Pay

York   26th February, 1820 "Late Glengy, Lt. Infantry"

Petition, James Secord, Military Pension - 1823
To enhance his family's income, James Secord also pursued a military compensation petition to the Lieutenant Governor Sir Peregrine Maitland in 1823. He wrote:
"Upper Canada
I hereby declare that I have not received or applied for any Gratuity or Allowance whatsoever on account of a Wound received by me in Action with the Enemy at Queenston on the thirteenth day of October one thousand eight hundred and twelve, through any other channel except that of His Excellency Sir Peregrine Maitland to the Earl of Dalhousie.
James Secord Senr.
Capt. 1st Reg't Militia
Queenston, 18th February 1823".

As a result, Maitland sent the following memorandum to Colonel Darling, the Military Secretary:
"York, Upper Canada, 8 March 1823
Sir,
I have the Honor to forward to you the certificates necessary in order to the issue of one years pay to Captain James Secord of the 1st Regt. Of Lincoln Militia, as authorized by the Secretary at War's letter of the 20 August last No. 167784.
I have the honor to be etc.
P. Maitland
M.G. Comm'g U.C."

Petition, FitzGibbon Certificate - 1827
In the Public Archives of Canada is the second certificate from FitzGibbon, which Laura Secord sent to the Lieutenant-Governor's office (in error) without making a copy. It was rediscovered by Henry Cartwright Secord and published in the Mail & Empire in 1934, although the Niagara Historical Society had informed its readers of the certificate's existence a decade earlier. It states that Laura Secord communicated with FitzGibbon on the evening of 22 June 1813, which was before the main contingent of Americans troops had left Fort George:
"York, 11 May 1827

I do hereby Certify that on the 22d. day of June 1813, Mrs. Secord, Wife of James Secord, Esqr. then of St. David's, came to me at the Beaver Dam after SunSet, having come from her House at St. David's by a circuitous route a distance of twelve miles, and informed me that her Husband had learnt from an American officer the preceding night that a Detachment from the American Army then at Fort George would be sent out on the following morning (the 23rd.) for the purpose of Surprising and capturing a Detachment of the 49th Regt. then at the Beaver Dam under my command. In Consequence of this information I placed the Indians under Norton together with my own Detachment in a Situation to intercept the American Detachment, and we occupied it during the night of the 22d. – but the Enemy did not come until the morning of the 24th when his Detachment was captured.

Colonel Boerstler, their commander, in a conversation with me confirmed fully the information communicated to me by Mrs. Secord, and accounted for the attempt not having been made on the 23rd, as at first intended.

The weather on the 22d. was very hot, and Mrs. Secord whose person was slight and delicate appeared to have been and no doubt was very much exhausted by the exertion She made in coming to me, and I have ever since held myself personally indebted to her for her conduct upon that occasion, and I consider it an imperative duty on my part humbly and earnestly to recommend her to the favourable consideration of His Majesty's Provincial Government.

I beg leave to add that Mrs. Secord and her Family were entire Strangers to me before the 22d. of June 1813, her exertions therefore could have been made from public motives only.
[signed] James Fitzgibbon
[Endorsed] Mrs. Secord. 11 May 1827"

Petition, James Secord, Militia Pension - 1832

In 1832 James Secord realized, rather belatedly, that he could potentially use his Captaincy of the Militia to seek further remuneration from the Government. He wrote:

"To His Excellency Sir John Colborne K.C.B. Lieutenant Governor of the Province of Upper Canada, and Major General Commanding His Majesty's Forces therein. Etc. etc. etc.
The Petition of James Secord Senior, formerly a Captain in the 1st Regiment of Lincoln Militia.
Humbly Sheweth
That your Excellency's Petitioner was a Captain in the 1st Regiment of Lincoln Militia in the year of our Lord, One Thousand Eight hundred and twelve, when the Government of the United States of America declared war against Great Britain, that his residence being on the Frontier, he was one of those, who were peculiarly liable both in person and property to injury from the hostility of the Enemy.
That on the 13th of October in the year of our Lord, One thousand Eight hundred and twelve, when the attack was made on Queenston, he was with His Majesty's Troops, and the Militia engaged in its defence and during the Action of that day he received a severe wound and remained many months confined to his house, and still remains disabled in his left shoulder. But during the War, the Enemy having possession of the Frontier, from time to time gained possession of his residence and plundered him of every article they thought fit to carry away. That his losses in this way were considerable but being then in easy circumstances he cheerfully bore them.
That he devoted himself much to the Public Service, and principally in securing secret and confidential information for the general, and other Officers from time to time, acting on the frontier.
That he then never contemplated asking for or accepting remuneration for those services, but that the events attendant on a state of Warfare on the Frontier for three years had a most injurious effect on his affairs, which in connection with other circumstances, and the effect of his wound, have brought him with a numerous family into very distressed circumstances.
That as many Militia Officers, who belonged to the particular Corps to whom Land has been graciously granted, by the late Prince Regent in the year, One Thousand, Eight Hundred and twenty, have not performed so much service as your Excellency's Petitioner, nor suffered from wounds as he has, he is emboldened to hope that now in his present distressed

circumstances, and upon a review of his Services your Excellency may be pleased to consider favourably the prayer of this Petition, which is that your Excellency will be pleased to grant him Land as a Captain under the Militia General Order of the 21st January, 1820, but should your Excellency be restrained from granting him Land under that order, He prays that you will be pleased to recommend his case to the favourable consideration of His Majesty's Government in England, and as in duty bound, your Petitioner will ever pray.

J. Secord, Senr.
Late Capt. 1st Regt. Lincoln Militia
Queenston 18th July 1832

Copy of Minute of Council on the above Petition –
Recommended in consequence of his great Services, during the late War, as testified by the Adjutant General of Militia to the special consideration of His Excellency the Lieut. Governor.
J. Baby
Presiding Councillor
13 September 1832".

Award, Collector Customs for Chippawa, James Secord - 1835
In July 1835, James obtained the best-paying job of his life – as the Collector of Customs in Chippawa, which he held until his death in 1841 at the age of 67.
"Queenston, 18th July 1835
Sir,
I have the honor to acknowledge the receipt of your Letter of the 9th Inst. notifying me of my appointment to the Collectorship of the Port of Chippawa and, in consequence of that appointment, respectfully beg leave to resign my situation as Judge of the Niagara District Surrogate Court.
I have the honor to be Sir,
Your most ob'dt Ser't,
J. Secord Senr,

Col. Wm. Rowan
Sec'y L.G. etc. etc.
Toronto".

Petition, FitzGibbon Certificate - 1837

Ten years after writing the second certificate on behalf of Laura Secord, and awaiting another promotion, this time to Colonel of the Militia, FitzGibbon penned and signed this third certificate, the original of which was kept by Laura Secord:

Toronto, 23 February 1837.

"I do hereby Certify that Mrs. Secord, the Wife of James Secord of Chippawa Esquire, did in the month of June 1813 walk from her House in the village of St. David's to Decows House in Thorold by a circuitous rout[e], of about 20 miles partly through the Woods to acquaint me that the enemy intended to attempt by surprise to capture a detachment of the 49th Regiment then under my command she having obtained such knowledge from good authority as the event proved.

Mrs. Secord was a person of slight and delicate frame & made this effort in weather excessively warm & I dreaded at the time that she must suffer in health in consequence of fatigue and anxiety she having been exposed to danger from the enemy, through whose line of communication she had to pass. The attempt was made on my detachment, by the enemy and his detachment, consisting of upwards of 500 Men and with 2 field pieces and fifty Dragoons were captured in consequence.

I write this Certificate in a moment of much hurry and from memory, and it is therefore thus brief.

[Signed] James FitzGibbon

Formerly Lieut. in 49th Regiment"

Petition, Laura Secord, Queenston Ferry - 1839

In late 1839, Laura sent a petition seeking the Queenston ferry concession. As was common practice of the day, Laura embellished this petition in an attempt to increase the potential for a positive outcome. The text is as follows:

"To His Excellency Sir George Arthur K. C. H., Lieutenant Governor of Upper Canada, Major General commanding His Majesty's forces thereon, etc etc etc

In Council

The Memorial of Laura Secord of Chippawa

Respectfully Sheweth

That your Excellency's Memorialist did in the Month of June 1813 as the following Certificate of Colonel FitzGibbon will fully cor[r]oborate, did at great Risk, peril and danger travelling on foot & partly at Night by a circuitous rout(e), through woods, mountains, enemy's lines and Indian Encampments to give important intelligence of a meditated attack by the Americans upon our troops & by which means 550 of the enemy were captured with two field Pieces and which circumstance has been the foundation of a desease from which the foes never recovered & for which performance your Excellency's Memorialist has never Received the smallest compensation being now informed that the Ferry at Queenston is unoccupied she your Memorialist will take your Excellency's Memorialist Case into Kind consideration & grant her the Ferry at Queenston for a term of years, say from 7, 14 or 21 years.
Your Excellency's Memorialist would not now presume to ask any remuneration but from the circumstance of having a large family of Daughters and Grand-Daughters to provide for & for which the small means of Husband Captain James Secord Sen'r. with not meet & also from the circumstance of the Ferry of Fort Erie having been given the widow of the late Colonel Warren & your Excellency's Memorialist presumes to say for far less services than your Excellency's Memorialist has performed, however should your Excellency not se(e) fit to grant to your Memorialist the said Ferry at Queenston without Rent free that your Excellency will be pleased to offer a small Rent upon the same as you in your Judgment may seem Just & right leaving my £50 pension. Therefore all herein stated and considering her great claim & your Memorialist in different circumstances your Excellency will give her case just and equitable consideration. & as in Duty bound will ever pray,
Laura Secord"

Petition, Laura Secord, in support of her son Charles - 1841
A few days after James' burial, Laura penned a petition to Lieutenant-Governor Sydenham requesting that her son, Charles be appointed Collector of Customs in Chippawa to succeed her husband. Charles, married and living in the Secord homestead in Queenston, had already succeeded his father as Registrar of

the Niagara Surrogate Court in 1835. He was also a practicing attorney by this time.

"To His Excellency the Right Honorable Charles Baron Sydenham of Sydenham in the County of Kent and Toronto in Canada, and of His Majesty's Most Honorable Privy, Colonial Governor General of British North America and Captain General and Governor in Charge in and over our Province of Canada, Nova Scotia, New Brunswick and the Island of Prince Edward, and Vice Admiral of the same.
Memorial of Laura Secord of the village of Chippawa, widow of the late James Secord Sen.
Humbly represents
That your Memorialist's late husband held in his life time the office of Collector of Customs for Port Chippawa which becoming vacant by his death has left your Memorialist without any means of support and with two daughters and several grand-children depending entirely upon her. Your Memorialist has moved into this Province from the United States of America during the Revolutionary War and was all her life a firm supporter of the British Sovereign which the whole County will attest.
That your Memorialist has therefore ventured to apply to your Excellency for the appointment of Collector for her only son Charles that he will render her much assistance.
That your Memorialist is now an old woman and incapable of working or entering into any kind of business to support herself and those who could live with her for support.
That the services your Memorialist has rendered the British Government in this Province are well known and, as they have been already laid before the Government, being unnecessary to [re]state them at this time to your Excellency well, knowing that His Excellency Sir George Arthur will feel great pleasure in giving Your Excellency such information connected with the Memorialist and her dear late husband as may your Excellency in possession of all the facts which your Excellency may be desirous to know imparting their loyalty and respectability. Your Memorialist therefore trusts your Excellency will be pleased to take this case into consideration and in duty bound will ever pray.

Laura Secord
Chippawa 27th Feb'y 1841".

As a covering letter to this petition, Laura's son, Charles Secord
wrote:
"Queenston, 1 March 1841
Sir,
I have the honor herewith to carbon you a memorial from my
mother to His Excellency the Governor General praying His
Excellency to appoint me to the office of Collector at Port
Chippawa, vacant by the death of my much lamented father
which you will be so good as lay before His Excellency the
Deputy Governor that it may by him brought before His
Excellency the Governor General.
I have the honor to be Sir,
Your Meek and Humble Servant,
Charles B. Secord

for Samuel B. Harrison
Secretary to His Excellency the Deputy Governor".

Petition, Laura Secord, Pension - 1841
So, on 10 May 1841, Laura wrote a second petition to Sydenham
asking this time for a pension:
"Application for a Pension on the ground that her husband's
death was hastened by a wound injured at the battle of
Queenston, with a request that it may be submitted to the
Legislature. 17 June 1841.
To the Right Honorable Charles Baron Sydenham of Sydenham
in the County of Kent and Toronto in Canada, Governor General
of British North America and Captain General and Governor in
Charge in and over our Province of Canada, Nova Scotia, New
Brunswick and the Island of Prince Edward, and Vice Admiral of
the same.
The petition of Laura Secord widow of the late James Secord of
Chippawa deceased, formerly of the first Reg't of Lincoln Militia
of Upper Canada.
Humbly Sheweth

That your Excellency's Petitioner has been left by the decease of her husband without means of sup-port that she is now far advanced in years and consequently is unable to make much exertion for her own maintenance.

That but for her indigence your Excellency's Petitioner would never have prayed for any allowance for the Legislature however great her ground of application may have been, but now as she has been made wholly deprived of the death of husband and left totally unprovided for, her dear late husband not having had the means of working a provision for her support, your Excellency's Petitioner is compelled to apply to the Legislature for relief,

That your Excellency's Petitioner's late husband was a Captain in the first Reg't of Lincoln Militia in the year 1812.

That on the 13th day of October in that year he received a wound when in action with the enemy at Queenston in the said Province that your Excellency's Petitioner's late husband had for a long time previous to his death suffered severely from the effects of the said wound which not only materially injured his shoulder but also his general health, a certificate of which is hereunto appended.

That your Excellency's Petitioner did herself embrace an opportunity of rendering useful service at the risk of her life in going through the enemies lines to communicate information to a Detachment of Her Majesties Troops at the Beaver Dam in this district in the month of June 1813, a certificate of which is also hereunto appended which your Petitioner accomplished not without suffering great bodily fatigue on account of the circuitous route she was compelled to take and the difficulty she had to encounter with the Indians, and it was only with the greatest persua(s)ion and exertion that she was allowed by them to pass to the British Station to appraise the British troops of the intention of the Enemy and but for such information your Excellency's Petitioner was fully convinced the British troops must have been captured and by that means would have took an important Station, for which Service your Excellency's Petitioner has never received the slightest remuneration nor has she ever claimed any until now, and if her dear late husband could have but spared to his widow for years longer she would never have prayed for any compensation.

That therefore under all the circumstances of her means your Excellency's Petitioner hopes and trusts your Excellency will be graciously pleased to have her application laid before the Honorable the Commons House of Assembly at this ensuing session of Parliament for consideration and trust the legislature will view her case favourably and thereby grant her a Pension and your Excellency's petitioner is in duty bound will ever pray.
Laura Secord
Chippawa, 10 May 1841".

The two attachments to this petition were a copy of the third FitzGibbon certificate of 1837 and a certificate from Captain Isaac Swayze that James had been wounded in the battle of Queenston Heights. In her ignorance of government bureaucracy in earlier submissions, the 1837 document was the only original FitzGibbon certificate that she had kept.

During the probate proceedings after James Secord's death, the Coroner from Danby House, Stamford also wrote:
"I have been requested by Mrs. Secord, the widow of the late James Secord Esq. Collector of Customs of Chippawa to give a certificate on her behalf relating to the death of her deceased husband, which I must respectfully recommend to the consideration of His Excellency the Governor General. Although I cannot conscientiously say death was caused by the effects of the gunshot wound only, yet I can with safety declare my opinion that it ha(d) material effect on hastening the fatal result. I have the honor to remain Sir,
Your obedient Servant,
John Mewburn"

Petition, Charles Secord, Collector Customs, Chippawa - 1841
In 1841, a month after his father's death, Charles B. Secord sent a petition to Lord Sydenham, Governor of British North America, requesting the position of Collector of Customs at the Chippawa Port of Customs:
"Queenston 4th March 1841
Dear Sir,
The situation of Collector having become vacant by the death of my much lamented father, my mother has in consequence made an application to His Excellency the Governor General praying that His Excellency would appoint me to the vacant office. As he ha(s) had an opportunity of knowing my poor father when Collector, although I myself have had the pleasure of not a slight acquaintance with him, I feel confident that he would not have taken to certifying to my dear father's conduct in business and the functioning with which the office was conducted in his life time. He no doubt would meet a defence in recommending me to fill the vacant office. Indeed I cannot ask it with preference, but still I feel a denial that the general functioning with which my poor dear father discharged the duties of the office while Collector may come from the ex Inspector General. As it may have some weight in my favor and perhaps it may not be improper to add that my father during his illness expressed a wish that a letter should be written to him upon the subject impressing upon the Governor the great desire he felt that I should succeed him. However this letter never was written, in account of great weakness nor did I "press" it upon him, trusting that he will excuse the liberty I have taken.
I am Dear Sir Yours with great respect
Chas. B. Secord".

The reference from Macaulay was circumspect:
"Inspector General's Office, 6th March 1841
I enclose a communication from the son of the late Collector of Chippawa, who appears to be a candidate for the vacant Office. The late Mr. Secord, though not very energetic, was yet a very conscientious officer.
I am, Dear Sir, Yours truly
JW Macaulay".

Petition, Charles Secord, Collector Customs, Chippawa - 1842

At the time, Lord Sydenham was not well and probably diverted by his ill health; he died within the year. The tenure of James Secord as Collector had not been without its problems, which had caught the attention of the government. As a result it remained unclear whether the position should pass to his son, who had already been given one of his father's former positions and was an attorney with his own business. With the position of Collector of Customs for Chippawa remaining vacant for more than a year, and to raise his mother's cause with the then-present administration, Charles Secord wrote again in 1842 after the next Governor General had been sworn in:

To the Right Honorable Sir Charles Bagot Governor General of British North America – etc., etc., etc.

May it Please Your Excellency.

The office of Collector of Customs having become vacant by the death of my much lamented father, and no successor yet having been appointed to succeed him, I am particularly desirous to impress upon Your Excellency's consideration [of] my great anxiety in coincidence with the wish of my dear departed parent expressing upon his dying bed, that the office might be given to me, to solicit at the hands of Your Excellency this favour, and when Your Excellency learns that my father was an old servant of the Crown, and all his life a steady and firm supporter of this Government, and that my mother during the late War with the United States performed useful service at the margin of her life in the cause of the British, a certificate of which I take the liberty herewith to annex, and who is now by the decease of my father without means of support. I feel a confidence that Your Excellency will convey to this County as Your Excellency does under the auspices of a Ministry desirous of rewarding the loyalty of English Canadian subjects, duly consider our claim as far as Your Excellency can with propriety. I therefore trust Your Excellency will be graciously pleased to take the whole of these circumstances into consideration and thus Your Excellency will decide accordingly. With respect to the popular feeling in the County it is almost universally in my favour. I did not however think it necessary to get up a Petition to Your Excellency, but beg to refer Your Excellency to the Honorable Mr. Dunn the Receiver General and also to Mr. Cartwright a member of the Assembly, also to the Hon. Mr. MacAulay Inspector General, all of whom I am convinced if referred to would give Your Excellency every wanted information, more particulars of my dear late father, character for honesty and loyalty.

I have the honor to be Your Excellency's Humble Servant

Charles B. Secord

Queenston 20th January 1842".

The reference from Cartwright was also circumspect:

"Hon. Cartwright Esq., Kingston, 10 Febr'y 1842

recommends Mr. Charles Secord for Collectorship of Chippawa."

Petition, Charles Secord, in support of FitzGibbon - 1845

Seven years after FitzGibbon's last of three certificates was penned on behalf of the Secords, a proposal to grant Colonel FitzGibbon, then Chief Clerk of the Legislative Council, the sum of £1000, in lieu of a former grant for five thousand acres of crown lands, subsequently disallowed as illegal, was strongly opposed in the Legislative Assembly by Mr. Aylwin of Quebec. Learning this, it was the Secords' turn to support FitzGibbon, one of their most respected supporters and the extraordinary victor at the Battle of Beaver Dams. Charles B. Secord addressed a letter to a religious periodical, called "The Church," published at Cobourg, Ontario, which was printed in that paper in April, 1845.

"To the Editor of the 'Church'

Queenston, 11th April 1845

Sir. – In the course of the late debate in the House of Assembly, relative to the propriety of granting Col. FitzGibbon £1000 for his services, in lieu of a grant of land, Mr. Aylwin said 'he strongly opposed the grant, and gave as one reason that Col. FitzGibbon had monopolized honour which did not rightfully belong to him. He had received credit for the affair at the Beaver Dam, whilst in point of fact, the party to whom that credit was due was Major Delorimier, a relative of his own, and a native of Lower Canada, but instead of being rewarded for his services Major Delorimier could not obtain the life of his son when he afterwards solicited it.' [One of his sons was executed for participation in the insurrection of 1837-8 in Lower Canada.]

Now I think it proper that Mr. Aylwin should be informed and that the country in general should know in what way Col. FitzGibbon achieved so much honour for the affair at the Beaver Dam. My mother, living on the frontier the whole of the late American war, a warm supporter of the British cause, frequently met with the American officers and upon the occasion of the capture of the American troops at the Beaver Dam, after our troops, consisting of a small detachment under Col. FitzGibbon, the Lieut. FitzGibbon of the 49th Regiment, and some Indians, had taken up their position at that place, overheard an American officer say to other of the officers that they intended to surprise and capture the British troops at the Beaver Dam. Without waiting for further information my mother, a lone woman, at once left her house to apprise the British troops of what she had heard, and travelled on foot the whole of the way, passing all the American guards and many of the Indian scouts who were placed along the road, until she arrived at the Beaver Dam, and enquiring for the officer in command was introduced to Col. FitzGibbon (then Lieut. FitzGibbon, as I said before) as the officer in command; she then told him what she had come for, and all she had heard – that the Americans intended to make an attack upon them and would no doubt, from their superior numbers, capture them all. Col. FitzGibbon in consequence of this information prepared himself to meet the enemy, and soon after the attack being made the American troops were captured and one or two field-pieces taken – as the Colonel's certificate of my mother's services on that occasion, accompanying this communication, will shew. It might perhaps be as well for me while upon this subject further to state that I never heard my mother speak of Major Delorimier or any other officer being at the Beaver Dam at that time. Col. FitzGibbon was the only officer who appeared to be in command, to whom my mother gave the information, and who acted the part he so nobly did on that occasion.

I am, Sir, your most obedient servant,

Chas. B. Secord"

Resolution 143:

Resolved, That it is the opinion of the committee that a sum not exceeding one thousand pounds currency, be granted to Her

Majesty or Lt.-Col FitzGibbon in lieu of the grant of land recommended to be made to him by the Legislature of Upper Canada.
Yeas - 38 Nays - 24
Mr. Aylwin opposed the motion.

Petition, Laura Secord, Prince of Wales - 1860
In the Niagara Mail of 8 Aug 1860, under "Laura Secord. A Canadian Heroine" was published:
"A respectable, aged lady of this county, one of the loyal stock, presented herself at the office of the Clerk Of The Peace at Niagara, to sign the address to H.R.H. the Prince of Wales, along with the old soldiers of 1812. The Clerk demurred to taking so novel a signature, although the lady insisted on her right, having done her country more signal service than half the soldiers and militiamen engaged in the war. We do not give the venerable lady's name, as she might not like the notoriety, but she is the same person who..." The article goes on to tell of her walk to Beaver Dams to give warning, and closes with:
"We say the brave, loyal, old lady ought not only to be allowed to sign the address, but she deserved a special introduction to the Prince of Wales as a worthy example of the War of 1812, when both men and women vied alike in their resolution to defend the country."
In 1860, for the Prince of Wales tour of Canada, and specifically the Niagara River region, Laura Secord provided the Prince with this introductory, appealing memorandum in her own words:
"His Royal Highness the Prince of Wales.
May it please your Royal Highness.
Having the privilege accorded me this day of presenting myself before your Royal Highness I beg to assure you that I do so with the greatest gratification to my feelings. I am confident your Royal Highness will pardon the liberty I have taken when your Royal Highness is informed of the circumstances which have led me to do so.
In the war of 1812 being strongly attached to the British cause I took every opportunity to watch its progress, and living on the Frontier during the whole of the war I had frequent opportunities of knowing the moves of the American forces. I thus was enabled to obtain important information which I

deemed proper to communicate to the British Commander Colonel FitzGibbon, then lieut. FitzGibbon of the 49th Regt. whose certificate of my services upon the occasion of the capture of the American troops in 1813 – herewith appended – will show. I shall commence at the battle of Queenston, where I was at the time the cannon balls were flying around me in every direction. I left the place during the engagement. After the battle I returned to Queenston, and then found that my husband had been wounded; my house plundered and property destroyed. It was while the Americans had possession of the frontier, that I learned the plans of the American commander, and determined to put the British troops under Fitzgibbon in possession of them, and if possible, to save the British troops from capture, or, perhaps, total destruction. In doing so I found I should have great difficulty in getting through the American guards, which were out ten miles in the country. Determined to persevere, however, I left early in the morning, walked nineteen miles in the month of June, over a rough and difficult part of the country, when I came to a field belonging to a Mr. Decamp [DeCew], in the neighbourhood of the Beaver Dam. By this time daylight had left me. Here I found all the Indians encamped; by moonlight the scene was terrifying, and to those accustomed to such scenes, might be considered grand. Upon advancing to the Indians they all rose, and, with some yells, said "Woman," which made me tremble. I cannot express the awful feeling it gave me; but I did not lose my presence of mind. I was determined to persevere. I went up to one of the chiefs, made him understand that I had great news for Capt. Fitzgibbon, and that he must let me pass to his camp, or that he and his party would be all taken. The chief at first objected to let me pass, but finally consented, after some hesitation, to go with me and accompany me to Fitzgibbon's station, which was at the Beaver Dam, where I had an interview with him. I then told him what I had come for, and what I had heard – that the Americans intended to make an attack upon the troops under his command, and would, from their superior numbers, capture them all. Benefiting by this information Capt. Fitzgibbon formed his plan accordingly, and captured about five hundred American infantry, about fifty mounted dragoons, and a fieldpiece or two was taken from the enemy. I returned home next day, exhausted and fatigued. I am now advanced in years, and when I look back I wonder how I could have gone through so much fatigue, with the fortitude to accomplish it.

I am now a very old woman – a widow many years. A few short years even if I should so long live will see me no more upon this earth. I feel that it will be gratifying to my family and a pleasure to myself that your Royal Parent the Queen should know that the services which I performed were truly loyal and that no gain or hope of reward influenced me in doing what I did.

I request that your Royal Highness will be pleased to convey to your Royal Parent Her Majesty the Queen the name of one who in the hour of trial and danger – as well as my departed husband who fought and bled on Queenston Heights in the ever memorable battle of 13th Oct. 1812 – stood ever ready and willing to defend this Country against every invasion come what might."

With this memorandum was enclosed a copy of Fitzgibbon's 1837 Certificate.

Letters – and reminiscences

Letter of James Secord to Mrs. Hitchcock (Laura's sister)
                                    Queenston, December 20, 1829
Dear Mira, -- We have received two letters from you lately, and
am truly happy to hear of your health and happiness, although
we have not answered your letters heretofore, it has not been
from want of affection, but from not knowing where to direct a
letter to you. That obstacle is now removed and I will endeavor
in future to be a better correspondent. I do assure you that you
are alive in our remembrance and age, and the troubles of the
world increases the love of our relations, and friends are still
more endearing. Rest satisfied, therefore, my dear Mira, that we
all love you and yours.
With respect to our own family, and as you will be anxious to
know how many there are and so forth, I will briefly give you a
sketch. Well, in the first place we have six daughters and one
son, -- Mary, Charlotte, [Harriet, Appolonia], Laura, Hannah,
and Charles. Mary is married and is now a widow. She has an
estate in Ireland, and a pension from the British Government of
about $400 a year. She goes next year to Ireland in the months of
June or July. Charlotte goes with her and is unmarried. Harriet
is married to a lawyer by the name of Smith and lives in St.
Catharines and has two daughters. Poor dear Appy is no more.
She died rejoicing in her Redeemer and left a glorious example
for elder people. Laura and Hannah are at home, and good
children they are. Charles has been bred to the law and will
commence to practice next spring. He is at present at York, and
is writing in the House of Parliament. I forgot to tell you that
Mary Trumble has two daughters, Elizabeth and Mary. With
respect to our worldly affairs I am sorry to say we are not very
prosperous. We make out to live and have clothing and food,
but riches, my dear woman, it seems to me, is not for James
Secord, therefore, you have a true account of my squad. At this
moment all the little family is around the table on which I am
writing, and Harriet and little Louisa are singing a song.
Elizabeth and Mary, Hannah and Laura are drawing, Mary
Trumble and Charlotte sewing and preparing for their voyage to

Ireland. Among the number I cannot forget the loss of our good useful black girl Fanny, who died about a month ago. Your sister Laura never had health better. She bears her age most remarkably considering her former delicate state of body. We are, however, Mira, getting old and grey heads, and now and then a tremor of the body. The Almighty is looking for us. May He grant us the pardon for our sins and enable us all to meet death cheerfully and with Christian resignation. My dear Mira it is hardly necessary to tell you that we love you all.
Your loving brother, J. Secord, Senr.
M. Hitchcock,
Lebanon, County of Madison
[As this has no postmark it was probably sent by private hands.]

Letters from Laura Secord

Chippawa, July 2nd, 1841

My Dear Sister, --
You must think that I have forgotten you, far from that. My grief has been such that I could not write. I was so disappointed in my anticipations. What a change. My dear James and myself thought to pay you a visit. My pleasure has changed to sorrow and grief. God sees fit to take My Dear Husband. You can not think what grief we are in. Such a loss is great – you – my dear Sister, know his worth. One of the best of Fathers and Husbands. I never knew any one so much lamented as he is by every one that knew him. He suffered very much in his sickness – but died very easy. He took the sacrament in the morning and died at eight o'clock in the evening. My dear Sister, how I wish to see you. I fear I never shall. If God so decrees I hope to meet in a better world. I often think that if I could be with you what a consolation it would be to me. This world has no pleasure for me. I only hope I may soon meet my Dear Husband in Heaven never to part.
Before I could finish I have new grief – I have heard my youngest daughter's child lays at the point of death. I fear she is no more. My Dear Sister, my grief is so great I do not know what to say or do.
I hope, my dear sister, you will come and see me once more, and your daughters. Our sisters would be so happy to once more see

you. Do come and let us once more meet in this world. If God so decrees that we are not to meet here I hope to meet in Heaven never to part.

Give my love to your family and tell them that I love them and wish to see them.

I remain your loving sister till death,
Laura Secord

Chippawa, August 1st, 1843

My Dear Sister, --

I received your letter last week. I was very unhappy to hear of your ill-health. What is this world to us if we do not enjoy our health – nothing. I know that by experience. I hope, my dear Sister, to hear that you are well when I hear from you again. I was in hopes that I should have paid you a visit this summer. I fear I will not, as many things prevent.

My dear Sister, I am very much agitated this moment, at the sudden Death of Mrs. ---. What is life; all is vanity. I fear that she was not prepared to meet her God. She thought so little of a future state. Her belief was that all would be saved at the last day, let them be bad or good, that Death is the punishment. She was a kind-hearted woman, always kind to the poor. I hope she is at rest is my most sincere wish.

I received a letter from our brother James; he says the Brothers and Sisters are all well. Thomas has moved from Oxford about Fifteen miles and has bought Mills. I hope that he may do well. Our Brothers and Sisters all wish very much to see you.

I could wish we could once more meet in this world together, it would be a happy meeting. My dear Sister, how often I wish I could be near you to tell you my griefs. I feel so lonely; all will soon be in the grave. I only hope that I may be prepared to meet my God, is all I ask.

You know I would like to hear from my family. Harriet is with me, and her family. We are well, which is the greatest blessing in this life. My love to you and all your family. Tell them that I love them and would wish to see them.

I remain your affectionate sister,
Laura Secord
Postage 18 ½ cents.

Mrs. Julius Hitchcock, Lebanon Post Office, Madison County,
New York State

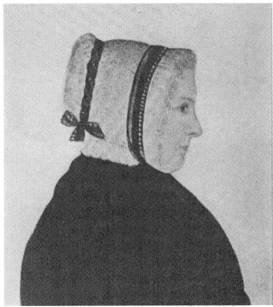

Myra Ingersoll, Mrs. Julius Hitchcock
Courtesy: Hitchcock Family

Myra Ingersoll Hitchcock's home in Lebanon, Madison Co., New York
Courtesy: Hitchcock Family

Chippawa, June 17th, 1844

My Dear Sister, --

I was glad, my dear Mira, to hear from you and should have
answered it immediately. I was waiting to hear from my son,
while he was waiting to hear from headquarters to know how to
proceed. He finds that it will be attended with a great deal of
trouble and expense, and when got you know not where to take
it up, as the lands are mostly sold to the Canada Company. I
have given up the idea of trying to do anything about mine. If
you would still wish to go on with trying you will have to send a
power of attorney. I was very much pleased to hear that your
health is better. I much wish to see you once more, I fear I never
shall without you should the trouble to come and see us. We
should be happy to see you, the family always talking about you.
You wrote that your family are all married. I hope that they may
be a pleasure and a blessing to you. I feel so unhappy, my dear
sister, that I know not what to write, to think we are the only
ones of our family on earth. We must soon expect our summons.
My only hope is to be prepared. How often I do wish to be with
you and think what a pleasure it would be to us. I have always
thought I should have the happiness of paying you a visit. I now
despair, it is a great grief to me, indeed. I hope, my dear sister,
that you will come and see us. Your friends at Oxford wish it
very much. I wish you could come and we would go and see
them together. What a happy meeting it would be. I think it
would almost be heaven on earth. Do not let me dwell too long
on such anticipations. It is too much for a poor unworthy person
like me. My family are all well and send love to you and all your
family. You will accept mine.

I remain your affectionate sister,

Laura Secord

Postage 18 ½ cents.

Mrs. Julius Hitchcock, Lebanon Post Office, Madison County,
New York State

Last Will and Testament, Laura Secord - 1857

Laura Secord died on 17 October 1868 in her house on Water`
Street in Chippawa. Her last will and testament reads:
"In the Name of God Amen.

I Laura Secord of Chippawa in the County of Welland Relict of
James Secord late of the same place Esquire deceased. Being of
sound mind and memory. Do make this my Last Will and
Testament in manner following,

First, I give and devise unto my two Daughters Charlotte Secord
and Harriet Smith widow of David Smith late of St Catharines
Esquire deceased as Tenants in Common all and singular my
whole messuage and Tenement situate lying and being in the
Village of Chippawa in the County of Welland whereon I now
reside. To Have and to Hold to my said two Daughters Charlotte
Secord and Harriet Smith as Tenants in Common their heirs and
assigns forever.

Secondly, All the rest residue and remainder of all my Estate and
effects, real and personal whatsoever and wheresoever, not
hereinbefore disposed of after payment of my debts and funeral
expenses, I do give devise and bequeath unto my Two Daughters
aforesaid share and share alike.

Lastly, I do hereby constitute and appoint my said Daughter
Charlotte Secord sole Executrix of this my Last Will and
Testament hereby revoking all former Wills by one made.

In Witness Whereof I have hereunto set my hand and seal the
Twenty sixth day of November in the year of our Lord one
thousand eight hundred and fifty seven.

Signed Sealed and Declared by the Testatrix as for her Last Will
and Testament

In presence of (signed) Anne Hepleane, Wm. M. Christie.
(Signed) Laura Secord "

This Will, No. 3632, was prepared for probate in the Surrogate
Court of the County of Welland, Province of Ontario and
registered on 15 January 1869 by D.D. Everard of the said Court.
It recognized Charlotte Secord, spinster, as the sole Executrix of
the Will. Thus Charlotte had remained unmarried.

Letter from Elizabeth Ann Stewart Secord (Mrs. Gregory; 1826-1893) to Mary Magdalen Secord (Mrs. Dunn; 1844-1936) – 1884 – about their mutual great aunt, Laura Ingersoll Secord. It was written 16 years after Laura's death, and contains some excellent first hand knowledge about the heroine.

First, the cast of characters:

The writer (married to William Gregory; 1816-1872) was the daughter of David Secord (1790-1846); her aunt Elizabeth Secord (1793-1814) walked through St Catharines with Laura. Capt. Richard Henry Secord (1799-1866) and Esther Magdalen Secord (married Capt. George II Sr. Keefer; 1795-1871) helped Laura financially after her husband James Secord died in 1841 in Chippawa. David, Elizabeth, Esther and Richard were all children of Stephen Secord (the miller; 1757-1808) and Hannah (Annatie) DeFreest (the miller's wife, 1767-1841). Stephen was Laura's brother in-law. This letter is between cousins, Mary Magdalen Secord (married to Lt.Col. Orlando Dunn; 1844-1936) being the daughter of Capt. Richard Henry Secord. Both the writer and the recipient were great nieces of Laura.

Charles Ingersoll (1791-1832) was Laura's half-brother, being her father's eldest child by his third wife. One of Charles' daughters was Mary Anne Ingersoll (1817-1877) who married Hon. Senator James Rae Benson (1807-1885).

Mary and Charlotte Secord were Laura's eldest two children. Mrs Smith was Harriet Hopkins Secord, of whom we now have a photograph in this Newsletter.

Reference: Canadian Methodist magazine, 19, 20 (April, May 1884), p.350-9, 426-33.

"Aunt Laura's maiden name was Ingersoll one of the good old families who preferred poverty and privation in the then wilderness of Canada to remaining in care and comfort under the wings of the Almighty Eagle. Aunt's family alited where the town of Ingersoll now stands. Her brother Charles Ingersoll father of the late Hon. Mrs James Benson married a sister of the late Hon. William Hamilton Merritt. Uncle James Secord was a merchant and lived in the Village of Queenston. He was very dangerously wounded (from the effects of which he never entirely recovered) at the Battle of Queenston heights or at Niagara, I do not remember which. Aunt Laura left her home on that ever to be remembered morning before daylight (the cow and the milk pail are a fable) and came to St David's, and rested at Grandma's for a few minutes and then left Aunt Elizabeth Secord accompanying her as far as St Catharines then called Shipman's Corners, after which she proceeded on her way alone. I never heard Mrs Neville's name in connection with the affair until I read it in a sketch copied from the Methodist magazine. I remember well of sitting in childish astonishment and horror listening to Aunt and Grandma talking over the affair and of hearing her relate the fears she entertained of meeting and being taken prisoner by the American Indians before she had reached the British lines and given the information she was perilling freedom and life itself to give. She did not seem to think she had done any thing more than a sacred duty. Mary was the name of her oldest daughter, who married a regimental surgeon a Dr Trumbull [Trumble] who at the close of the war went to Indies where he died leaving her with two young Daughters one of whom the eldest was heiress in right of her Father to a large landed Estate in County Sligo Ireland. I will remember when cousin Mary and her Daughters came home from Indies and of her again leaving to go and take possession of the estate where I presume the Daughters are still living. I remember well the facts connected with the affair, but I can not remember dates. I never heard that Uncle James was an officer at all. I know he was not a Major. Uncle David of old St Davids, cousin Phillip's Father was the Major Secord who fought in all the principal battles of that campaign and whom the poor Indian thought must bear a charmed life. But you did not ask me for the Major's history so I will close that subject for the present and tell what more I can of Aunt's and Uncle's history. They continued living in Queenston for several years. When the family compact that then ruled the land gave him the Princely appointment of Collector of Customs at Chippawa where he died shortly after the close of the rebellion having Aunt in very poor circumstances which would have been very much worse had it not been for your Dear Father and Aunt Keefer. She never received any thing from the Government. A few years before her death the Prince of Wales made her a present of one hundred pounds, which sum must have been a perfect Godsend to her and her two Daughters, the one a widow and the other a maiden lady. You will remember Dear Mary the

148

visit you and I made her just three days before her death. She was then in her 97th year and she was still in possession of her memory. Mrs Smith told me that the Clergyman in charge was often astonished at her remarkable memory. Did you know that Charlotte died at Guelph sometime in 1881? I think that Mrs Smith is still living with her two daughters, who have for years taught in private school.

Tell Col. Dunn that the account contained in the Methodist magazine as to the number of prisoners taken is very near correct. I always hear that between six and seven hundred were taken through information she gave the British. Tell Mr Dunn that as a historian I shall be a very poor success – these are so many things I have heard from the dear ones now no more in regard to that eventful period and what one own family had to undergo that I know not what to write first.

(sgd.) Elizabeth
Mrs Elizabeth Gregory
Aylmer   Mrs Orlando Dunn
Oct 27, 1884.   Hayden House
                                     Bloor Street West
                                     Toronto, Ontario."

Recollections of Miss Augusta Smith, of Guelph, Granddaughter of Laura Secord – abt. 1900

My grandmother was ever sensible and courageous. Her great fortitude and courage were exhibited under all circumstances. Mr. Secord was a customs-house official at Chippawa. During the summer months there was a daily steamer from Chippawa to Buffalo. At all seasons of the year there was traffic between the two countries. Mr. Secord had been notified that a party of smugglers would be in a certain direction at night. My grandmother at once said: "There are only two of you and there will be great danger. I will represent the third person." She dressed herself in an overcoat and cap of my grandfather's, his boots also, and went to the boat with them. She stood by when the seizure was made, which was very valuable. When there was an alarm of burglars at the house she would say, "Now, James, you stand back with the light and let me go forward – they will not injure a woman as they would a man."

She was an excellent nurse. On two occasions – one of three months and another of six weeks, – she never undressed at night, and sat beside the bed in an armchair. She was a remarkably fine needle-woman, for it was an accomplishment and one of the fine arts of those early days. I remember seeing her sit working on a little white dress one time when I was ill. It was put together with open work stitches. In their prosperous days she was called extravagant. When her daughters attended the balls at Niagara or elsewhere she took great pride in having their satin boots or slippers to match their dress. These she made with her own hands. She also made their long gloves, as there was nothing of the kind to be had nearer than Montreal. She was hospitable and every one had a welcome. A relative told me of her gifts as a cook; that she had the happy faculty of making everything "tastey" from limited materials.

People wondered how she could leave her home and children and go into danger she knew not what. The few letters she has left tell of her strong religious principles, her strong affections, and the "sacred duty" foremost in her mind of doing good. Last, but not least, was her strong faith in God. My dear sister and myself often referred to the beautiful prayer she would make upon our departure after making her a visit. These are some instances of her private life. Her motto was, "It is ever the darkest hour just before the daylight."

[In the Smith family there was one brother and two sisters – Louisa and Augusta. Miss Louisa died in 1908. The brother died in 1904 in Minnesota. Laura Ingersoll Secord was remarkably reticent in regard to herself – never boastful – a quality reflected in the communications about her from the grandchildren.

Recollections of Miss Laura Secord Clarke – 1928
(Reprinted courtesy of The Chippawa Times, Page 12, Don's Attic, by Don Ede)
Laura Secord Clark, a granddaughter of the Laura Secord famous in Canadian history, was born in Guelph, Ontario, and lived much of her adult life at 6 Clarendon Crescent, Toronto. "At the age of six years I was placed in boarding school there. The lady principal was a Miss Wild, a Quakeress. It was the first private school established there in pioneer days.

[Miss Clark's] father was a medical man", she said when recalling her childhood days, and her mother had died when she was very young.

"I very seldom had holidays from school, " said Miss Clark, "but I do remember wen I was eight, being taken to spend the summer with my Grandmother Secord, and I certainly enjoyed the visit.

I can remember going to my grandmother to do the marketing for the family, and I also remember being taken to the Anglican Church, and I think the officiating clergyman was a Mr. Leeming.

When I was fourteen I was sent to a boarding school in Coburg, and the lady principal was a Miss Dean, a most charming person, and we all loved her and were anxious to please her.

I had the pleasure of staying with my Secord cousins, the Cockburns. I stayed with Mrs. Cockburn while she lived in St. Catharines. She was the daughter of Charles Secord and a granddaughter of Laura Secord. Mrs. Cockburn was buried in St. Mark's churchyard, Niagara."

The other Secord cousins are Morden Carthew, who lives in Thornbury, Ontario, where he is practicing law; William Carthew, who lives in Waterloo, Ontario, and Charles Carthew, a medical man in Edmonton, Alberta.

Mrs. Young, another granddaughter, lives in Cornwall, Ontario, and Mrs. Brock is in Guelph.

Miss Clark has a pleasant 'remembrance' of several weeks spent in Chester, England, with a Secord aunt, Mrs. Trumble; she went from there to stay with some of her relations in Ireland and the hospitality of her Irish friends was pleasant to look back upon. From Ireland she went to Edinburgh and enjoyed prowling about there. Having been an ardent reader of Walter Scott's novels, she was able 'to locate a great many places of interest.'

Tributes to the Memory of Laura Secord – 1890s

Mrs. Agnes Chamberlin, whose first husband was Col. FitzGibbon, wrote: "I heard quite often from Colonel FitzGibbon about Mrs. Secord. In my eyes she was more of a heroine than is generally known. Like Lady Godiva, her journey was performed not without clothing, but next to nothing, being only a flannel petticoat and what old people called a bed-gown, or short dress worn over the petticoat."

Harriet Smith (1803-1892), Laura Secord's third daughter, said: "I remember seeing my mother leave the house on that fateful morning, but neither I nor my sisters knew on what errand she was bent. A flowered print gown, I think it was brown with orange flowers, at least a yellow tint, is connected with that particular morning."

Probably another contemporary reminiscence from Harriet Smith, Sarah-Ann Curzon passed this communication with Harriet on to the reader about the quickness of Laura Secord's speech: "Three Americans called at her house in Queenston to ask for water. One of them said, 'When we come for good to this country we'll divide the land, and I'll take this here for my share.' Mrs. Secord was so nettled by the thought expressed that, although the men were civil and respectful, she replied sharply, 'You scoundrel, all you'll ever get here will be six feet of earth.' When they were gone her heart reproached her for her heat, because the men had not molested her property. Two days after the men returned. They said to Mrs. Secord, 'You were right about the six feet of earth, missus.' The third man had been killed." H.C. Mewburn, of Stamford, also heard Laura Secord tell the same story.

Another incident, related by her granddaughter, Alicia Cockburn, probably occurred about this time: "Mr. Secord had received quite a large sum of money, which by some means must have become known. One night soon after, when she was alone with her young children, and only a colored boy called Bob and a coloured girl called Fan in the house, a man appeared asking admittance, saying he was pursued. My grandmother refused to admit him at that time of night. Then he said he could and

152

would come in. Changing her voice to an Irish brogue, she threatened to set the dog upon him. The coloured boy was told to growl like a dog, which it seems he could do to perfection. The man went away, but soon returned, when my grandmother presented an old horse-pistol, telling him she would shoot if he did not leave. He went off declaring he would yet get in. Grandmother afterwards heard that a desperate character had been seen around the village at the time the money was received."

An incident of Laura Secord's life in Chippawa is also related by her granddaughter, Alicia Cockburn :
"My grandmother was a woman of strong personality and character, and her word carried great weight with it, as the following incident will show. Upon one occasion a negro in whom she was interested was very ill with the smallpox. Of course there were no isolated hospitals in those days, the patient having to be treated at home, precautions being taken to prevent the contagion from spreading. Grandma heard that the doctor intended smothering the poor negro, and accordingly challenged him as to those reports. He admitted the charge, saying at the same time: 'He is only a nigger and not much account anyway.' 'As sure as you do,' my grandmother answered, 'I will have you indicted for murder.' This seemed to set him thinking, and putting forth renewed efforts he pulled the poor fellow through, who, in after years, testified his gratitude in many ways for the saving his life. She was a great favourite with young people, who, on returning from school for their holidays, would say, after a brief time in the house, 'Now, we must go and see Mrs. Secord.' "

Matilda Ridout, Lady Edgar (1844-1910), in her "Ten Years of Peace and War, 1805-1815" in telling Laura Secord's story says: "As to Laura Secord's reward, it has come to her in the fame that rests on her name wherever the story of 1812 is told. The heroine lived until 1868, and sleeps now in that old cemetery at Drummondville, where lie so many of our brave soldiers."

Hon. Albertina Agnes Mary Denison (1854-1929), the wife of Ivor Herbert, 1st Baron Treowen and General Officer Commanding the Militia of Canada in 1890-1895, says: It gave General Herbert the greatest pleasure to visit Niagara and its ever memorable surroundings, especially the field of Lundy's Lane. I trust the spot where Laura Secord rests will be marked by a monument worthy of the brave and noble spirit we all must honour."

Laura Louisa Smith, said upon the death of her grandmother: "I feel a nation's gratitude should have appreciated the noble act of Laura Secord, and have raised a monument to her memory on the spot selected by her husband as their last resting-place."

Laura's Legacy rises later in the Berkshires, Massachusetts
In the early 1970s, the author of "Laura Secord, The Legend and The Lady" (1971), Ruth McKenzie communicated several times with Gerard Chapman of Great Barrington, Massachusetts – Laura Ingersoll's town of birth. Chapman wrote: "I find, upon casual inquiry, that few persons around here know of, or have any clear idea of, Laura Ingersoll Secord or what she did...". Indeed, Charles J. Taylor and his son-in-law, George E. MacLean published the second edition of the "History of Great Barrington" (1882) in 1928, and there did not appear a single reference to Laura Ingersoll, although she was known to the author. Chapman, who later became a Pittsfield resident, published a long essay, "Berkshire-born Canadian Patriot", in The Berkshire Courier in 1975. This work by Chapman was the beginning of a more modern view of Laura Ingersoll in the Great Barrington area, followed shortly by a plaque to her memory beside the front entrance of the Mason Library there.

Publicity – early writings

Auchinleck - 1853

A 'History of the War of 1812', by Gilbert Auchinleck, was the first publication detailing Laura Secord's heroism for a public audience. It was printed in 1853 as a serial in the Anglo-American Magazine, Vol. III, November 1853, No. 5, p. 467 which afterwards appeared in a book. In a note to the November instalment, he stated the following:

"The circumstances connected with the affair at the Beaver Dam, where Col. FitzGibbon (then Lieut. FitzGibbon) gained so much praise for the victory achieved by him over the Americans, was owing to information which Mrs. Secord, the widow of James Secord, Esq., deceased, formally of Queenston, who was wounded at the battle of that place (13th October, 1812,) obtained from private sources of the intention of the American troops to surround and take Fitz Gibbon and party, which consisted at that time of a detachment of the 49th Regiment, some few militia, and a small body of Indians, to oppose some 500 of the American infantry and a detachment of some 50 of mounted American dragoons. The difficulty in reaching Lieut. Fitz Gibbon's post is thus related in Mrs. Secord's own words:

"I shall commence at the battle of Queenston, where I was at the time the cannon balls were flying around me in every direction. I left the place during the engagement. After the battle I returned to Queenston, and then found that my husband had been wounded; my house plundered and property destroyed. It was while the Americans had possession of the frontier, that I learned the plans of the American commander, and determined to put the British troops under Fitzgibbon in possession of them, and if possible, to save the British troops from capture, or, perhaps, total destruction. In doing so I found I should have great difficulty in getting through the American guards, which were out ten miles in the country. Determined to persevere, however, I left early in the morning, walked nineteen miles in the month of June, over a rough and difficult part of the country, when I came to a field belonging to a Mr. Decamp [DeCew], in the

neighbourhood of the Beaver Dam. By this time daylight had left me. Here I found all the Indians encamped; by moonlight the scene was terrifying, and to those accustomed to such scenes, might be considered grand. Upon advancing to the Indians they all rose, and, with some yells, said "Woman," which made me tremble. I cannot express the awful feeling it gave me; but I did not lose my presence of mind. I was determined to persevere. I went up to one of the chiefs, made him understand that I had great news for Capt. Fitzgibbon, and that he must let me pass to his camp, or that he and his party would be all taken. The chief at first objected to let me pass, but finally consented, after some hesitation, to go with me and accompany me to Fitzgibbon's station, which was at the Beaver Dam, where I had an interview with him. I then told him what I had come for, and what I had heard – that the Americans intended to make an attack upon the troops under his command, and would, from their superior numbers, capture them all. Benefitting by this information Capt. Fitzgibbon formed his plan accordingly, and captured about five hundred American infantry, about fifty mounted dragoons, and a fieldpiece or two was taken from the enemy. I returned home next day, exhausted and fatigued. I am now advanced in years, and when I look back I wonder how I could have gone through so much fatigue, with the fortitude to accomplish it.
Laura Secord"

Gilbert Auchinleck then added FitzGibbon's Certificate to Laura Secord, as written in 1837.

Lossing - 1861
In summer of 1860, the American artist and writer, Benson J. Lossing, visited Canada to collect material for his 'Pictorial Fieldbook of the War of 1812', which was not published until 1869 – the year after Laura Secord died. Although they did not meet, he corresponded with her, and on page 621 of the book in a footnote he printed an extract of a letter from her:

"After going to St. David's, and the recovery of Mr. Secord, we returned again to Queenston, where my courage was again much tried. It was then I gained the secret plan laid to capture Captain

156

Fitzgibbon and his party. I was determined, if possible to save them. I had much difficulty in getting through the American guards. They were ten miles out in the country. When I came to a field belonging to Mr. Decoo, in the neighbourhood of the Beaver Dams, I then had walked nineteen miles. By that time daylight had left me. I yet had a swift stream of water to cross over an old fallen tree (Twelve-mile Creek,) and to climb a high hill, which fatigued me very much.

Before I arrived at the encampment of the Indians, as I approached they all arose with one of their war-yells, which indeed awed me. You may imagine what my feelings were to behold so many savages. With forced courage I went to one of the chiefs, told him I gad great news from his commander, and that he must take me to him, or they would be all lost. He if not understand me, but said, 'Woman, what does woman want here?' The scene by the moonlight might have been grand, but to a weak woman, certainly terrifying. With difficulty I got one of the chides to go with me to their commander. With the intelligence I gave him he formed his plans and saved his country. I have ever found the brave and noble Colonel Fitzgibbon a friend to me, may he prosper in the world to come as he has done in this.

Laura Secord.

Chippawa, U. C. February 18th, 1861."

Laura Secord still possessed the original in December 1863.

Coffin - 1864
In 1864, a former sheriff of the Montréal District and staff officer in the militia, William F. Coffin published his '1812; The War and its Moral'. On pages 147-9, he described Laura Secord's journey. Coffin holds the notoriety of being the first to introduce the cow into the story of Laura's walk:

"In despite of all precautions, rumours of the intended expedition leaked out, and reached the ears of James Secord, a British militia soldier, who resided at Queenston, then within American lines. He had been badly wounded the preceding autumn at Queenston Heights, and was a cripple. He hobbled home to his wife with the news. The pair were in consternation; they were loyal Canadians — their hearts were in the cause. If the design succeeded; if Fitzgibbon was surprised, De Haren in the rear would follow. Burlington Heights might be carried, and their country would be lost. Mrs. Mary (sic.) Secord, the wide, at the age of 88, still lives in the village of Chippawa, to tell the story, and wakes up into young life as she does so. What was to be done, Fitzgibbon must be warned. The husband in his crippled state could not move, and moreover no man could pass the line of American sentries. She spoke out, she would go herself, would he let her? She could get past the sentries; she knew the way to St. David's, and there she could get guidance. She would go, and out her trust in God. He consented.

At three in the morning she was up, got ready the children's breakfast, and taking a cracker and a cup of coffee, started after daybreak. To have left earlier would have aroused suspension. her first difficulty was the American advanced sentry. He was hard to deal with, but she pointed to he farm building a little in advance of his post, insisted she was going for milk; told him he could watch her, and was allowed to pass on. She did milk a cow, which was very contrary, and would persist in moving onwards to the edge of the opposite bushes, into which she and the cow disappeared. Once out of sight, she pushed on rapidly. She knew the way for miles, but fear rose within her, in despite of herself, and what 'scared' her most was the distant cry of the wolf, they were abundant in those days; and twice she encountered a rattlesnake, they are not infrequent even now. She did not care much for them, as she knew they would run from a stick or stone, and she did not wait for any such exorcism. At length she reached a brook. It was very hot, and the water refreshed her, but she had some difficulty in crossing. At last she found a log and shortly after got to the mill. The miller's wife was an old friend, and tried to dissuade her from going on. Spoke of the danger, spoke of her children; the latter was a sore trial, for she was weary and thoughtful, but the thing had to be done, so she was resolute, and having rested and refreshed, proceeded on. Her next trouble was the British outlying sentry, but she soon re-assured him and he sent her on, with a kind word, warning her to beware of the Indians. This scared her again, but she was scared still more, when the cracking of the dead branches under footsteps roused from their cover a party of red skins. The chief, who first sprang to his feet, confronted her, and demanded, 'Woman, what you want?' the other yelled awful. The chief silenced them with his hand. She told him, at once that she wanted to see Fitzgibbon, and why. 'Ah' said the Indian, 'me go with you,' and with a few words to his people, who remained, he accompanied her to Fitzgibbon's quarters, which she reached about nine in the evening of the 23rd. A few words sufficed to satisfy him. He sent off, forthwith, to his Major De Haren, in the rear and made his own preparations. She found friends in a farm house near, for in those days everybody knew everybody. She slept right off, for she had journeyed in for twenty miles, and safely, God be praised. 'Here are many new details, assembled with considerable skill, for which the writer gives no authority, but the narrative seems to imply that they were derived in some way from Mrs. Secord herself, despite the unfortunate blunder in gibing her Christian name as Mary. Elsewhere he acknowledges his obligations to Colonel James Clark of St. Catharines. I have endeavored to bring together here all the firsthand authorities, stating the circumstances of Mrs. Secord's patriotic deed. Certain discrepancies will be observed, which it is difficult to reconcile, and can only be attributed to lapses of memory.

The statement was made that "The Mohawks did the fighting, the Caughnawagas got the plunder and Fitzgibbon got the praise." Frankly, as FitzGibbon later attested, it had been the Indians under Captains William J. Kerr and Dominique Ducharme who had won the Battle of Beaver Dams for the British.

Coffin embellished the story of Laura Secord's walk. The use of the cow as a ruse for the American guard was first mentioned in his account. The additions of an ill-defined ruse for the British sentry and the rattlesnake encounters were enticements to the Victorian reader.

FitzGibbon - 1894
"Thus," wrote Mary Agnes FitzGibbon in the biography of her father, 'Veteran of 1812', in 1894, "did a young, delicate woman

brave the terrors of the forest in a time of such desultory warfare that the dangers were increased tenfold, to do her duty to her country, and by timely warning save much bloodshed and disaster."

Curzon and Currie – 1883-1913

The woman suffrage movement in Canada had its beginning in 1878 under the leadership of Dr. Emily Howard Stowe. The Canadian Women's Suffrage Association was the outcome of a meeting of the Toronto Women's Literary and Social Progress Club in the city council chamber in 1883, to discuss the question of woman suffrage. A change in the Electoral Act, which made the Dominion and provincial voters' lists coincide, rendered efforts useless in the Dominion legislature, and made of woman suffrage a provincial issue. The first municipal franchise was granted to widows and spinsters in Ontario in 1884. However, it was not until the 1920s that woman suffrage in Canadian provinces gained some traction and it was not until the 1980s that the Canadian Charter of Rights was enacted. It had taken a hundred years.

Two leading lights of the woman suffrage movement were Sarah Ann Vincent Curzon (1833-1898) and Emma Currie. In 1887 Curzon had her verse drama, "Laura Secord, the heroine of 1812", published by C. Blackett Robinson in Toronto; this was followed in July 1891 by "The Story of Laura Secord", published by the Lundy's Lane Historical Society. Her efforts to raise the profile of Laura Secord as a heroine was helped by her communication with Harriet Hopkins Secord Smith, Laura's daughter and witness to the Walk in June 1813, who died in 1892. In 1895, Curzon co-founded the Women's Canadian Historical Society in Toronto with Mary Agnes Fitzgibbon, Lady Matilda Edgar, and others. One of Curzon's friends Emma Augusta Currie (1829-1913) later wrote "The Story of Laura Secord and Canadian Reminiscences", published by William Briggs in Toronto in 1900. Currie was a leading light in the establishment of the Woman's Literary Club in St. Catharines, formed in 1892.

Plaques

Plaque, House at Great Barrington, Massachusetts
The plaque on the former Ingersoll land in Great Barrington,
Massachusetts, just outside the town's Mason Library, was
dedicated on 18 October 1997. It states:
"LAURA INGERSOLL SECORD
Laura Ingersoll was born in a dwelling which stood on this site
until 1913, when Mason Library was built. She was the daughter
of Elizabeth (Dewey) and Thomas Ingersoll, a hatter and miller
with privilege nearby on the Housatonic River. Looking for new
opportunity, the Ingersolls relocated to Upper Canada in 1795.
Laura married James Secord, a United Empire Loyalist. They
were living in Queenston, Ontario at the outbreak of the War of
1812. Alerted to an impending American attack at Beaver Dams,
Laura Secord in June 1813 undertook an arduous 19 mile journey
through woods and swamp to warn British troops. Her tenacity
and courage made her a heroine. Laura Secord was honoured on
a Canadian postage stamp in 1992."
Great Barrington Historic District Commission, 1997.

Plaque, Queenston Village, Ontario
Queenston held many memories for the Secords who had
struggled through the long post-war period in difficult
circumstances and ignored petitions for assistance. However,
had become an important commercial destination during these
days, as stated on the town's plaque:
"THE FOUNDING OF QUEENSTON
Following the loss, after the American Revolution of the Niagara
River's east bank, a new portage around Niagara Falls was
established in the 1780s' with Queenston its northern terminous.
Wharves, storehouses and a block-house were built. Robert
Hamilton, a prominent merchant considered the village's
founder, operated a thriving trans-shipment business. Known as
the "Lower Landing" it was named "Queenston" by Lieut.-
Governor Simcoe. During the war of 1812 the village was badly
damaged. Here lived such well-known figures as Laura Secord

and William Lyon Mackenzie. Despite loss of commerce following the opening of the Welland Canal in 1829, Queenston later served as a terminus for the province's first horse-drawn railway. Queenston was incorporated into the town of Niagara-on-the-Lake in 1970."
This plaque was erected by the Archaeological and Historic Sites Board, Ministry of Colleges and Universities.

Plaque, House at Queenston, Ontario
The plaque outside the Laura Secord Homestead in Queenston, Ontario, reads:
"LAURA INGERSOLL SECORD 1775-1868
Born in Great Barrington, Massachusetts, Laura Ingersoll came to Upper Canada with her father in 1795 and settled in this area. About two years later she married James Secord, a United Empire Loyalist, and within seven years they had moved to this site from nearby St. David's. From here, during the War of 1812, Laura Secord set out on an arduous 19-mile journey to warn the local British commander, Lieutenant James FitzGibbon, of an impending American attack. The courage and tenacity displayed on this occasion in June 1813 placed her in the forefront of the province's heroines. Mrs. Secord's house, a simple frame building, was restored (1971-72), and remains as a memorial to this exceptional act of patriotism."

Plaque, Homestead at Queenston, Ontario
Right beside the above plaque in Queenston is another that reads:
"This marker was placed in 1901, by the Women's Literary Club of St. Catherine's to honour Laura Secord and was re-dedicated in 1972 by members of the club on the occasion of their 80th annual pilgrimage."

Laura Secord Homestead museum is located at 29 Queenston Street in the village of Queenston, Ontario, close to the Niagara River. It is a beautiful, 15 minute drive along the Niagara Parkway from Niagara Falls to the south or from Niagara-on-the-Lake to the north.

Plaque, Beaver Dams Battlefield Park, Ontario
Also in Beaver Dams Park is a plaque that reads:
"LAURA INGERSOLL SECORD, 1775-1868
Who set out from home in Queenston early in the morning of
June 22, 1813, to walk an arduous nineteen miles to warn the
British outpost at DeCew Falls of an impending American attack.
The information enabled the local commander, Lieutenant James
FitzGibbon, and his detachment to surprise and capture the
entire enemy force at the Battle of Beaver Dams on June 24, 1813,
thereby marking the turning point in the War of 1812.
To perpetuate her memory."

Plaque, Beaver Dams Battlefield Park, Ontario
There is a plaque on a cairn in the Battle of Beaver Dams park
behind the school on South Pine Street in downtown Thorold,
which summarizes the events nearby in the summer of 1813:
"BEAVER DAMS
Following their repulse at Stoney Creek the Americans sent a
force from Fort George to destroy a British advanced post at
Beaver Dams. Warned of their approach by an Indian scout and
by Laura Secord, a force of Iroquois from Caughnawaga and the
Grand River, led by Captains Dominique Ducharme and William
Kerr, ambushed the attackers near here on 24 June 1813, and
compelled them to surrender to Lieutenant James Fitzgibbon of
the regular British army. After this defeat the Americans did not
again venture out in force, leaving the British in control of the
area. "

Plaque, House at Chippawa, Ontario
The small plaque outside 3800 Bridgewater Street, near Adelaide
Street (now Laura Secord Place), which is just across the road
from the cottage's private access to Chippawa Creek, reads:
"LAURA SECORD HOME
Laura Ingersoll Secord resided at this Chippawa home for 27
years. A heroine of the War of 1812, Mrs. Secord had, in the
summer of 1813, walked 19 miles through swamp and bush from
Queenston to DeCew Falls to warn the British of an impending

American attack. In 1861 the Prince of Wales rewarded her with a gift of 100 pounds for her bravery; however, she never met the Prince. Laura Secord attended Holy Trinity Church. She died here October 17, 1868 at the age of 93 and was buried in the Drummond Hill Cemetery."

This plaque was erected in 1996 by the Village of Chippawa Citizens' Committee with the assistance of the Ontario heritage Foundation.

Laura Secord's house in later life at 3800 Bridgewater Street in Chippawa village is down the Parkway from Niagara Falls about 10 minutes. Immediately after crossing Chippawa Creek, going south, it is due west of Cummington Square along the creek bank and accessed by driving along Laura Secord Place.

Plaque, Church at Chippawa, Ontario
When the Prince of Wales worshipped, he did so at the Church of the Holy Trinity in Chippawa, where Laura Secord was a parishioner. The plaque at this church, at 7820 Portage Rd. S., Chippawa, reads:
"CHURCH OF THE HOLY TRINITY
A frame church was built here following the arrival in 1820 of an Anglican missionary, the Reverend William Leeming. It was burned on the night of September 12-13, 1839, by supporters of William Lyon Mackenzie who crossed the Niagara River from New York State. The present church was designed by John Howard and built with the aid of private subscriptions and government assistance. The corner-stone was laid in 1841 by Bishop John Strachan. Among the well known persons who worshipped here were: Jenny Lind, the famous singer, in 1851; Edward, Prince of Wales (later King Edward VII), in 1860; and Laura Secord, a parishioner, who died in 1868."

The plaque was erected by the Archaeological and Historic Sites Board of Ontario.

War Claim

War Claim, James Secord of Queenston – after 1815
A statement of losses sustained by James Secord of Queenston, Merchant, during the late war between Great Britain and the United States of America.
Losses sustained by his Majesty's troops -

3 Pair shutters with hinges and bolts	£ 6. 0.0
9 panel doors with hinges and locks	£28. 0.0
10 – 24 Lights or sash and glass	£30. 0.0
1100 feet 1½ inch flooring boards, nails and labor included	£14. 2.0
133 Yds Lathing & plastering for kitchen	£26. 8.0
1 mantlepiece	£ 4. 0.0
Store shelves and counter	£20. 0.0
1 Room 20x16 Lathing and plastering	£45.12.0
Lathing and plastering, a room 24x9 feet	£ 9.12.0
1 porch	£ 8. 0.0
1 stable	£35. 0.0
Store house	£36. 0.0
Repairing chimneys	£25. 0.0
500 rails @ 40/- pr. Hundred	£10. 0.0
1 Horse waggon destroyed on the retreat of General Vincent from Niagara	£30. 0.0
1 horse waggon on retreat of army from Fort Erie	£40. 0.0
6 months House Rent	£30. 0.0

N.Y.C. £397.14.0

I, James Secord of Queenston do hereby solemnly declare that I have actually sustained the damage in the accompanying Claim set forth and that I have not received any remuneration whatever either from his Majesty's Government, from the Individuals who committed the damage claimed for or from any person or persons for them.
J. Secord

What happened 50 years ago?

Fifty years ago, the residents of the Niagara Peninsula had an earlier Walk Commemoration. Recognition of that anniversary was sponsored by the St. Catharines and Lincoln Historical Society. The celebration was held on the closest Sunday to June 22 (but in the wrong year).

Although the Niagara Historical Society had already published the only daguerreotype photograph of Laura Ingersoll Secord, the lady in the program's photograph was an image of Mary (Polly) Page, Major David Secord's third wife - the sister-in-law of the heroine, Laura Secord.

The "Laura Secord Walk" Commemoration, 1812-1962

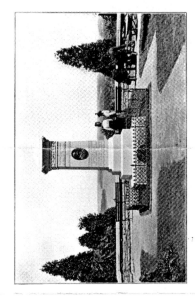

THE
"LAURA SECORD WALK"
COMMEMORATION

1812 - 1962

SUNDAY

JUNE 24, 1962

THE MAPLE LEAF FOREVER

1. In days of yore, from Britain's shore,
   Wolfe, the dauntless hero came,
   And planted firm Britannia's flag,
   On Canada's fair domain.
   Here may it wave, our boast, our pride,
   And join in love to-gether,
   The Thistle, Shamrock, Rose entwine,
   The Maple Leaf Forever!

Chorus
   The Maple Leaf, our emblem dear,
   The Maple Leaf Forever!
   God save our Queen and Heaven bless,
   The Maple Leaf Forever!

2. At Queenston Heights and Lundy's Lane,
   Our brave fathers, side by side,
   For freedom, homes, and loved ones dear,
   Firmly stood and nobly died;
   And those dear rights which they maintained,
   We swear to yield them never!
   Our watchword ever more shall be,
   The Maple Leaf Forever!

Sponsored by St. Catharines and Lincoln Historical Society

Courtesy: Author's Collection

Some Belongings related to Laura Secord

After her death in 1868, at the age of 93, the belongings of Laura Ingersoll Secord were scattered among her family and friends. Of course, in fact, there were few heirlooms left because Laura and James Secord's house in Queenston had been plundered twice by marauding American soldiers in 1813-14. However, some of the remaining belongings can now be located here:

1. Niagara Historical Society Museum

Photographs of Laura Secord
Bust of Laura Secord, by Mildred Peel, as grave monument
Engraving of the Ingersoll home in Great Barrington, MA
Three panels from mantel in Great Barrington house
Three bricks from fireplace in Great Barrington house
Sample of the handwriting of James Secord
Copper tea kettle in which gold coins were hidden for safety
Large hamper;   Small trunk
Glass sugar bowl;   Lid of china sugar bowl
Marble markers for prayer book
Yarn winder;   Beadwork purse
Jet necklace
Silver sugar tongs;   Two silver tablespoons
Small tray
Quilt jointly made by granddaughter Louisa, and Laura Secord
Large butterfly of coloured beads on black cloth (copy)
Flower wreath made of hair of different colours by daughter
Illuminated copy of the Lord's Prayer owned by Laura Secord

[Also at this museum:
Map showing her Walk from Queenston to DeCew house;
photocopy of FitzGibbon's Certificate regarding the Walk; a

Commemorative medal of her Walk to DeCew Falls; and a Poem written by Janet Carnochan about Laura Secord.]

Silver sugar tongs of Laura Ingersoll Secord ('LIS')
Courtesy: Niagara Historical Society

2. St. Mary's Museum, Ontario
Photo of Eugenia Mary Sparks MacPherson, who was the great-niece of Laura Secord, wearing Laura Secord's shawl.

3. Royal Museum, British Columbia
Laura's bonnet, as passed down through the family and donated.

4. Lundy's Lane Historical Museum in Niagara Falls, Ontario
A cup and saucer from the family.

5. Fort York warehouse, Toronto
Laura Secord's two black shawls, and a lock of hair.

Most of these belongings can only be attributed to Laura Secord. Their provenance and authenticity would need to be successfully achieved. Other family heirlooms are either still in the descendant families or in locations which shall remain nameless for security reasons.

Ancestors of Laura Ingersoll Secord

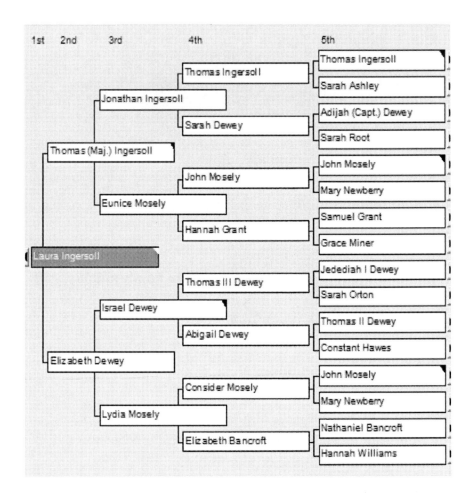

1st	2nd	3rd	4th	5th
				Thomas Ingersoll
			Thomas Ingersoll	Sarah Ashley
		Jonathan Ingersoll		Adijah (Capt.) Dewey
			Sarah Dewey	Sarah Root
	Thomas (Maj.) Ingersoll			John Mosely
			John Mosely	Mary Newberry
		Eunice Mosely		Samuel Grant
			Hannah Grant	Grace Miner
Laura Ingersoll				Jedediah I Dewey
			Thomas III Dewey	Sarah Orton
		Israel Dewey		Thomas II Dewey
			Abigail Dewey	Constant Hawes
	Elizabeth Dewey			John Mosely
			Consider Mosely	Mary Newberry
		Lydia Mosely		Nathaniel Bancroft
			Elizabeth Bancroft	Hannah Williams

170

Descendants of Laura Ingersoll Secord

Laura Ingersoll's birth and marriage records are missing, probably destroyed with other records in the Revolutionary and 1812 Wars, respectively. It is possible that Laura Ingersoll and James Secord were married by either James' brother, David, or by Major David Secord, both of whom were Justices of the Peace in St. David's. The approximate date of her marriage is known from circumstantial evidence. Two birth dates have appeared in biographies and family histories – 13 September and 19 December 1775. The first of these was confirmed as correct by Laura Secord's granddaughter, Laura Louisa Smith, in E.J. Thompson's 1913 article, "Laura Ingersoll Secord," in a 1913 Niagara Historical Society publication. Laura Ingersoll Secord's burial record is also missing because the sexton at Drummond Hill Cemetery was elderly and forgetful of his duty.

In the Descendant list below, a child with a "+" sign on the left sign is a parent in the next generation. "Ontario" is used for the province formerly known as Upper Canada. "BNA" means British North America. "Married" may also mean "partnered with" in common law. Dates and places are omitted from the 5th, 6th, 7th and 8th generations. Finally, the Descendant list is presented as a biological family tree, including only those who are biological children of descendants of Laura Ingersoll Secord. The Index at the end of this book excludes this family tree.

If the reader can contribute further to this descendants' listing below, the author would be grateful for any adds, omissions or changes by email communication to: bygonespublishing@gmail.com .

1. **Laura₁ Ingersoll**, born 13 Sep 1775 in Great Barrington, Berkshire, Massachusetts, BNA; died 17 Oct 1868 in Chippawa, Niagara Falls, Ontario, Canada; buried in Drummond Hill Cem., Lundy's Lane, Ontario, Canada, daughter of Thomas (Maj.) Ingersoll and Elizabeth Dewey. She married in 1797 in Niagara Twp., Lincoln Co., Ontario, Canada **James (Capt.; Sgt.) Secord**, born 7 Jul 1773 in New Rochelle, Westchester Co., New York, BNA; died 22 Feb 1841 in Chippawa, Ontario, Canada; buried in Drummond Hill Cem., Lundy's Lane, Ontario, Canada, son of Jacques (James) (Lt.) Secord and Madeline (Magdelaine) Badeau.

Children of Laura Ingersoll and James (Capt.; Sgt.) Secord were as follows:

+ 2   i   **Mary Lawrence₂ Secord**, born 1799 in St. David's, Lincoln, Ontario, Canada; died 11 Mar 1876 in Dublin, Ireland; buried in Mount Jerome Cem., Dublin, Ireland. She married **William H. (Dr.) Trumble**.

  3   ii   **Charlotte₂ Secord**, born 1801 in Queenston, Lincoln, Ontario, Canada; died 14 Oct 1880 in Guelph, Wellington, Ontario, Canada; buried 16 Oct 1880 in Bk. N-397, Woodlawn Cem., Guelph, Wellington, Ontario, Canada.

+ 4   iii **Harriet Hopkins₂ Secord**, born 10 Feb 1803 in St. David's, Lincoln, Ontario, Canada; died 20 Jan 1892 in Guelph, Wellington, Ontario, Canada; buried in Bk. N-397, Woodlawn Cem., Guelph, Wellington, Ontario, Canada. She married **David William Smith**.

+ 5   iv   **Charles Badeau₂ Secord**, born 1809 in Queenston, Ontario, Canada; christened 18 Apr 1816 in Niagara Twp., Lincoln, Ontario, Canada; died 7 Nov 1872 in Lincoln, Ontario, Canada; buried in St. Mark's Ch. Cem., Niagara-on-the-Lake, Lincoln, Ontario, Canada. He married **Margaret Ann Robins**.

  6   v   **Appolonia₂ Secord**, born 1810 in Queenston, Lincoln, Ontario, Canada; died 20 Dec 1828 in Queenston, Lincoln, Ontario, Canada.

+ 7   vi   **Laura Ann₂ Secord**, born 20 Oct 1815 in Queenston, Lincoln, Ontario, Canada; christened 18 Apr 1816 in Niagara Twp., Lincoln Co., Ontario, Canada; died 18 Aug 1852 in Guelph, Wellington, Ontario, Canada; buried in Bk. N-397, Woodlawn Cem.,

Guelph, Wellington, Ontario, Canada. She married
(1) **John (Capt.) Poore**; (2) **William (Dr.) Clarke**.

+ 8   vii   **Hannah Cartwright**2 **Secord**, born 1817 in
Queenston, Lincoln, Ontario, Canada; christened 31
Jul 1820 in Niagara Twp., Lincoln Co., Ontario,
Canada; died 21 Nov 1877 in Guelph, Wellington,
Ontario, Canada; buried in Bk. O-194, Woodlawn
Cem., Guelph, Wellington, Ontario, Canada. She
married (1) **Howley Williams**; (2) **Edward Pyke
Carthew**.

Generation 2

2. **Mary Lawrence**2 **Secord**, born 1799 in St. David's, Lincoln, Ontario,
Canada; died 11 Mar 1876 in Dublin, Ireland; buried in Mount Jerome
Cem., Dublin, Ireland. She married on 18 Apr 1816 in Queenston,
Lincoln, Ontario, Canada **William H. (Dr.) Trumble**, born 1794 in
Kilmorgan, Co. Sligo, Ireland; died 1821 in Belize, British Honduras,
son of Harloe Trumble and Elizabeth Sodan.
Children of Mary Lawrence Secord and William H. (Dr.) Trumble
were as follows:

+ 9   i   **Elizabeth**3 **Trumble**, born 27 Mar 1817 in Kingston,
Jamaica; christened 18 Apr 1817 in Kingston,
Jamaica; died 1893 in Dungannon, Co. Tyrone,
Ireland. She married **William Henry Davis**.

   10   ii   **Mary**3 **Trumble**, born abt 1820 in Belize, British
Honduras; died Mar 1890 in Camberwell, London,
England.

4. **Harriet Hopkins**2 **Secord**, born 10 Feb 1803 in St. David's, Lincoln,
Ontario, Canada; died 20 Jan 1892 in Guelph, Wellington, Ontario,
Canada; buried in Bk. N-397, Woodlawn Cem., Guelph, Wellington,
Ontario, Canada. She married on 23 Nov 1824 in Queenston, Ontario,
Canada **David William Smith**, born 1801 in Fort Erie, Welland,
Ontario, Canada; died 23 May 1842 in St Catharines, Lincoln, Ontario,
Canada; buried 25 May 1842 in St. Paul's Ch. Cem., Fort Erie, Welland,
Ontario, Canada, son of William Smith and Mary (---).
Children of Harriet Hopkins Secord and David William Smith were
as follows:

   11   i   **Laura Louisa**3 **Smith**, born 11 Sep 1825 in Lincoln,
Ontario, Canada; died 7 Jan 1904 in Guelph,
Wellington, Ontario, Canada; buried in Woodlawn
Cem., Guelph, Wellington, Ontario, Canada.

12   ii   **Mary Augusta**3 **Smith**, born 9 Nov 1828 in Lincoln, Ontario, Canada; died 16 Apr 1911 in Guelph, Wellington, Ontario, Canada; buried in Bk. N-397, Woodlawn Cem., Guelph, Wellington, Ontario, Canada.

+   13   iii   **William James**3 **Smith**, born Oct 1829 in Lincoln, Ontario, Canada; died 1901 in Montevideo, Minnesota, USA. He married **Elizabeth Bresnahan**.

5. **Charles Badeau**2 **Secord**, born 1809 in Queenston, Ontario, Canada; christened 18 Apr 1816 in Niagara Twp., Lincoln, Ontario, Canada; died 7 Nov 1872 in Lincoln, Ontario, Canada; buried in St. Mark's Ch. Cem., Niagara-on-the-Lake, Lincoln, Ontario, Canada. He married on 26 Nov 1830 in Kingston, Frontenac, Ontario, Canada **Margaret Ann Robins**, born 1813 in Kingston, Frontenac, Ontario, Canada; died 1872 in Lincoln, Ontario, Canada; buried in St. Mark's Ch. Cem., Niagara-on-the-Lake, Lincoln, Ontario, Canada, daughter of W. Robins.

Children of Charles Badeau Secord and Margaret Ann Robins were as follows:

+   14   i   **Charles Forsyth (Prof.)**3 **Secord**, born 9 May 1833 in St. Charles, Welland, Ontario, Canada; christened 21 Jul 1834 in Queenston Ch., Lincoln, Ontario, Canada; died 7 Jul 1899 in Omaha, Douglas, Nebraska, USA; buried in Cedar Dales Cem., Papillion, Sarpy, Nebraska, USA. He married (1) **Elizabeth Ellis**; (2) **Elizabeth (Liza) Nancy Neff**.

15   ii   **James Badeau**3 **Secord**, born 1836 in Queenston, Lincoln, Ontario, Canada; died 16 Aug 1899 in Niagara, Lincoln, Ontario, Canada; buried 19 Aug 1899 in Niagara, Lincoln, Ontario, Canada. He married on 27 Jun 1888 in York, Ontario, Canada **Clara Flint**, born 1862 in Toronto, York, Ontario, Canada; died 26 Dec 1927 in Middlesex, Canada, daughter of George Henry Flint and Charlotte F. Warren.

16   iii   **Alicia**3 **Secord**, born 26 Dec 1838 in Queenston, Lincoln, Ontario, Canada; died 1926 in Niagara Twp., Lincoln, Ontario, Canada; buried in St. Mark's Ch., Niagara-on-the-Lake, Ontario, Canada. She married (1) **Joseph Clayton**; (2) on 13 Apr 1876 in Toronto, Ontario, Canada **Isaac Cockburn**, born

1841 in Berwick, Ontario, Canada; died 8 May 1927 in Winnipeg, Manitoba, Canada; buried in Gravenhurst, Muskoka, Ontario, Canada, son of Peter Clayton Cockburn and Mary (---).

7. **Laura Ann**2 **Secord**, born 20 Oct 1815 in Queenston, Lincoln, Ontario, Canada; christened 18 Apr 1816 in Niagara Twp., Lincoln Co., Ontario, Canada; died 18 Aug 1852 in Guelph, Wellington, Ontario, Canada; buried in Bk. N-397, Woodlawn Cem., Guelph, Wellington, Ontario, Canada. She married (1) on 17 Oct 1833 in Queenston Ch., Lincoln, Ontario, Canada **John (Capt.) Poore**, born 20 Nov 1808 in Dorchester, England; died 11 Feb 1842 in Hamilton Barracks, Ontario, Canada, son of John Poore and Mary DeLisle; (2) on 11 Jul 1843 in Guelph, Wellington, Ontario, Canada **William (Dr.) Clarke**, born 1810 in Maryborough, Queens, Ireland; christened 30 Dec 1810 in Coolbanagher Parish, Queens, Ireland; died 7 Oct 1887 in Guelph, Wellington, Ontario, Canada; buried in Bk. O, Woodlawn Cem., Guelph, Wellington, Ontario, Canada, son of Thomas Clarke and Elizabeth Wilkinson.

Children of Laura Ann Secord and John (Capt.) Poore were as follows:

+ 17	i	**John**3 **Poore**, born 28 Oct 1835 in Guelph, Wellington, Ontario, Canada; died 22 Mar 1902 Of Stonewall, Selkirk, Manitoba, Canada. He married **Flora Leitch**.
18	ii	**Albert James de Lisle**3 **Poore**, born 1 Nov 1836 in Guelph, Wellington, Ontario, Canada; died 17 Jan 1837 in Guelph, Wellington, Ontario, Canada.

Children of Laura Ann Secord and William (Dr.) Clarke were as follows:

19	i	**William**3 **Clarke**, born 2 Jul 1844 in Guelph, Wellington, Ontario, Canada; christened 12 May 1845 in Guelph, Wellington, Ontario, Canada; died abt 1845 in Guelph, Wellington, Ontario, Canada; buried in Woodlawn Cem., Guelph, Wellington, Ontario, Canada.
20	ii	**Laura Secord**3 **Clarke**, born 23 Oct 1846 in Guelph, Wellington, Ontario, Canada; christened 26 Apr 1847 in Guelph, Wellington, Ontario, Canada; died 4 May 1936 in Toronto, Ontario, Canada; buried in Bk. N-397, Woodlawn Cem., Guelph, Wellington, Ontario, Canada.

21   iii   **Millicent**3 **Clarke**, born Oct 1849 in Guelph,
Wellington, Ontario, Canada; died 21 Aug 1850 in
Guelph, Wellington, Ontario, Canada; buried in
Woodlawn Cem., Guelph, Wellington, Ontario,
Canada.

8. **Hannah Cartwright**2 **Secord**, born 1817 in Queenston, Lincoln,
Ontario, Canada; christened 31 Jul 1820 in Niagara Twp., Lincoln Co.,
Ontario, Canada; died 21 Nov 1877 in Guelph, Wellington, Ontario,
Canada; buried in Bk. O-194, Woodlawn Cem., Guelph, Wellington,
Ontario, Canada. She married (1) on 22 Aug 1833 in Queenston Ch.,
Lincoln, Ontario, Canada **Howley Williams**, born 21 Dec 1810 in
Clapham, London, England; died 10 Aug 1844 in Guelph, Wellington,
Ontario, Canada; buried in Bk. O, Woodlawn Cem., Guelph,
Wellington, Ontario, Canada; (2) on 17 Mar 1847 in Guelph, Wellington,
Ontario, Canada **Edward Pyke Carthew**, born 22 May 1808 in
Mattishall, Norfolk, England; died 8 Apr 1879 in Guelph, Wellington,
Ontario, Canada; buried 10 Apr 1879 in Bk. O-194, Woodlawn Cem.,
Guelph, Wellington, Ontario, Canada, son of Morden (Rector) Carthew
and Emily Tweed-Pyke.
      Children of Hannah Cartwright Secord and Howley Williams were
as follows:
+   22   i   **Katherine Emma**3 **Williams**, born 1841 in Guelph,
Wellington, Ontario, Canada; died 18 Mar 1883 in
Guelph, Wellington, Ontario, Canada; buried in Bk.
O, Woodlawn Cem., Guelph, Wellington, Ontario,
Canada. She married **John Andrews Lamprey**.
    23   ii   **Caroline**3 **Williams**, born 24 Jul 1843 in Guelph,
Wellington, Ontario, Canada; died 1848 in Guelph,
Wellington, Ontario, Canada; buried in Woodlawn
Cem., Guelph, Wellington, Ontario, Canada.
      Children of Hannah Cartwright Secord and Edward Pyke Carthew
were as follows:
+   24   i   **Hannah**3 **Carthew**, born 24 Jan 1848 in Guelph,
Wellington, Ontario, Canada; died 8 Apr 1929 in
Elliott Home, Guelph, Wellington, Ontario,
Canada; buried 10 Apr 1929 in Guelph, Wellington,
Ontario, Canada. She married **Llewellyn (Dr.)
Brock**.
+   25   ii   **James Morden**3 **Carthew**, born 17 Nov 1849 in
Guelph, Ontario, Canada; died 1 Jan 1929 in
Thornbury, Grey, Ontario, Canada. He married
Adeline Pauline Maud Chisholm.

+ 26   iii   **Caroline**3 **Carthew**, born 13 Aug 1851 in Guelph,
                Ontario, Canada; died 11 Mar 1931 in 24 Adolphus
                St., Cornwall, Stormont, Ontario, Canada; buried
                12 Mar 1931 in Woodlawn Cem., Cornwall,
                Ontario, Canada. She married **Charles William
                Young**.
+ 27   iv   **Charles Edward (Dr.)**3 **Carthew**, born 20 Nov 1853
                in Guelph, Ontario, Canada; died 28 Apr 1931 in
                Edmonton West, Alberta, Canada. He married
                Angelica Caroline Elizabeth Harvey.
+ 28   v   **William**3 **Carthew**, born 29 Mar 1856 in Guelph,
                Ontario, Canada; died 30 Jun 1934 in Waterloo,
                Waterloo Co., Ontario, Canada. He married **Jessie
                Tremain Innes**.

Generation 3

9. **Elizabeth**3 **Trumble**, born 27 Mar 1817 in Kingston, Jamaica;
christened 18 Apr 1817 in Kingston, Jamaica; died 1893 in Dungannon,
Co. Tyrone, Ireland. She married on 4 Jun 1844 in Lisnagore Ch., nr
Sligo, Co. Sligo, Ireland **William Henry Davis**, born Jun 1815 in
Belturbet, Co. Cavan, Ireland; died Apr 1894 in Belfast, Ireland, son of
Richard Davis and Jane Beck.

William Henry Davis & Gertrude.   William Henry Newland Davis
Courtesy: Eldrid Ingebjørg Mageli

Children of Elizabeth Trumble and William Henry Davis were as follows:

+ 29   i   **William Henry Newland**4 **Davis**, born Apr 1845 in Avon Lodge, Armagh, Ireland; died 14 Oct 1917 in GlenRock Twp., Converse, Wyoming, USA. He married **Amelia Elizabeth Protzman**.

+ 30   ii   **Laura Mary**4 **Davis**, born 8 Oct 1847 in Avon Lodge, Armagh, Ireland; died 27 Oct 1932 in Oslo, Norway. She married **Henrik Martin Fredrik Mack**.

   31   iii   **Edith**4 **Davis**, born abt 1850 in Avon Lodge, Armagh, Ireland; died 1919 in 21 Malone Park, Belfast, Ireland.

   32   iv   **Gertrude**4 **Davis**, born abt 1852 in Dungannon, Ireland; died aft 1932 in 21 Malone Park, Belfast, Ireland.

   33   v   **Robert Evans Stuart (Lt-Col., Dr.)**4 **Davis**, born 1855 in Dungannon, Ireland; died 29 Nov 1925 in Belfast, Ireland.

L->R: Robert, Frederick & William
Courtesy: Eldrid Ingebjørg Mageli

   34   vi   **Frederick**4 **Davis**, born abt 1858 in Dungannon, Ireland; died aft 1932.

13. William James3 **Smith**, born Oct 1829 in Lincoln, Ontario, Canada; died 1901 in Montevideo, Minnesota, USA. He married abt 1856 in Chicago, Cook, Illinois, USA **Elizabeth Bresnahan**, born 1839 in Milford, Ireland; died 1887 in Browns Valley, Minnesota, USA.

Children of William James Smith and Elizabeth Bresnahan were as follows:

+ 35   i   **William James Jr.**4 **Smith**, born 12 Mar 1857 in Lake Street, Chicago, Illinois, USA; died 9 Dec 1943 in Montevideo, Minnesota, USA; buried 12 Dec 1943 in Montevideo Cem., Minnesota, USA. He married **Edith Henriette Benson**.

178

Smith Farms, Minnesota, established in 1877.
Courtesy: Sandra DiNanni

+ 36 ii **Charles Secord₄ Smith**, born 12 Sep 1860 in
Ellsworth, Wisconsin, USA; died 1902. He married
Annie Lynch.

+ 37 iii **Francis (Frank) David₄ Smith**, born 28 Oct 1862 in
Ellsworth, Wisconsin, USA; died 14 Jul 1934 in
Browns Valley, Minnesota, USA. He married
Serena Fossen Anderson.

38 iv **Arthur George₄ Smith**, born 24 Jun 1864 in
Prescott, Wisconsin, USA; died 18 Jun 1865 in
Prescott, Wisconsin, USA.

+ 39 v **George Arthur₄ Smith**, born 28 Jun 1868 in
Prescott, Wisconsin, USA; died 14 Oct 1956 in
Koochiching Co., Minnesota, USA. He married
Minnie Austa Belle Jewett.

14. **Charles Forsyth (Prof.)₃ Secord**, born 9 May 1833 in St. Charles,
Welland, Ontario, Canada; christened 21 Jul 1834 in Queenston Ch.,
Lincoln, Ontario, Canada; died 7 Jul 1899 in Omaha, Douglas,
Nebraska, USA; buried in Cedar Dales Cem., Papillion, Sarpy,
Nebraska, USA. He married (1) abt 1855 **Elizabeth Ellis**, born 1835 in
Ontario, Canada; died abt 1871 in DeWitt, Saline, Nebraska, USA; (2) in
1872 in Ontario, Canada **Elizabeth (Liza) Nancy Neff**, born 4 Feb 1844

in Humberstone, Welland, Ontario, Canada; died 20 Oct 1931 in Omaha, Nebraska, USA, daughter of Abraham Neff and Mary Burger.

Children of Charles Forsyth (Prof.) Secord and Elizabeth Ellis were as follows:

40 i **Charles Frederick**4 **Secord**, born 1856 in Ontario, Canada; died 1872 in Phoenix, Arizona, USA.

+ 41 ii **Agnes Elizabeth**4 **Secord**, born 25 Jun 1858 in Ontario, Canada; died 26 Apr 1923 in Los Angeles, California, USA. She married (1) **Henry Clinton Smith**; (2) **Charles Rogers**.

+ 42 iii **Appalonia (Lona) Josepha**4 **Secord**, born 16 Jun 1860 in Ontario, Canada; died 8 Mar 1948 in St. Edward, Nebraska, USA; buried 10 Mar 1948 in Sunset Cem., Cedar Rapids, Nebraska, USA. She married **William Riley Hackney**.

+ 43 iv **William Henry**4 **Secord**, born 25 Sep 1862 in DeWitt, Saline, Nebraska, USA; died 9 Jul 1904 in Collins, Iowa, USA. He married **Iona A. Van Loan**.

+ 44 v **Frank Alexander**4 **Secord**, born 6 Dec 1866 in DeWitt, Saline, Nebraska, USA; died 27 Mar 1954 in Omaha, Douglas, Nebraska, USA. He married **Winifred Mayfield**.

45 vi **Anna**4 **Secord**, born in DeWitt, Saline, Nebraska, USA.

46 vii **Claude**4 **Secord**, born 17 Apr 1869 in DeWitt, Saline, Nebraska, USA; died 10 Jan 1870.

47 viii **Jesse**4 **Secord**, born in DeWitt, Saline, Nebraska, USA.

+ 48 ix **Margaret (Ella)**4 **Secord**, born 4 Feb 1871 in Dorchester, Saline, Nebraska, USA; died 13 Jul 1931 in Omaha, Douglas, Nebraska, USA. She married **Osmos C. Higbee**.

Children of Charles Forsyth (Prof.) Secord and Elizabeth (Liza) Nancy Neff were as follows:

+ 49 i **Clayton (Carlos) Forsythe (Dr.)**4 **Secord**, born 22 Jun 1874 in Blair, Dorchester, Saline, Nebraska, USA; died 28 Jan 1955 in Central, Alleghany, Maryland, USA. He married (1) **Susan Hazel James**; (2) **Cristina Alvarado Mota**.

+ 50 ii **Harold R.**4 **Secord**, born 27 Apr 1877 in Dorchester, Saline, Nebraska, USA; died 9 Aug 1938 in Gretna, Sarpy, Nebraska, USA. He married **Rachel Curley**.

| 51 | iii | **Ross Horace**[4] **Secord**, born 12 Jun 1879 in Dorchester, Saline, Nebraska, USA; died 27 Oct 1939 in Omaha, Douglas, Nebraska, USA. He married on 5 May 1905 in Omaha, Douglas, Nebraska, USA **Lola Edna Snyde (Snide)**, born 5 May 1884 in Papillion, Sarpy, Nebraska, USA; died 17 Nov 1948 in Denver, Colorado, USA. |

Cyril Paul Secord & Elizabeth Nancy Neff
Courtesy: Betty Secord Deaton

| + | 52 | iv | **Cyril Paul**[4] **Secord**, born 1 Sep 1883 in DeWitt, Saline, Nebraska, USA; died 20 Oct 1962 in Omaha, Douglas, Nebraska, USA. He married **Florence Margaret Peterson**. |
| | 53 | v | **Geraldine A.**[4] **Secord**, born 10 Aug 1887 in DeWitt, Saline, Nebraska, USA; died 2 Oct 1904 in Papillion, Sarpy, Nebraska, USA. |

17. **John**[3] **Poore**, born 28 Oct 1835 in Guelph, Wellington, Ontario, Canada; died 22 Mar 1902 Of Stonewall, Selkirk, Manitoba, Canada. He married **Flora Leitch**, born 28 Nov 1837; died 11 Sep 1872 in Guelph, Wellington, Ontario, Canada, daughter of Dougald Leitch and Elizabeth (---).

Children of John Poore and Flora Leitch were as follows:

+	54	i	**John Frederick DeLisle**[4] **Poore**, born 5 Jul 1861 in Ontario, Canada; died 24 Jan 1932 in Portland, Oregon, USA. He married **Mary Ann Gordon**.
+	55	ii	**Laura Mary Madeline**[4] **Poore**, born 17 Oct 1862 in Guelph, Wellington, Ontario, Canada; died 13 Nov 1947 Of Stonewall, Manitoba, Canada. She married **Isaac Riley**.
+	56	iii	**Elizabeth**[4] **Poore**, born 28 Dec 1868 in Ontario, Canada; died Of Portland, Oregon, USA. She married (1) **Robert Gossman**; (2) **David C. Burns**.

22. Katherine Emma3 **Williams**, born 1841 in Guelph, Wellington, Ontario, Canada; died 18 Mar 1883 in Guelph, Wellington, Ontario, Canada; buried in Bk. O, Woodlawn Cem., Guelph, Wellington, Ontario, Canada. She married in 1864 in Guelph, Wellington, Ontario, Canada **John Andrews Lamprey**, born 1831; died 24 May 1913 in Guelph, Wellington, Ontario, Canada; buried in Bk. O, Woodlawn Cem., Guelph, Wellington, Ontario, Canada, son of Gregory (Capt.) Lamprey and Jane (---).

Children of Katherine Emma Williams and John Andrews Lamprey were as follows:

57	i	**Alice Jane Caroline**4 **Lamprey**, born 9 May 1865 in Guelph, Wellington, Ontario, Canada; died 15 Jul 1884 in Guelph, Wellington, Ontario, Canada; buried in Bk. O, Woodlawn Cem., Guelph, Wellington, Ontario, Canada.
58	ii	**George Sidney**4 **Lamprey**, born 22 Oct 1866 in Guelph, Wellington, Ontario, Canada; died 27 Dec 1898 in Guelph, Wellington, Ontario, Canada; buried in Bk. O, Woodlawn Cem., Guelph, Wellington, Ontario, Canada.
59	iii	**Edward Howley**4 **Lamprey**, born 9 Feb 1869 in Guelph, Wellington, Ontario, Canada; died 20 Jan 1900 in Mobile, Alabama, USA.
60	iv	**Frederick**4 **Lamprey**, born abt 1872 in Guelph, Wellington, Ontario, Canada; died bef 1881 Of Guelph, Wellington, Ontario, Canada.
+ 61	v	**Ernest Williams**4 **Lamprey**, born 12 Oct 1875 in Guelph, Wellington, Ontario, Canada; died 1967 in Vancouver, British Columbia, Canada. He married **Helen Gertrude Collins**.

24. Hannah3 **Carthew**, born 24 Jan 1848 in Guelph, Wellington, Ontario, Canada; died 8 Apr 1929 in Elliott Home, Guelph, Wellington, Ontario, Canada; buried 10 Apr 1929 in Guelph, Wellington, Ontario, Canada. She married abt 1880 **Llewellyn (Dr.) Brock**, born 24 Aug 1839 in Guelph, Wellington, Ontario, Canada; died 11 Dec 1914 in Guelph, Wellington, Ontario, Canada; buried in Bk. O, Woodlawn Cem., Guelph, Wellington, Ontario, Canada, son of Thomas Rees Brock and Eleanor Thompson.

Children of Hannah Carthew and Llewellyn (Dr.) Brock were as follows:

| 62 | i | **Edward Carthew4 Brock**, born abt 1887 in Guelph, Wellington, Ontario, Canada; died 1887 in Guelph, Wellington, Ontario, Canada. |
| 63 | ii | **George Carthew4 Brock**, born 1 Jan 1889 in Guelph, Wellington, Ontario, Canada; died 25 Dec 1893 in Guelph, Wellington, Ontario, Canada; buried in Bk. O, Woodlawn Cem., Guelph, Wellington, Ontario, Canada. |

25. James Morden3 Carthew, born 17 Nov 1849 in Guelph, Ontario, Canada; died 1 Jan 1929 in Thornbury, Grey, Ontario, Canada. He married on 4 Feb 1879 in Ontario, Canada **Adeline Pauline Maud Chisholm**, born 10 Jan 1853 in Burlington, Ontario, Canada; died 12 Jan 1929 in Thornbury, Grey, Ontario, Canada, daughter of William Davis Chisholm and Mary Land.

Children of James Morden Carthew and Adeline Pauline Maud Chisholm were as follows:

+	64	i	**Mary Hannah4 Carthew**, born 26 Oct 1879 in Ridgetown, Kent, Ontario, Canada; died 30 May 1948 in Larwood Nursing Home, 3838 Sekirk St., Vancouver, British Columbia, Canada. She married **George Weatherall Hemmans**.
	65	ii	**Edith Adeline4 Carthew**, born 22 Jan 1881 in Kent, Ontario, Canada; died 31 Aug 1954 in Ontario, Canada.
+	66	iii	**Alfred Morden4 Carthew**, born 27 Jul 1883 in Thamesville, Ontario, Canada; died 18 Sep 1962 in Hamilton, Ontario, Canada. He married (1) **Ethel Margaret McIntyre**; (2) **Helen Beatrice Peterson**.
+	67	iv	**Caroline Cartwright4 Carthew**, born 2 Sep 1884 in Gravenhurst, Ontario, Canada; died 23 Dec 1933 in Clarksburg, Ontario, Canada. She married **George Herbert McCaroll Mitchell**.
+	68	v	**William Thomas4 Carthew**, born 9 Dec 1888 in Palmerston, Wellington, Ontario, Canada; died 10 Mar 1974 in Walkerville, Ontario, Canada. He married (1) **Elizabeth Isabel Marshall**; (2) **Helen May Harvey**.
+	69	vi	**Laura Secord4 Carthew**, born 4 May 1890 in Palmerston, Wellington, Ontario, Canada; died 18 Mar 1979. She married **Clayton L. Jackson**.

James Morden Carthew & Adeline Pauline Maud Chisholm
with their children in c. 1905: Back Row: Caroline, Alfred, Mary,
William. Front Row: Edith, James Morden, Adeline Pauline, Laura.
Courtesy: Cheryl Daskaluk Sutherland

26. **Caroline**3 **Carthew**, born 13 Aug 1851 in Guelph, Ontario, Canada;
died 11 Mar 1931 in 24 Adolphus St., Cornwall, Stormont, Ontario,
Canada; buried 12 Mar 1931 in Woodlawn Cem., Cornwall, Ontario,
Canada. She married on 17 Dec 1879 in Wellington South, Guelph,
Ontario, Canada **Charles William Young**, born 15 May 1849 in
Georgetown, Stratford, Ontario, Canada; died 6 Apr 1927 in 24
Adolphus St., Cornwall, Stormont, Ontario, Canada; buried 8 Apr 1927
in Woodlawn Cem., Cornwall, Ontario, Canada, son of James Young
and Hester Phillips.

Children of Caroline Carthew and Charles William Young were as
follows:

70	i	**Carthew**4 **Young**, born abt 1881 in Ontario, Canada; died 1885 in Ontario, Canada.
71	ii	**George**4 **Young**, born abt 1882 in Ontario, Canada.
72	iii	**Joseph Edward**4 **Young**, born 30 Oct 1883 in Perth, Ontario, Canada; died 1889 in Ontario, Canada.
73	iv	**Blanche Caroline**4 **Young**, born 11 Nov 1887 in Ontario, Canada; died aft Apr 1927 Of Cornwall, Ontario, Canada.
74	v	**William Robert**4 **Young**, born 22 Oct 1888 in Ontario, Canada; died aft 1931 Of Cornwall, Ontario, Canada. He married on 5 Sep 1936 in

Sacre Coeur Ch., Ottawa, Ontario, Canada **Marie Leda Lemieux**, born 1903, daughter of Jean Mathias Lemieux and Blanche Gandelive Marquis.

75   vi   **Clarence4 Young**, born abt 1890 in Ontario, Canada; died young.

76   vii   **Edith4 Young**, born abt 1892 in Ontario, Canada; died young.

27. Charles Edward (Dr.)3 Carthew, born 20 Nov 1853 in Guelph, Ontario, Canada; died 28 Apr 1931 in Edmonton West, Alberta, Canada. He married on 25 May 1884 in Qu'Appelle, Assiniboia, The Territories, Canada **Angelica Caroline Elizabeth Harvey**, born 19 Feb 1861 Of Kinnettles, Fergus, Ontario, Canada; died 15 Aug 1945 in Edmonton West, Alberta, Canada, daughter of Alexander Harvey and Angelica Dingwall-Fordyce.

Children of Charles Edward (Dr.) Carthew and Angelica Caroline Elizabeth Harvey were as follows:

+   77   i   **Edward4 Carthew**, born 10 May 1885 in Qu'Appelle, Assiniboia, The Territories, Canada; died 20 Oct 1946 Of Vancouver, British Columbia, Canada. He married **Bertha Emily Lagee**.

+   78   ii   **Hannah Caroline4 Carthew**, born 13 Nov 1894 in Qu'Appelle, Assiniboia, Saskatchewan, Canada; died aft 1911 in Toronto, Ontario, Canada. She married **Sidney Warner Eakins**.

    79   iii   **James Harvey4 Carthew**, born 1 Jan 1897 in Qu'Appelle, Assiniboia, The Territories, Canada; died 3 May 1918 in R.A.F., Western Europe.

+   80   iv   **Angelica Isabella4 Carthew**, born 27 Nov 1900 in Qu'Appelle, Assiniboia, The Territories, Canada; died aft 1916 Of Edmonton West, Alberta, Canada. She married **Francis Herbert (Frank) Thomas**.

    81   v   **Alicia4 Carthew**, born 29 Jul 1903. She married in Aug 1922 **William J. Purdy**, born abt 1900.

28. William3 Carthew, born 29 Mar 1856 in Guelph, Ontario, Canada; died 30 Jun 1934 in Waterloo, Waterloo Co., Ontario, Canada. He married on 12 Jun 1882 in Grafton, Ontario, Canada **Jessie Tremain Innes**, born 16 Jul 1862 in Grafton, Ontario, Canada; died 13 Aug 1933 in Waterloo, Waterloo Co., Ontario, Canada, daughter of John Stewart Innes and Joan Cunningham Lawrie Laurie.

L -> R: Jessie Tremain Innes Carthew, Marjorie Drummond Carthew, William Carthew, Adeline Pauline Maud Carthew. Plus: Edward Horace Carthew, Charles Innes Carthew. Courtesy: Barbara I. March

Children of William Carthew and Jessie Tremain Innes were as follows:

+ 82 i **Gertrude Alice4 Carthew**, born 16 Jul 1883 in Waterloo North, Waterloo Co., Ontario, Canada; died abt 1955. She married **Charles Ada Boehm**.

83 ii **Edward Horace4 Carthew**, born 25 Oct 1884 in Palmerston, Waterloo, Ontario, Canada; died 30 Jan 1957 in Waterloo, Wellington, Ontario, Canada; buried in Waterloo, Wellington, Ontario, Canada.

84 iii **Jessie Georgina4 Carthew**, born 7 Jan 1886 in Palmerston, Wellington, Ontario, Canada; died 17 Sep 1886 in Waterloo, Wellington, Ontario, Canada.

85 iv **Charles Innes (Pte.)4 Carthew**, born 25 Nov 1888 in Waterloo North, Waterloo Co., Ontario, Canada; died 30 Jun 1919 in Waterloo, Ontario, Canada; buried in Mount Hope Cem. Sec. G, Kitchener, Waterloo, Ontario, Canada.

+ 86 v **Frederick George4 Carthew**, born 15 Aug 1892 in Waterloo North, Waterloo Co., Ontario, Canada; died 1918. He married **Mary Eleanor Berlet**.

+ 87 vi **Marjorie Drummond4 Carthew**, born 22 Nov 1896 in Waterloo North, Waterloo Co., Ontario, Canada; died 10 May 1983 in Waterloo, Ontario, Canada. She married **Dudley Brooke March**.

Generation 4

29. William Henry Newland⁴ Davis, born Apr 1845 in Avon Lodge, Armagh, Ireland; died 14 Oct 1917 in GlenRock Twp., Converse, Wyoming, USA. He married on 9 Jun 1881 in USA **Amelia Elizabeth Protzman**, born 1849 in Center, Marion, Indiana, USA; died 1932 in Crook, Logan, Colorado, USA, daughter of Andrew J. Protzman and Henrietta Elizabeth Lisette Krumpanitzky.

Children of William Henry Newland Davis and Amelia Elizabeth Protzman were as follows:

+ 88   i   **Elizabeth (Bessie)⁵ Davis**, born Jun 1884 in GlenRock Twp., Converse, Wyoming, USA; died Jul 1969 in Sheridan, Sheridan, Wyoming, USA. She married **Guy Tresingleon George**.

   89   ii   **Frank Stewart⁵ Davis**, born 13 Mar 1886 in GlenRock Twp., Converse, Wyoming, USA; died aft 1920.

+ 90   iii   **Eric F.⁵ Davis**, born 17 Feb 1889 in GlenRock Twp., Converse, Wyoming, USA; died Jul 1980 in Casper, Natrona, Wyoming, USA. He married **Susie F. Uriens**.

   91   iv   **Rollo William⁵ Davis**, born 17 Feb 1889 in GlenRock Twp., Converse, Wyoming, USA; died aft 1920.

30. Laura Mary⁴ Davis, born 8 Oct 1847 in Avon Lodge, Armagh, Ireland; died 27 Oct 1932 in Oslo, Norway. She married on 25 Sep 1872 in Belfast, Co. Antrim, Ireland **Henrik Martin Fredrik Mack**, born 24 Jun 1843 in Tromsø, Troms, Norway; christened 27 Aug 1843 in Tromsø, Troms, Norway; died 11 Aug 1914 in Kristiania, Norway, son of Johan Fredrik Daniel Mack and Nanna Sabine Klerk.

Children of Laura Mary Davis and Henrik Martin Fredrik Mack were as follows:

+ 92   i   **Harald⁵ Mack**, born 24 Jul 1873 in Tromsø, Troms, Norway; died 12 Jan 1947 in Oslo, Norway. He married **Ragnhild Petersen**.

+ 93   ii   **Edith⁵ Mack**, born 28 Oct 1874 in Tromsø, Troms, Norway; died 11 Nov 1960 in Narvik, Norway. She married **Nils Astrup**.

+ 94   iii   **Nanna Elisabeth⁵ Mack**, born 24 May 1877 in Tromsø, Troms, Norway; christened 5 Aug 1877 in

Tromsø, Troms, Norway; died 14 Feb 1931 in Oslo, Norway. She married **Fin Meier**.

+ 95 iv **Dermot5 Mack**, born 4 Dec 1883 in Oslo, Norway; died 26 Jun 1957 in Bergen, Norway. He married **Effie Anne Rieber**.

+ 96 v **Fredrik Wilhelm Stuart (Freddy)5 Mack**, born 19 Jan 1890 in Oslo, Norway; died 27 Aug 1960 in Oslo, Norway. He married **Olga Sørsdal**.

97 vi **Gerda5 Mack**, died young.

Freddy Mack, Astrid & Olga Sørsdal

Nanna Elisabeth Mack

Laura Mary Davis Mack, Harald Mack &
Ragnhild Petersen
Courtesy: Eldrid Ingebjørg Mageli

35. William James Jr.4 Smith, born 12 Mar 1857 in Lake Street, Chicago, Illinois, USA; died 9 Dec 1943 in Montevideo, Minnesota, USA; buried 12 Dec 1943 in Montevideo Cem., Minnesota, USA. He married on 20 Aug 1888 in Montevideo, Minnesota, USA **Edith Henriette Benson**, born 20 Aug 1862 in Gloucester, Massachusetts, USA; died 21 Dec 1960 Of Browns Valley, Minnesota, USA, daughter of Andrew Benson and Caroline Burrowson.

Children of William James Jr. Smith and Edith Henriette Benson were as follows:

+ 98   i   **Kenneth Vernon (Dr.)5 Smith**, born 11 Jun 1889 in Telegraph office, Willow City, North Dakota, USA; died 9 Jan 1966 in Pompano Beach, Florida, USA; buried in Lakewood Cem., Minneapolis, Minnesota, USA. He married **Helen Constance Stebbins**.

+ 99   ii   **Howard Raymond5 Smith**, born 17 Apr 1892 in Browns Valley, Minnesota, USA; died 13 Nov 1971 in Wadena, Minnesota, USA. He married **Adele Louise MacDonald**.

36. Charles Secord4 Smith, born 12 Sep 1860 in Ellsworth, Wisconsin, USA; died 1902. He married in 1884 **Annie Lynch**.

Children of Charles Secord Smith and Annie Lynch were as follows:

100   i   **George5 Smith**, born 1885; died 3 Dec 1908.

37. Francis (Frank) David4 Smith, born 28 Oct 1862 in Ellsworth, Wisconsin, USA; died 14 Jul 1934 in Browns Valley, Minnesota, USA. He married in 1890 in Browns Valley, Minnesota, USA **Serena Fossen Anderson**, born 2 May 1866 in Ringsaker, Hedmark, Norway; died 30 Aug 1937 in Browns Valley, Minnesota, USA, daughter of Andrew Anderson and Lena Larson.

Children of Francis (Frank) David Smith and Serena Fossen Anderson were as follows:

+ 101   i   **Arthur William5 Smith**, born 26 May 1891 in Windsor Twp., Minnesota, USA; died 1 Oct 1959 in Windsor Twp., Minnesota, USA. He married **Emily May Moland**.

+ 102   ii   **Francis Elmer5 Smith**, born 2 Sep 1892 in Windsor Twp., Minnesota, USA; died 2 Sep 2002 in Pierre, South Dakota, USA. He married **Mary De Spiegler**.

| 103 | iii | Harry George5 Smith, born 26 Mar 1894 in Windsor Twp., Minnesota, USA; died 8 Jul 1932 in Browns Valley, Minnesota, USA. |

+ 104   iv   **Laura Elizabeth5 Smith**, born 8 Oct 1897 in Windsor Twp., Minnesota, USA; died 20 Jan 1956 in Los Angeles, California, USA. She married (1) **Joseph Strasburg**; (2) **Eugene M. Martin**.

+ 105   v   **Charles Ludwig5 Smith**, born 6 Dec 1899 in Windsor Twp., Minnesota, USA; died 29 Jul 1937. He married **Thelma Anderson**.

106   vi   **Louise Juliet5 Smith**, born 12 Jul 1901 in Windsor Twp., Minnesota, USA; died 30 Dec 1964 in Sheridan, Sheridan, Wyoming, USA. She married on 25 Jul 1929 **Leon McVean**, born 13 Sep 1900 in Minnesota, USA; died Oct 1972 in Sheridan, Sheridan, Wyoming, USA.

107   vii   **Louis Romeo5 Smith**, born 12 Jul 1901 in Windsor Twp., Minnesota, USA; died 13 May 1919.

108   viii   **Alwyn Octavious5 Smith**, born 12 Oct 1904 in Browns Valley, Minnesota, USA; died 16 Feb 1935 in Browns Valley, Minnesota, USA.

109   ix   **Harriett Georgia5 Smith**, born 17 Apr 1911 in Browns Valley, Minnesota, USA; died 17 Apr 1929 in Graceville, Minnesota, USA.

39. George Arthur4 Smith, born 28 Jun 1868 in Prescott, Wisconsin, USA; died 14 Oct 1956 in Koochiching Co., Minnesota, USA. He married on 25 Dec 1891 **Minnie Augusta Belle Jewett**, born 6 Mar 1864; died 24 Jun 1954, daughter of Henry Franklin Jewett and Elizabeth C. Pullman.

Children of George Arthur Smith and Minnie Augusta Belle Jewett were as follows:

+ 110   i   **Rollin Jewett5 Smith**, born Jan 1893 in Minnesota, USA; died Of Belfair, Washington, USA. He married (1) **Mabel Erickson**; (2) unknown.

+ 111   ii   **Elizabeth Hazel5 Smith**, born 9 Mar 1895; died in International Falls, Minnesota, USA. She married **Dorr Albert Young**.

41. Agnes Elizabeth4 Secord, born 25 Jun 1858 in Ontario, Canada; died 26 Apr 1923 in Los Angeles, California, USA. She married (1) on 21 Dec 1878 **Henry Clinton Smith**, born 17 Oct 1855; died 21 Apr 1935 in Los

Angeles, California, USA, son of Clinton Smith and Mariah Miller; (2) **Charles Rogers**.

Children of Agnes Elizabeth Secord and Henry Clinton Smith were as follows:

+ 112   i   **Pearl Alicia5 Smith**, born 10 Mar 1880. She married **Arthur Thomas Lunn**.

+ 113   ii   **Helen Agnes5 Smith**, born 11 Dec 1883; died Jul 1975 in Halethorpe, Baltimore, Maryland, USA. She married (1) **Vernon Clair Bennett**; (2) **Louis Redmond**.

    114   iii   **Paul5 Smith**, born 1884; died young.

    115   iv   **Bernice5 Smith**, born 1886; died 11 Oct 1892.

+ 116   v   **Elizabeth Josephine5 Smith**, born 17 Jun 1888 in Nebraska, USA; died Of Huntington Park, California, USA. She married **Carl A. Wallin**.

    117   vi   **Charles Henry5 Smith**, born 9 May 1890; died Oct 1918 in Huntington Park, California, USA. He married **May Benton**, daughter of Frederick Benton and Marie Sanstrom.

42. **Appalonia (Lona) Josepha4 Secord**, born 16 Jun 1860 in Ontario, Canada; died 8 Mar 1948 in St. Edward, Nebraska, USA; buried 10 Mar 1948 in Sunset Cem., Cedar Rapids, Nebraska, USA. She married on 27 Nov 1884 in Albion, Boone, Nebraska, USA **William Riley Hackney**, born 19 Nov 1854 in Tennessee or Kentucky, USA; died Of St. Edward, Nebraska, USA; buried in Sunset Cem., Cedar Rapids, Nebraska, USA, son of Benjamin Hackney and Janetta (---).

Children of Appalonia (Lona) Josepha Secord and William Riley Hackney were as follows:

+ 118   i   **Gladys Ione5 Hackney**, born 2 Aug 1887 in Nebraska, USA; died Of Laguna Beach, California, USA. She married **Howard Bernard Marshall**.

+ 119   ii   **Bethine Doris5 Hackney**, born 28 Sep 1889 in Nebraska, USA; died Mar 1967 in Tulsa, Oklahoma, USA. She married **Clyde A. Hacke**.

+ 120   iii   **Leda5 Hackney**, born 10 Sep 1891 in Cedar Rapids, Nebraska, USA; died 25 Nov 1963 in Boone Memorial Hosp., Boone, Nebraska, USA. She married **William Edward Nearhood**.

+ 121   iv   **Ronald Earle5 Hackney**, born 23 Feb 1894 in Nebraska, USA; died 11 Oct 1961 in Albuquerque, Bernalillo, New Mexico, USA; buried in Santa Fe

National Cem., Santa Fe, New Mexico, USA. He married **Georgia Lutz**.

122   v   **Mary5 Hackney**, born 8 Nov 1895 in Cedar Rapids, Nebraska, USA; died 23 Mar 1983 in Hooper Care center, Hooper, Nebraska, USA.

+ 123   vi   **Dorothy Agnes5 Hackney**, born 19 Dec 1899 in Nebraska, USA; died 8 Oct 1935 in Cedar Rapids, Nebraska, USA. She married **Ernest Vear Downs**.

124   vii   **Kenneth R.5 Hackney**, born 23 Apr 1905 in Nebraska, USA; died 28 Jul 1973 in Great Falls, Cascade, Montana, USA; buried in New Highland Cem., Great Falls, Cascade, Montana, USA. He married **Hilda P. Sappington**, died 13 Dec 1944 in Great Falls, Cascade, Montana, USA, buried in New Highland Cem., Great Falls, Cascade, Montana, USA.

43. **William Henry4 Secord**, born 25 Sep 1862 in DeWitt, Saline, Nebraska, USA; died 9 Jul 1904 in Collins, Iowa, USA. He married in 1888 **Iona A. Van Loan**, born 1868 in Iowa, USA; died aft 1900.

Children of William Henry Secord and Iona A. Van Loan were as follows:

125   i   **William R.5 Secord**, born Jan 1889 in Nebraska, USA; died aft 1911. She married on 17 Jan 1911 in Coeur d'Alene, Kootenai, Idaho, USA **Charles McAfee**.

126   ii   **Jessie M.5 Secord**, born 14 Dec 1893 in Nebraska, USA; died 22 Apr 1974 in Fond Du Lac, Fond Du Lac, Wisconsin, USA.

44. **Frank Alexander4 Secord**, born 6 Dec 1866 in DeWitt, Saline, Nebraska, USA; died 27 Mar 1954 in Omaha, Douglas, Nebraska, USA. He married **Winifred Mayfield**, born 22 Mar 1863 in Cass, Michigan, USA; died 20 Jan 1943, daughter of George W. Mayfield and Emmaline T. Todd.

Children of Frank Alexander Secord and Winifred Mayfield were as follows:

127   i   **LeRhea5 Secord**, born 1884; died 18 Jan 1932. She married on 8 Dec 1912 in Jackson, Kansas City, Missouri, USA **Richard R. Grotte**, born abt 1877.

128   ii   **Blanche5 Secord**, born 1886; died 2 Mar 1944. She married **A.E. Sciple**.

48. **Margaret (Ella)**4 **Secord**, born 4 Feb 1871 in Dorchester, Saline, Nebraska, USA; died 13 Jul 1931 in Omaha, Douglas, Nebraska, USA. She married in 1889 **Osmos C. Higbee**, born 10 Apr 1865; died Jul 1925 in Omaha, Douglas, Nebraska, USA.

Children of Margaret (Ella) Secord and Osmos C. Higbee were as follows:

129	i	**Margaret Irene**5 **Higbee**, born 9 Nov 1890 in Unadilla, Otoe, Nebraska, USA; died 15 Dec 1975 in Omaha, Douglas, Nebraska, USA.
130	ii	**Don Charles**5 **Higbee**, born 29 May 1893 in Kansas, USA; died 18 Aug 1963 in Orange, California, USA. He married (1) abt 1918 in Nebraska, USA, divorced **Alice F. Winder**, born 12 Feb 1896 in Iowa, USA; died 12 Nov 1966 in San Francisco, California, USA; (2) abt 1953 in California, USA **Hazel D. (---)**, born 7 Feb 1895 in California, USA; died 17 May 1971 in Orange, California, USA.

49. **Clayton (Carlos) Forsythe (Dr.)**4 **Secord**, born 22 Jun 1874 in Blair, Dorchester, Saline, Nebraska, USA; died 28 Jan 1955 in Guatemala City, Guatemala. He married (1) in 1898 **Susan Hazel James**, born 7 Nov 1874 in Searsboro, Iowa, USA; died aft 1920, kidnapped and disappeared, Mexico, daughter of Henry Bascom James; (2) in 1929 in Guatemala City, Guatemala **Cristina Alvarado Mota**, born 25 Jul 1909 in Guatemala City, Guatemala; died 1967 in Guatemala City, Guatemala, daughter of Joseph A. Alvarado and Jeanne Mota.

Children of Clayton (Carlos) Forsythe (Dr.) Secord and Susan Hazel James were as follows:

131	i	**Carl J.**5 **Secord**, born 31 Aug 1910 in Chichicastenango, Guatemala; died young in Texas, USA.
132	ii	**Rachael**5 **Secord**, born 2 Oct 1912 in Chichicastenango, Guatemala; died aft 1920 in Mexico.

Children of Clayton (Carlos) Forsythe (Dr.) Secord and Cristina Alvarado Mota were as follows:

133	i	**Clayton Charles**5 **Secord**, born 15 Aug 1931 in Chichicastenango, Guatemala. He married in Macon, Georgia, USA **Mary Agnes Williams**.
+ 134	ii	**Roberto Edgar**5 **Secord Mota**, born 19 Sep 1932 in Chichicastenango, Guatemala; died abt 1990 in

Guatemala. He married **Sarah Contreras-Quimonez**.

+ 135 iii **Arnold Franklyn5 Secord**, born 9 Jan 1934 in Chichicastenango, Guatemala. He married **Ana Marie Valle**.

+ 136 iv **Frederick Albert5 Secord**, born 29 Oct 1936 in Chichicastenango, Guatemala. He married **Luz Marina Porres**.

137 v **George Edward5 Secord**, born 29 Oct 1936 in Chichicastenango, Guatemala; died May 1937 in Chichicastenango, Guatemala.

+ 138 vi **Milton Paul (Dr.)5 Secord**, born 19 Apr 1943 in Guatemala City, Guatemala. He married **Marie Ofelia Pineda**.

50. **Harold R.4 Secord**, born 27 Apr 1877 in Dorchester, Saline, Nebraska, USA; died 9 Aug 1938 in Gretna, Sarpy, Nebraska, USA. He married in 1900 in Papillion, Sarpy, Nebraska, USA **Rachel Curley**, born 12 Aug 1877 in Papillion, Sarpy, Nebraska, USA; died 15 May 1969 in Omaha, Douglas, Nebraska, USA, daughter of James Curley and Fanny Cook.

Children of Harold R. Secord and Rachel Curley were as follows:

139 i **Thelma5 Secord**, born 8 Aug 1900 in Forest, Sarpy, Nebraska, USA; died 1961 in Omaha, Douglas, Nebraska, USA. She married on 10 Oct 1928 in Omaha, Nebraska, USA **Gerald Everett Collins**, born 11 Oct 1903 in Fort Crook, Nebraska, USA; died 9 Jan 2002 in Omaha, Douglas, Nebraska, USA, son of Harvey Collins and Daisy E. Crocker.

52. **Cyril Paul4 Secord**, born 1 Sep 1883 in DeWitt, Saline, Nebraska, USA; died 20 Oct 1962 in Omaha, Douglas, Nebraska, USA. He married on 14 Sep 1916 in Nebraska, USA **Florence Margaret Peterson**, born 21 Nov 1894 in Nebraska, USA; died 30 Dec 1991 in Lincoln, Lancaster, Nebraska, USA, daughter of Charles Peterson and Matena (---).

Children of Cyril Paul Secord and Florence Margaret Peterson were as follows:

140 i **James Charles5 Secord**, born 26 Apr 1920 in Nebraska, USA; died 28 Jan 1986 in Mansfield, Richland, Ohio, USA.

+   141   ii   **Betty Louise**5 **Secord**, born 7 Sep 1923 in Omaha, Douglas, Nebraska, USA. She married **Raymond Charles Deaton.**

+   142   iii   **Jeanne C.**5 **Secord**, born 6 Oct 1926 in Omaha, Douglas, Nebraska, USA. She married **Robert (Bob) B. Dillman.**

54. **John Frederick DeLisle**4 **Poore**, born 5 Jul 1861 in Ontario, Canada; died 24 Jan 1932 in Portland, Oregon, USA. He married **Mary Ann Gordon**, born 1868 in Ireland; died 18 Jan 1940 in Portland, Oregon, USA.

Children of John Frederick DeLisle Poore and Mary Ann Gordon were as follows:

143   i   **John W. Gordon**5 **Poore**, born 1892 in Winnipeg, Manitoba, Canada; died 1892 in Winnipeg, Manitoba, Canada.

+   144   ii   **Flora May**5 **Poore**, born 18 Jul 1893 in Winnipeg, Manitoba, Canada; died aft 1918. She married **Charles Frederick Yates.**

+   145   iii   **Laura Elizabeth**5 **Poore**, born 1895 in Winnipeg, Manitoba, Canada; died aft 1918 in Portland, Oregon, USA. She married **Richard Thomas Crake.**

55. **Laura Mary Madeline**4 **Poore**, born 17 Oct 1862 in Guelph, Wellington, Ontario, Canada; died 13 Nov 1947 Of Stonewall, Manitoba, Canada. She married on 20 Dec 1881 **Isaac Riley**, born Oct 1853; died 8 Jul 1926 Of Stonewall, Manitoba, Canada.

Children of Laura Mary Madeline Poore and Isaac Riley were as follows:

+   146   i   **John Melville**5 **Riley**, born 10 Feb 1883; died in St. Paul, Minnesota, USA. He married **Jane Holden Beamish.**

147   ii   **William Dyson**5 **Riley**, born 7 Jun 1886; died in Detroit, Michigan, USA. He married on 4 Sep 1916 **Elda Williamson.**

+   148   iii   **Mary Irene**5 **Riley**, born 5 May 1888; died 12 Nov 1913 in Nelson, British Columbia, Canada. She married **James Arthur Bracken.**

149   iv   **Grace Helena**5 **Riley**, born 1894; died 1922 in Montreal, Quebec, Canada. She married on 17 Sep 1922 **George Merry.**

56. Elizabeth4 Poore, born 28 Dec 1868 in Ontario, Canada; died Of Portland, Oregon, USA. She married (1) on 3 Dec 1899 **Robert Gossman**, born in Iowa, USA; (2) on 18 Mar 1903 **David C. Burns**, born 28 Nov 1860 in Scotland; died 19 Feb 1918 in Portland, Oregon, USA, son of Thomas Burns and Agnes Hasty.

Children of Elizabeth Poore and Robert Gossman were as follows:

+   150   i   **Arthur Delyle5 Gossman**, born 31 Dec 1890 in Portland, Multnomah, Oregon, USA; died 23 Jan 1958 in Portland, Multnomah, Oregon, USA. He married **Annette (Nettie) GeBotte**.

61. Ernest Williams4 Lamprey, born 12 Oct 1875 in Guelph, Wellington, Ontario, Canada; died 1967 in Vancouver, British Columbia, Canada. He married on 26 Jun 1907 in Durham, Ontario, Canada **Helen Gertrude Collins**, born 17 Oct 1884 in Millbrook, Ontario, Canada; died aft 1911 Of Westmount, Montreal, Quebec, Canada, daughter of Thomas B. Collins and Frances Armstrong.

Children of Ernest Williams Lamprey and Helen Gertrude Collins were as follows:

+   151   i   **John (Jack) Howard Montgomery5 Lamprey**, born 22 Feb 1909 in Montreal, Quebec, Canada; died 2 Oct 1962 in Vancouver, British Columbia, Canada. He married **Marjorie Joan Arbuckle**.
+   152   ii   **Frances Patricia Secord5 Lamprey**, born 19 May 1912 in Montreal, Quebec, Canada; died in Vancouver, British Columbia, Canada. She married **Peter Marsden Downes**.

64. Mary Hannah4 Carthew, born 26 Oct 1879 in Ridgetown, Kent, Ontario, Canada; died 30 May 1948 in Larwood Nursing Home, 3838 Sekirk St., Vancouver, British Columbia, Canada. She married on 26 Jan 1907 in Perth, Ontario, Canada **George Weatherall Hemmans**, born 27 Feb 1877 in Devon, England; died 2 Oct 1945 in Vancouver, British Columbia, Canada, son of Samuel Edward William Weatherall Hemmans and Ethel Phyllis Little.

Children of Mary Hannah Carthew and George Weatherall Hemmans were as follows:

+   153   i   **Edith Phyllis Adeline5 Hemmans**, born 12 Jan 1910; died 8 Jun 1983 in Vancouver, British Columbia, Canada. She married **Francis William Gauntlett Fladgate**.

| 154 | ii | **Elizabeth Gwendolyn**5 **Hemmans**, born 1 Aug 1912; died 1985 in Vancouver, British Columbia, Canada. She married on 10 Nov 1941 **Joseph Gordon Hall**, born 12 May 1915, son of Charles A. Hall and Ruby M. Bartliff. |

+ 155   iii   **George Edward Weatherall (Ted)**5 **Hemmans**, born 19 Jul 1914; died 2000 in Vancouver, British Columbia, Canada. He married **Gwendolyn Frances Haskins**.

66. Alfred Morden4 **Carthew**, born 27 Jul 1883 in Thamesville, Ontario, Canada; died 18 Sep 1962 in Hamilton, Ontario, Canada. He married (1) on 21 Jun 1911 in Owen Sound, Grey, Ontario, Canada **Ethel Margaret McIntyre**, born 1884 in Owen Sound, Grey, Ontario, Canada; died 24 Mar 1917 in Owen Sound, Grey, Ontario, Canada, daughter of Archibald L. McIntyre and Mary Fleming; (2) on 10 Sep 1919 in York, Ontario, Canada **Helen Beatrice Peterson**, born 28 Aug 1891 in Hawkesville, Ontario, Canada; buried in Woodland Cem, Flamborough East, Wentworth, Ontario, Canada, daughter of James Albert Peterson and Annie Joyner.

Children of Alfred Morden Carthew and Ethel Margaret McIntyre were as follows:

156   i   **Mary Adeline**5 **Carthew**, born 15 Mar 1912 in Moorefield, nr. Palmerston, Ontario, Canada; died 14 Nov 2008 in Toronto, Ontario, Canada.

+ 157   ii   **Edward Morden**5 **Carthew**, born 20 Nov 1913; died 19 Dec 1998 Of Humberstone, Ontario, Canada. He married **Hazel Edith Doidge**.

Mary Adeline Carthew - or Sister Mary Adela Courtesy: Barbara I. March

+ 158   iii   **Melvil McIntyre (Pete)**5 **Carthew**, born 6 Mar 1917; died 4 Jul 1990 in Beamsville, Ontario, Canada. He married (1) **Marie Theresa Parker**; (2) **Marilyn Lumley Stewart**.

Children of Alfred Morden Carthew and Helen Beatrice Peterson were as follows:

+ 159 i **Alice Ann5 Carthew**, born 20 Jun 1924 in Dundalk, Ontario, Canada; died 2 Nov 1991 in Burlington, Ontario, Canada. She married **Hugh Alexander Sutherland**.

67. Caroline Cartwright4 Carthew (James Morden3, Hannah Cartwright2 Secord, Laura1 Ingersoll), born 2 Sep 1884 in Gravenhurst, Ontario, Canada; died 23 Dec 1933 in Clarksburg, Ontario, Canada. She married on 15 Apr 1908 in Perth, Ontario, Canada **George Herbert McCaroll Mitchell**, born 18 Mar 1887 in Clarksburg, Thornbury, Ontario, Canada; died Jul 1964 in Clarksburg, Ontario, Canada, son of John Gillespie Mitchell and Mary Ann McCarroll.

Children of Caroline Cartwright Carthew and George Herbert McCaroll Mitchell were as follows:

+ 160 i **John (Jack) Carthew5 Mitchell**, born 18 Dec 1909; died in Thornbury, Ontario, Canada. He married **Helen G. Armstrong**.

+ 161 ii **Richard Morden (Col.)5 Mitchell**, born 2 Nov 1911; died 2009 in Toronto, Ontario, Canada. He married **Helen K. Chapman**.

+ 162 iii **Edith Adeline (Peter)5 Mitchell**, born 17 Nov 1912; died in Montreal, Quebec, Canada. She married **William Kenneth Braithwaite**.

+ 163 iv **Mary McCaroll (Carol)5 Mitchell**, born 15 Dec 1913; died Of Peterborough, Ontario, Canada. She married **George Ross Davidson**.

+ 164 v **Alan George5 Mitchell**, born 23 Apr 1920 in Clarksburg, Thornbury, Ontario, Canada. He married **Alice Maxine Headland**.

68. William Thomas4 Carthew, born 9 Dec 1888 in Palmerston, Wellington, Ontario, Canada; died 10 Mar 1974 in Walkerville, Ontario, Canada. He married (1) on 18 Sep 1912 in Wellington, Ontario, Canada **Elizabeth Isabel Marshall**, born 14 May 1886 in Fergus, Ontario, Canada; died 26 Apr 1924, daughter of Samuel Marshall and Jessie Dinwoodie Hunter; (2) on 30 Jul 1932 **Helen May Harvey**, born 14 Oct 1894, daughter of William Henry Harvey and Mary C. Clement.

Children of William Thomas Carthew and Elizabeth Isabel
Marshall were as follows:
> 165   i   **Ina Margaret**5 **Carthew**, born 25 Sep 1913 in
>   Fergus, Ontario, Canada; died in Toronto, Ontario,
>   Canada. She married on 7 Sep 1944 **Joseph Kniep**,
>   born 25 Jun 1904, son of Mathias K. Kniep and
>   Barbara Theis.
> 166   ii   **John Marshall**5 **Carthew**, born 1915 in Fergus,
>   Ontario, Canada; died 15 Feb 1922.
> + 167 iii   **Charles William Ingersoll**5 **Carthew**, born 14 Dec
>   1919 in Fergus, Ontario, Canada. He married
>   **Audrey Lund Pickell.**

69. Laura Secord4 **Carthew**, born 4 May 1890 in Palmerston, Wellington,
Ontario, Canada; died 18 Mar 1979. She married on 1 Aug 1914
Clayton L. Jackson, born 1 Apr 1885 in Simcoe, Ontario, Canada, son of
Charles R. Jackson and Margaret (Maggie) S. Ferguson.
Children of Laura Secord Carthew and Clayton L. Jackson were as
follows:
> + 168 i   **Morden Alexander (Jack)**5 **Jackson**, born 27 Sep
>   1916. He married **Elizabeth Barry.**
> + 169 ii   **Walter Charles**5 **Jackson**, born 25 Jun 1919; died 26
>   Feb 1976 in Edmonton, Alberta, Canada. He
>   married **Elizabeth Agnes Ellinger.**
> + 170 iii   **Laura Secord**5 **Jackson**, born 9 Sep 1920; died 10
>   Mar 1995. She married **Charles Ray (Dr.) Giles.**
> + 171 iv   **Nancy Barbara**5 **Jackson**, born 12 Sep 1924 in
>   Edmonton, Alberta, Canada; died Apr 1965. She
>   married **Lloyd George McDonald.**

77. Edward4 **Carthew**, born 10 May 1885 in Qu'Appelle, Assiniboia, The
Territories, Canada; died 20 Oct 1946 Of Vancouver, British Columbia,
Canada. He married **Bertha Emily Lagee**, born 12 Aug 1895 Of
Vancouver, British Columbia, Canada; died Jan 1985 in Hemet,
Riverside, California, USA, daughter of Ole Lagee and Belle Hansen.
Children of Edward Carthew and Bertha Emily Lagee were as
follows:
> 172   i   **Laura Evelyn**5 **Carthew**, born 19 Aug 1915 in
>   Langley, British Columbia, Canada; died 3 Apr
>   1933.

173	ii	**Jean Lagee**5 **Carthew**, born 19 Jul 1917 in Langley, British Columbia, Canada; died in New Westminster, British Columbia, Canada.
174	iii	**Marjorie Rosetta**5 **Carthew**, born 21 Jul 1919 in Langley, British Columbia, Canada; died 25 Dec 1983 in Orange, California, USA. She married, divorced **Donald A. Newton**.
175	iv	**Audrey Beatrice**5 **Carthew**, born 21 Oct 1925 in Langley, British Columbia, Canada; died in New Westminster, British Columbia, Canada.

78. **Hannah Caroline**4 **Carthew**, born 13 Nov 1894 in Qu'Appelle, Assiniboia, Saskatchewan, Canada; died aft 1911 in Toronto, Ontario, Canada. She married on 7 Aug 1912 Of Edmonton, Alberta, Canada **Sidney Warner Eakins**, born 21 Dec 1879 in Belleville, Ontario, Canada; died 14 Feb 1954, son of James Edward (Dr.) Eakins and Annetta Jane Warner.

Children of Hannah Caroline Carthew and Sidney Warner Eakins were as follows:

+	176	i	**Elizabeth Carthew**5 **Eakins**, born 27 Jul 1915 in Edmonton West, Alberta, Canada; died 1996 in Toronto, Ontario, Canada. She married **Norman Reeve Keene**.
+	177	ii	**James Edwin (Pete)**5 **Eakins**, born 4 Apr 1922; died 1976 in Baltimore, Maryland, USA. He married **Elsa (Hartle) McLeod**.
+	178	iii	**Mary Alicia**5 **Eakins**, born 18 Jul 1928 in Ontario, Canada; died 10 Mar 2009 in Guelph, Wellington, Ontario, Canada. She married **Hedley G. (Dr.) Dimock**.

80. **Angelica Isabella**4 **Carthew**, born 27 Nov 1900 in Qu'Appelle, Assiniboia, The Territories, Canada; died aft 1916 Of Edmonton West, Alberta, Canada. She married on 25 Jan 1924 **Francis Herbert (Frank) Thomas**, born 3 Jan 1896, son of George Herbert Thomas and Fanny Brooks Knight.

Children of Angelica Isabella Carthew and Francis Herbert (Frank) Thomas were as follows:

+	179	i	**Charles Arnold**5 **Thomas**, born 14 Feb 1935 in Regina, Saskatchewan, Canada. He married **Donalda (---)**.

82. Gertrude Alice₄ Carthew, born 16 Jul 1883 in Waterloo North, Waterloo Co., Ontario, Canada; died abt 1955. She married on 18 Oct 1905 in Waterloo, Ontario, Canada **Charles Ada Boehm**, born 1877 in Ontario, Canada; died 1927 in Waterloo, Ontario, Canada; buried in Mount Hope Cem., Waterloo, Ontario, Canada, son of Joseph Gonder Boehm and Mary Ann Tytherleigh.

Children of Gertrude Alice Carthew and Charles Ada Boehm were as follows:

180	i	**Mariam₅ Boehm**, born 1909 in Waterloo, Ontario, Canada; died 1913 in Waterloo, Ontario, Canada.
181	ii	**Alicia (Nesha)₅ Boehm**, born abt 1912 in Waterloo, Ontario, Canada; died 11 Mar 2007 in Kitchener, Waterloo, Ontario, Canada.
+ 182	iii	**Charles A.₅ Boehm**, born 1914 in Waterloo, Ontario, Canada; died in Halifax, Nova Scotia, Canada. He married **Elizabeth (Beth) Wilson**.

Alicia (Nesha) Boehm
Courtesy: Barbara I. March

86. Frederick George₄ Carthew, born 15 Aug 1892 in Waterloo North, Waterloo Co., Ontario, Canada; died 1918. He married on 20 Jan 1913 in York, Ontario, Canada **Mary Eleanor Berlet**, born 1891 in Linwood, Ontario, Canada; died 1918, daughter of Valentine Berlet and Mary Spahr.

Children of Frederick George Carthew and Mary Eleanor Berlet were as follows:

+ 183	i	**Edna Eloise₅ Carthew**, born 1915; died 1992 in Kitchener, Ontario, Canada. She married **Arnold Jack Blaney**.
+ 184	ii	**Frederick George₅ Carthew**, born 18 Dec 1916; died 18 Sep 2008

Edna Carthew
Courtesy: Barbara I. March

in Collingswood, Ontario, Canada. He married **Loraine Isabel Solomon**.

87. **Marjorie Drummond**[4] **Carthew**, born 22 Nov 1896 in Waterloo North, Waterloo Co., Ontario, Canada; died 10 May 1983 in Waterloo, Ontario, Canada. She married on 29 Aug 1922 in Waterloo, Ontario, Canada **Dudley Brooke March**, born 17 Mar 1897 in Partridge Island, nr. St. John, New Brunswick, Canada; died 15 Sep 1956 in Kitchener, Waterloo, Ontario, Canada, son of John Edgar (Dr.) March and Clymene Kaye.

Children of Marjorie Drummond Carthew and Dudley Brooke March were as follows:

Bill March

Courtesy: Barbara I. March

+ 185   i   **Joanne Kaye**[5] **March**, born 26 Aug 1924 in Waterloo, Ontario, Canada; died 18 Mar 2012 in Welland, Ontario, Canada. She married (1) **Arthur Charles Farwell Winslow**; (2) **James Eric Sutherland**.

186   ii   **William Dudley (Bill)**[5] **March**, born 13 May 1926 in Waterloo, Ontario, Canada; died 7 Oct 1998 in Kitchener, Waterloo, Ontario, Canada. He married abt 1958 in Ontario, Canada **Margaret Marsh**, born abt 1926.

+ 187   iii   **Barbara Innis**[5] **March**, born 28 May 1928 in Waterloo, Ontario, Canada. She married **Rudolph Paul Bellinger**.

Generation 5

88. Elizabeth (Bessie)5 **Davis**, born Jun 1884 in GlenRock Twp., Converse, Wyoming, USA; died Jul 1969 in Sheridan, Sheridan, Wyoming, USA. She married c. 1911 in Wyoming, USA **Guy Tresingleon George**, born 15 Dec 1883 in York, York, Nebraska, USA; died 7 Feb 1965 in Sheridan, Sheridan, Wyoming, USA, son of Fredrick George and Mary Ellen Copsey. Children:

188	i	**Helen**6 **George**.
189	ii	**Fredrick Henry**6 **George**.

90. Eric F.5 **Davis**, born 17 Feb 1889 in GlenRock Twp., Converse, Wyoming, USA; died Jul 1980 in Casper, Natrona, Wyoming, USA. He married in 1916 in Wyoming, USA **Susie F. Uriens**, born 13 Nov 1898 in Wyoming, Kent, Michigan, USA; died 15 Sep 1997 in Casper, Natrona, Wyoming, USA, daughter of Fredrick Uriens and Rosetta (Rosie) Brumbaugh. Children:

+	190	i	**Gertrude Lydia (Gertie; Pat)**6 **Davis**. She married (1) **Joseph H. Zentner**; (2) **(---) Hooker**; (3) **(---) Theron**; (4) **Albert Norrborn**.
+	191	ii	**Viola (Vi) Rose**6 **Davis**. She married **Donald L. Bell**.
	192	iii	**Robert (Bobby) R.**6 **Davis**.

92. Harald5 **Mack**, born 24 Jul 1873 in Tromsø, Troms, Norway; died 12 Jan 1947 in Oslo, Norway. He married on 1 Apr 1917 **Ragnhild Petersen**, born 21 Aug 1881 in Oslo, Norway. Children:

	193	i	**Ragnhild Laura**6 **Mack**.
	194	ii	**Fredrik**6 **Mack**.
	195	iii	**Nanna**6 **Mack**.
+	196	iv	**Harald William Davis**6 **Mack**. He married **Marit Hansen**.

93. Edith5 **Mack**, born 28 Oct 1874 in Tromsø, Troms, Norway; died 11 Nov 1960 in Narvik, Norway. She married on 8 Jul 1899 in Norway **Nils Astrup**, born 13 Sep 1870 in Sogndal, Norway; died 20 Nov 1941 in Narvik, Norway, son of Ole Christian Astrup and Henriette Magdalene (Jetta) Uchermann. Children:

+	197	i	**Henriette Laura (Etti)**6 **Astrup**. She married **Johan Wilhelm Fremming Egilsrud**.

+   198   ii   **Alf**6 **Astrup.** He married **Sigfried (Didi) Aass-Jacobsen.**

     199   iii   **Fredrik Mack (Kippi)**6 **Astrup.**

+   200   iv   **Ebbe Carsten**6 **Astrup.** He married **Bergljot Harlem.**

94. Nanna Elisabeth5 **Mack,** born 24 May 1877 in Tromsø, Troms, Norway; christened 5 Aug 1877 in Tromsø, Troms, Norway; died 14 Feb 1931 in Oslo, Norway. She married **Fin Meier,** born 8 Jul 1877 in Norway; died 16 May 1956 in Oslo, Norway. Children:

+   201   i   **Laura Elisabeth Secord**6 **Meier.** She married **Sverre Ellingsen.**

+   202   ii   **Agnes Klerck**6 **Meier.** She married (1) **Sigurd Johannessen;** (2) **Henrik Aggerholm.**

+   203   iii   **Ludvig Christian**6 **Meier.** He married **Karin Leganger Anisdahl.**

95. Dermot5 **Mack,** born 4 Dec 1883 in Oslo, Norway; died 26 Jun 1957 in Bergen, Norway. He married on 3 Jun 1911 **Effie Anne Rieber,** born 7 Mar 1887 in Bergen, Norway. Children:

+   204   i   **Johan Rieber**6 **Mack.** He married **Ilse Margarethe Kauschke.**

     205   ii   **Dermot Stuart**6 **Mack.**

+   206   iii   **Erik Klerck**6 **Mack.** He married (1) **Nina Skappel Jensen;** (2) **Ingrid Solberg.**

96. Fredrik Wilhelm Stuart (Freddy)5 **Mack,** born 19 Jan 1890 in Oslo, Norway; died 27 Aug 1960 in Oslo, Norway. He married **Olga Sørsdal,** born 23 Jan 1892 in Sor-Odal, Norway. Children:

+   207   i   **Edith Elisabeth**6 **Mack.** She married **Karsten Mageli.**

+   208   ii   **Gunnar Fredrik**6 **Mack.** He married **Randi Bjelke.**

98. Kenneth Vernon (Dr.)5 **Smith,** born 11 Jun 1889 in Telegraph Office, Willow City, North Dakota, USA; died 9 Jan 1966 in Pompano Beach, Florida, USA; buried in Lakewood Cem., Minneapolis, Minnesota, USA. He married **Helen Constance Stebbins,** born 5 Oct 1891 in Minneapolis, Minnesota, USA; died c. 1967 in Fort Lauderdale, Florida, USA; buried in Lakewood Cem., Minneapolis, Minnesota, USA, daughter of Henry Constante Stebbins and Augusta Schultz. Children:

+ 209   i   **Stanley (Stan) Stebbins6 Smith.** He married **Sara Dorothea (Thea) Dougherty.**
  210   ii   **Donald Langdon (Billie)6 Smith.**
+ 211   iii   **Helen Elizabeth (Betty)6 Smith.** She married (1) **Donald Milton Sandberg**; (2) **Robert (Bob) Frederic Straub.**

99. Howard Raymond5 Smith, born 17 Apr 1892 in Browns Valley, Minnesota, USA; died 13 Nov 1971 in Wadena, Minnesota, USA. He married on 8 Sep 1919 in Sisseton, South Dakota, USA **Adele Louise MacDonald**, born 25 Jan 1888 in Hastings, Minnesota, USA; died 24 Dec 1984 in Otter Tail, Minnesota, USA, daughter of Thomas MacDonald and Alice Jennison. Children:

+ 212   i   **Alice Adair6 Smith.** She married (1) **Jay Leland Kevern**; (2) unknown.
  213   ii   **Dorothy Grace6 Smith.**
  214   iii   **Shirley Mae6 Smith.**

101. Arthur William5 Smith, born 26 May 1891 in Windsor Twp., Minnesota, USA; died 1 Oct 1959 in Windsor Twp., Minnesota, USA. He married on 29 Oct 1918 in Buffalo, Wright Co., Minnesota, USA **Emily May Moland**, born 17 Apr 1896 in Silver Creek, Wright Co., Minnesota, USA; died 28 Feb 1975 in Beardsley, Minnesota, USA, daughter of Halvor Thomas Moland and Alice M. Bryant. Children:

+ 215   i   **William Moland6 Smith.** He married **Elaine Adair Akre.**
+ 216   ii   **James Secord6 Smith.** He married **Laura Catherine Bourland.**

102. Francis Elmer5 Smith, born 2 Sep 1892 in Windsor Twp., Minnesota, USA; died 2 Sep 2002 in Pierre, South Dakota, USA. He married on 14 Nov 1922 **Mary De Spiegler**, born 8 Sep 1900, daughter of Gustav De Spiegler and Theresa Jacomet. Children:

+ 217   i   **Betty Jane6 Smith.** She married (1) **Gabe Winters (Capt.) Potter**; (2) **Billy R. King.**
+ 218   ii   **Francis Eugene (Pete)6 Smith.** He married **Lorraine M. Asplund.**

104. Laura Elizabeth5 Smith, born 8 Oct 1897 in Windsor Twp., Minnesota, USA; died 20 Jan 1956 in Los Angeles, California, USA. She married (1) on 20 Nov 1916 in California, USA **Joseph Strasburg**, born Nov 1893 in Bryant, Roberts, Minnesota, USA; died bef 1934 Of

Minnesota, USA, son of Fred Strasburg and Pauline Bartz; (2) on 1 May 1934 in Watertown, Codington, South Dakota, USA **Eugene M. Martin**, born c. 1904 Of Los Angeles, California, USA. Children:

+ 219   i   **Lillian S.6 Strasburg**. She married **Arthur F. McCluskey**.
+ 220   ii   **Lawrence F.6 Strasburg**. He married **Mildred V. Thompson**.

105. Charles Ludwig5 Smith, born 6 Dec 1899 in Windsor Twp., Minnesota, USA; died 29 Jul 1937. He married on 6 Aug 1925 **Thelma Anderson**, born 6 Aug 1907, daughter of Andrew G. Anderson and Hattie Munson. Children:

+ 221   i   **Beverly Vesta Smith6 Pew**. She married **Bill Andersen**.
+ 222   ii   **Stanley Garrett Smith6 Pew**. He married **Adeline R. Schultz**.
+ 223   iii   **Shirley Nyota Smith6 Pew**. She married (1) **James G. (Jim) Schubin**; (2) **Alfred Barbero**.

110. Rollin Jewett5 Smith, born Jan 1893 in Minnesota, USA; died Of Belfair, Washington, USA. He married (1) on 2 May 1916 in Minnesota, USA **Mabel Erickson**, born 28 Feb 1894 in Minnesota, USA, daughter of Nels Erickson and Emma (---); (2) unknown. Children:

+ 224   i   **Lois Beverly6 Smith**. She married **Herman Mayse**.

111. Elizabeth Hazel5 Smith, born 9 Mar 1895; died in International Falls, Minnesota, USA. She married on 24 Jun 1918 in Minnesota, USA **Dorr Albert Young**, born 16 Nov 1880, son of Dwight Young and Ellen Hales. Children:

    225   i   **Robert Alan6 Young**. He married **Josephine Kava**.
    226   ii   **Patricia Anne6 Young**.

112. Pearl Alicia5 Smith, born 10 Mar 1880. She married on 1 Oct 1899 in California, USA **Arthur Thomas Lunn**, born 4 Sep 1876; died 28 May 1933 in Tarzana, California, USA, son of Thomas Lunn and Mary (---). Children:

+ 227   i   **William Albert6 Lunn**. He married **Marian Elizabeth Grebe**.
    228   ii   **Helen Theresa6 Lunn**.
+ 229   iii   **LaRhea Kathryn6 Lunn**. She married (1) **Frank Wilson Newton**; (2) **Herbert N. Young**.

230 iv   **Arthur Thomas**6 **Lunn**. He married **Cora May Love**.

231 v   **Lorraine Jeanice**6 **Lunn**.

113. **Helen Agnes**5 **Smith**, born 11 Dec 1883; died Jul 1975 in Halethorpe, Baltimore, Maryland, USA. She married (1) in Aug 1912 in California, USA **Vernon Clair Bennett**, son of Norman Bennett and Fanny Fleming; (2) **Louis Redmond**. Children:

232 i   **Verna Claire**6 **Bennett**.

233 ii   **Victor Chadwick**6 **Bennett**. He married **Ruth Schwartfager**.

116. **Elizabeth Josephine**5 **Smith**, born 17 Jun 1888 in Nebraska, USA; died Of Huntington Park, California, USA. She married on 27 Apr 1912 **Carl A. Wallin**, born 6 Aug 1886, son of Benjamin Wallin and Annette Johnson. Children:

+ 234 i   **Braton**6 **Wallin**. He married **Emily Keith Frazer**.

   235 ii   **Jack Robb**6 **Wallin**. He married **Mary Janet Melbus**.

118. **Gladys Ione**5 **Hackney**, born 2 Aug 1887 in Nebraska, USA; died Of Laguna Beach, California, USA. She married on 4 May 1910 in Nebraska, USA **Howard Bernard Marshall**, born 20 Sep 1885 in Union, Butler, Nebraska, USA; died 11 Aug 1980 in Huntington Beach, Orange, California, USA, son of Charles Marshall and Ellen T. Stewart. Children:

   236 i   **Harold Dean**6 **Marshall**.

+ 237 ii   **Helen Zelma**6 **Marshall**. She married **Henry Allen (Red) Gammel**.

+ 238 iii   **Mary Ilene**6 **Marshall**. She married **George A. McKinley**.

119. **Bethine Doris**5 **Hackney**, born 28 Sep 1889 in Nebraska, USA; died Mar 1967 in Tulsa, Oklahoma, USA. She married on 10 Apr 1913 **Clyde A. Hacke**, born 19 Feb 1888; died 20 Jul 1940 in Bexar, Texas, USA. Children:

   239 i   **Clyde A.**6 **Hacke**.

   240 ii   **Maxine R.**6 **Hack**.

120. **Leda**5 **Hackney**, born 10 Sep 1891 in Cedar Rapids, Nebraska, USA; died 25 Nov 1963 in Boone Memorial Hosp., Boone, Nebraska, USA.

She married on 24 Sep 1912 in Nebraska, USA **William Edward Nearhood**, born 3 Mar 1883 in Pennsylvania, USA; died aft 1930 Of Cedar Rapids, Boone, Nebraska, USA. Children:

+   241   i   **Gerald Edward (Lt.)**6 **Nearhood**. He married **Theresa Ann Wetovick**.

     242   ii   **Kenton Eugene (Capt.)**6 **Nearhood**. He married **Theresa Joan Somerville**.

+   243   iii **Corrine Bess (Corkie)**6 **Nearhood**. She married **Edward F. (Jeep) Micek**.

     244   iv   **Donald Earl**6 **Nearhood**.

+   245   v   **Marjory Jean (Margie)**6 **Nearhood**. She married **Walter Francis Frey**.

121. **Ronald Earle**5 **Hackney**, born 23 Feb 1894 in Nebraska, USA; died 11 Oct 1961 in Albuquerque, Bernalillo, New Mexico, USA; buried in Santa Fe National Cem., Santa Fe, New Mexico, USA. He married in 1919 **Georgia Lutz**, born 1893; died 1977 in Albuquerque, Bernalillo, New Mexico, USA; buried in Gate of Heaven Cem., Albuquerque, New Mexico, USA. Children:

     246   i   **John Kenneth**6 **Hackney**.

123. **Dorothy Agnes**5 **Hackney**, born 19 Dec 1899 in Nebraska, USA; died 8 Oct 1935 in Cedar Rapids, Nebraska, USA. She married **Ernest Vear Downs**, born 10 Oct. Children:

+   247   i   **Patricia Elizabeth**6 **Downs**. She married **Bernard Willis Gibb**.

     248   ii   **Dona Dorothy**6 **Downs**.

134. **Roberto Edgar**5 **Secord**, born 19 Sep 1932 in Guatemala City, Guatemala; died c. 1990 in Guatemala. He married on 20 Oct 1954 in Guatemala City, Guatemala **Sarah Contreras-Quimonez**, born 7 Nov 1936 in Guatemala City, Guatemala; died c. 1987 in Guatemala. Children:

     249   i   **Sarah Elizabeth**6 **Secord Contreras**.

+   250   ii   **Roberto Edgard**6 **Secord Contreras**. He married **Michelle M. (---)**.

     251   iii **Caroll Nova Janethe**6 **Secord Contreras**.

+   252   iv   **Madeline Charlotte**6 **Secord Contreras**. She married **Karim Hadweh**.

     253   v   **Winnie Harriet Emeline**6 **Secord Contreras**.

     254   vi   **Wendie Blanchie Apollonie**6 **Secord Contreras**.

| 255 | vii | Quinnie Magdalen Isabella6 Secord Contreras. |
| 256 | viii | Carlos Forsythe6 Secord Contreras. |

135. Arnold Franklin5 Secord, born 9 Jan 1934 in Guatemala City, Guatemala. He married in 1958 **Ana Marie Valle**. Children:

| + | 257 | i | Anna Maria6 Secord. She married Gert Gucciti. |
| + | 258 | ii | Christine Ingersoll6 Secord. She married Cesar Hernandez. |

136. Frederick Albert5 Secord, born 29 Oct 1936 in Guatemala City, Guatemala. He married **Luz Marina Porres**. Children:

| | 259 | i | Frederick Albert Jr.6 Secord. |
| + | 260 | ii | Nancy Jeannette6 Secord. She married Roberto Enriquez. |

138. Milton Paul (Dr.)5 Secord, born 19 Apr 1943 in Guatemala City, Guatemala. He married in 1977 in Gardena, California, USA **Marie Ofelia Pineda**, born 17 Oct 1953 in Guatemala. Children:

	261	i	Beverly Neff6 Secord. She married Marco A. Garcia.
	262	ii	Audrey Christine6 Secord.
	263	iii	Samantha Janie6 Secord.
	264	iv	Milton Paul Jr.6 Secord.

141. Betty Louise5 Secord, born 7 Sep 1923 in Omaha, Douglas, Nebraska, USA. She married in Jan 1946 in Omaha, Douglas, Nebraska, USA **Raymond Charles Deaton**, born 1922. Children:

| + | 265 | i | Linda6 Deaton. She married (1) Eugene Bittner; (2) Eddy Allen. |

142. Jeanne C.5 Secord, born 6 Oct 1926 in Omaha, Douglas, Nebraska, USA. She married **Robert (Bob) B. Dillman**. Children:

| + | 266 | i | Steven6 Dillman. He married Lianne Lance. |
| | 267 | ii | Lori6 Dillman. She married James (Jim) Swenson. |

144. Flora May5 Poore, born 18 Jul 1893 in Winnipeg, Manitoba, Canada; died aft 1918. She married on 16 Oct 1917 in Oregon, USA **Charles Frederick Yates**, born 4 May 1893; died 19 Nov 1941. Children:

| + | 268 | i | Bette Ann6 Yates. She married Howard Merle Sidwell. |

145. **Laura Elizabeth5 Poore**, born 1895 in Winnipeg, Manitoba, Canada; died aft 1918 in Portland, Oregon, USA. She married on 3 Jun 1922 in Portland, Oregon, USA **Richard Thomas Crake**, born 1894. Children:

269	i	**Richard Barrington6 Crake.**
270	ii	**Berurlie Jean6 Crake.**

146. **John Melville5 Riley**, born 10 Feb 1883; died in St. Paul, Minnesota, USA. He married on 6 Dec 1906 **Jane Holden Beamish**, born 17 Feb 1878. Children:

+	271	i	**Margaret Madeline6 Riley.** She married **George Joseph Rathbone Mountford.**

148. **Mary Irene5 Riley**, born 5 May 1888; died 12 Nov 1913 in Nelson, British Columbia, Canada. She married on 12 Nov 1913 **James Arthur Bracken**, born 10 Jan 1888. Children:

+	272	i	**Riley James6 Bracken.** He married **Mabel Alvilda Ellefson.**
+	273	ii	**William Ernest6 Bracken.** He married **Fern Margaret Butler.**

150. **Arthur Delyle5 Gossman**, born 31 Dec 1890 in Portland, Multnomah, Oregon, USA; died 23 Jan 1958 in Portland, Multnomah, Oregon, USA. He married on 9 Jul 1911 in Portland, Multnomah, Oregon, USA **Annette (Nettie) GeBotte**, born 5 Mar 1890 in Michigan, USA. Children:

+	274	i	**David William6 Gossman.** He married **Eleanor Roulston.**
+	275	ii	**Jeanne Dorothy6 Gossman.** She married **Paul Dennis Madigan.**
+	276	iii	**Kathryn Burns6 Gossman.** She married **Jerry Riebsamen.**

151. **John (Jack) Howard Montgomery5 Lamprey**, born 22 Feb 1909 in Montreal, Quebec, Canada; died 2 Oct 1962 in Vancouver, British Columbia, Canada. He married **Marjorie Joan Arbuckle**, born 25 Mar 1913 in Vernon, British Columbia, Canada; died 15 Aug 2006 in Marion Hospice, Vancouver, British Columbia, Canada. Children:

+	277	i	**Jillian Ann6 Lamprey.** She married **Philip Ferber.**

152. **Frances Patricia Secord**5 **Lamprey**, born 19 May 1912 in Montreal, Quebec, Canada; died in Vancouver, British Columbia, Canada. She married on 23 Sep 1939 **Peter Marsden Downes**, born 23 May 1914. Children:

> 278   i   **Susan Lamprey**6 **Downes**.

153. **Edith Phyllis Adeline**5 **Hemmans**, born 12 Jan 1910; died 8 Jun 1983 in Vancouver, British Columbia, Canada. She married on 24 Jun 1938 **Francis William Gauntlett Fladgate**, born 6 May 1908; died 13 Oct 1986 in Vancouver, British Columbia, Canada. Children:

> + 279   i   **Peter Francis Gauntlett**6 **Fladgate**. He married **Jeanette Ruth Woodford**.

155. **George Edward Weatherall (Ted)**5 **Hemmans**, born 19 Jul 1914; died 2000 in Vancouver, British Columbia, Canada. He married **Gwendolyn Frances Haskins**, born 31 Jul 1915 in Toronto, Ontario, Canada; died 14 Mar 2008 in Vancouver, British Columbia, Canada. Children:

> 280   i   **Gayden Ann**6 **Hemmans**. She married **Erik Kalaidzis**.
>
> + 281   ii   **Barbara Phyllis**6 **Hemmans**. She married **Jon Edward Turvey**.

157. **Edward Morden**5 **Carthew**, born 20 Nov 1913; died 19 Dec 1998 Of Humberstone, Ontario, Canada. He married on 14 Apr 1934 **Hazel Edith Doidge**, born 8 Jul 1916; died 21 Sep 1987. Children:

> 282   i   **Ethel Marlene**6 **Carthew**. She married **Anthony (Tony) Edwards**.
>
> + 283   ii   **Ellen Jacqueline (Jackie)**6 **Carthew**. She married **Alfred Marinelli**.
>
> + 284   iii   **James Morden**6 **Carthew**. He married (1) **Aileen Martin**; (2) **Caroline Gardner**.
>
> + 285   iv   **Richard Peter**6 **Carthew**. He married (1) **Marjorie Burger**; (2) **Claudia (---)**.
>
> 286   v   **William Edward**6 **Carthew**. He married **Susan Tarzwell**.

158. **Melvil McIntyre (Pete)**5 **Carthew**, born 6 Mar 1917; died 4 Jul 1990 in Beamsville, Ontario, Canada. He married (1) on 10 Nov 1945 **Marie Theresa Parker**, born 10 Sep 1925; died 1 Sep 1971; (2) aft 1971 **Marilyn Lumley Stewart**, born 12 Feb 1933. Children:

+ 287   i   Anne Marie6 Carthew. She married **Neil Heynemans**.

159. Alice Ann5 Carthew, born 20 Jun 1924 in Dundalk, Ontario, Canada; died 2 Nov 1991 in Burlington, Ontario, Canada. She married on 25 Oct 1947 **Hugh Alexander Sutherland**, born 22 Aug 1925. Children:
+ 288   i   **James Alexander6 Sutherland**. He married **Cheryl Lynn Daskaluk**.
+ 289   ii   **Jean Anne6 Sutherland**. She married **Emmerson Joseph McLaughlin**.

160. John (Jack) Carthew5 Mitchell, born 18 Dec 1909; died in Thornbury, Ontario, Canada. He married on 29 Jul 1933 **Helen G. Armstrong**, born 4 Apr 1912. Children:
  290   i   **Nancy Caroline6 Mitchell**. She married **William Kyle**.
  291   ii   **Mary Jane6 Mitchell**.
+ 292   iii   **Richard John Albert6 Mitchell**. He married (1) **Sherry Gardiner**; (2) **Leslie Bulmer**.

161. Richard Morden (Col.)5 Mitchell, born 2 Nov 1911; died 2009 in Toronto, Ontario, Canada. He married on 24 Mar 1945 **Helen K. Chapman**, born 17 Apr 1914. Children:
+ 293   i   **Peter Richard6 Mitchell**. He married **Dawna Hyde**.
  294   ii   **Graham Herbert6 Mitchell**.
  295   iii   **Lynn Leila6 Mitchell**.

162. Edith Adeline (Peter)5 Mitchell, born 17 Nov 1912; died in Montreal, Quebec, Canada. She married on 29 Jul 1938 **William Kenneth Braithwaite**, born 7 Nov 1915; died 15 Oct 1982. Children:
+ 296   i   **Suzanne6 Braithwaite**. She married (1) **Orval Thompson**; (2) **James Wylie**.
+ 297   ii   **Dianne6 Braithwaite**. She married (1) **Robert Froese**; (2) **Malcolm Burrows**; (3) **Denis Shackle**.

163. Mary McCaroll (Carol)5 Mitchell, born 15 Dec 1913; Of Peterborough, Ontario, Canada. She married on 30 Sep 1939 **George Ross Davidson**, born 24 Aug 1911. Children:

+ 298   i   **Bruce George Ross**6 **Davidson**. He married (1)
                            Heather Chadwick; (2) **Katherine Godden**.
+ 299   ii   **John Thomas (Dr.)**6 **Davidson**. He married **Judith**
                            (Dr.) Hall.
+ 300   iii   **Jane Anne**6 **Davidson**. She married **Joseph (Dr.)**
                            Niedoba.

164. **Alan George**5 **Mitchell**, born 23 Apr 1920 in Clarksburg, Thornbury, Ontario, Canada. He married on 29 Dec 1949 **Alice Maxine Headland**, born 31 Jul 1918 in Valley City, North Dakota, USA; died 1988. Children:

+ 301   i   **Roger Alan**6 **Mitchell**. He married **Coletta Ritter**.
+ 302   ii   **Caroline Winnifred**6 **Mitchell**. She married
                            Roderick (Roy) John McCormick.
   303   iii   **Alanna Marilyn**6 **Mitchell**. She married, divorced **Edward Hutchinson**.
+ 304   iv   **Elizabeth Gay**6 **Mitchell**. She married **Archibald W. McIntosh**.

167. **Charles William Ingersoll**5 **Carthew**, born 14 Dec 1919 in Fergus, Ontario, Canada. He married on 19 May 1945 **Audrey Lund Pickell**, born 23 Sep 1923. Children:

+ 305   i   **Victoria Isabel**6 **Carthew**. She married **Joseph Edward Campbell**.
+ 306   ii   **Audrey Marilyn**6 **Carthew**. She married **John Bennett (Dr.) Dickinson**.
+ 307   iii   **Richard William (Dr.)**6 **Carthew**. He married **Janet MacDermid**.
   308   iv   **Susan Lillian**6 **Carthew**. She married **Keith Naismith**.

168. **Morden Alexander (Jack)**5 **Jackson**, born 27 Sep 1916. He married on 18 Dec 1939 **Elizabeth Barry**, born 20 Apr 1918. Children:

   309   i   **William Arthur C.**6 **Jackson**. He married **Trixie Jeffels**.
   310   ii   **Robert Alexander**6 **Jackson**.
   311   iii   **Brian Christopher**6 **Jackson**.

169. **Walter Charles**5 **Jackson**, born 25 Jun 1919; died 26 Feb 1976 in Edmonton, Alberta, Canada. He married on 27 Sep 1947 **Elizabeth Agnes Ellinger**, born 20 Nov 1928. Children:

| 312 | i | Pamela Elizabeth6 Jackson. |
| 313 | ii | Peter Charles6 Jackson. |

170. **Laura Secord5 Jackson**, born 9 Sep 1920; died 10 Mar 1995. She married on 27 Dec 1943 **Charles Ray (Dr.) Giles**, born 30 May 1920; died Jan 1984. Children:

+	314	i	**Laura Secord6 Giles**. She married **David C. Somers**.
+	315	ii	**Susan Gladys6 Giles**. She married **Gerald A. (Gerry) Alexander**.
+	316	iii	**Michael Charles6 Giles**. He married (1) **Linda Devicq**; (2) **Anita Willis**.
+	317	iv	**Nancy Rae6 Giles**. She married (1) unknown; (2) **Donald Titus**.
+	318	v	**Mary Patricia6 Giles**. She married (1) **Doug Merrit**; (2) **Brett Anderson**.
	319	vi	**Clayton Thomas6 Giles**.
+	320	vii	**William Mark6 Giles**. He married **Donna Sharpe**.
	321	viii	**Pamela Ruth6 Giles**.
+	322	ix	**Matthew Dean Stonechild6 Giles**. He married **Mary (---)**.

171. **Nancy Barbara5 Jackson**, born 12 Sep 1924 in Edmonton, Alberta, Canada; died Apr 1965. She married **Lloyd George McDonald**. Children:

| 323 | i | **Richard Clayton6 McDonald**. He married unknown. |
| 324 | ii | **Robert James6 McDonald**. He married unknown. |

176. **Elizabeth Carthew5 Eakins**, born 27 Jul 1915 in Edmonton West, Alberta, Canada; died 1996 in Toronto, Ontario, Canada. She married on 29 Jun 1945 in Ontario, Canada **Norman Reeve Keene**, born 6 May 1910 Of London, Ontario, Canada; died 1993. Children:

| + | 325 | i | **Mary Elizabeth6 Keene**. She married **Stuart Robertson**. |
| | 326 | ii | **Susan Warner6 Keene**. She married **Peter Newman**. |

177. **James Edwin (Pete)5 Eakins**, born 4 Apr 1922; died 1976 in Baltimore, Maryland, USA. He married **Elsa (Hartle) McLeod**. Children:

327	i	**Gray6 Eakins.**
328	ii	**James Warner6 Eakins.**
+ 329	iii	**Elizabeth6 Eakins.** She married **James Bruwer.**

178. **Mary Alicia5 Eakins,** born 18 Jul 1928 in Ontario, Canada; died 10 Mar 2009 in Guelph, Wellington, Ontario, Canada. She married on 22 Jun 1951 **Hedley G. (Dr.) Dimock,** born 1928 in Ontario, Canada. Children:

+ 330	i	**Jane6 Dimock.** She married **Brian Mahoney.**
+ 331	ii	**Susan6 Dimock.** She married **Steven John Mulligan.**
332	iii	**Paul6 Dimock.** He married **Bridget Pannequin.**

179. **Charles Arnold5 Thomas,** born 14 Feb 1935 in Regina, Saskatchewan, Canada. He married **Donalda (---).** Children:

+ 333	i	**Alicia6 Thomas.** She married **Pierre Clement.**
334	ii	**Michael Charles6 Thomas.** He married **Claire Brown.**
335	iii	**Peter Francis6 Thomas.**
+ 336	iv	**Richard William6 Thomas.** He married **Kirsten Maxwell.**

182. **Charles A.5 Boehm,** born 1914 in Waterloo, Ontario, Canada; died in Halifax, Nova Scotia, Canada. He married in 1938 **Elizabeth (Beth) Wilson,** born in Vancouver, British Columbia, Canada. Children:

337	i	**Jennifer6 Boehm.** She married unknown.
338	ii	**Charles Richard (Dick)6 Boehm.**

183. **Edna Eloise5 Carthew** (Frederick George4, William3, Hannah Cartwright2 Secord, Laura1 Ingersoll), born 1915; died 1992 in Kitchener, Ontario, Canada. She married **Arnold Jack Blaney,** born 1915 in Ontario, Canada. Children:

339	i	**David6 Blaney.** He married **Donna Lander.**
+ 340	ii	**Douglas Arnold6 Blaney.** He married **Deborah Ann Double.**

184. **Frederick George5 Carthew** (Frederick George4, William3, Hannah Cartwright2 Secord, Laura1 Ingersoll), born 18 Dec 1916; died 18 Sep 2008 in Collingswood, Ontario, Canada. He married on 17 Apr 1943 **Loraine Isabel Solomon,** born 16 Apr 1920. Children:

| 341 | i | Frederick Charles6 Carthew. |
| 342 | ii | Scott Douglas6 Carthew. He married **Maridy Ayco**. |

185. Joanne Kaye5 March, born 26 Aug 1924 in Waterloo, Ontario, Canada; died 18 Mar 2012 in Welland, Ontario, Canada. She married (1) in 1948 in Ontario, Canada, divorced **Arthur Charles Farwell Winslow**, born abt 1924; (2) on 19 Jul 1963 in Ontario, Canada **James Eric Sutherland**, born abt 1925. Children (1):

| + | 343 | i | Susan Mary6 Winslow. She married **Murray Kropf**. |

187. Barbara Inniss5 March, born 28 May 1928 in Waterloo, Ontario, Canada. She married on 1 Oct 1948 in Waterloo, Ontario, Canada, divorced **Rudolph Paul Bellinger**, born 3 Jul 1926 in Windsor, Ontario, Canada. Children:

	344	i	Linda Tremain6 Bellinger. She married **Larry Galley**.
+	345	ii	Pamela Gale6 Bellinger. She married **Brian Carnell**.
+	346	iii	Debra Anne6 Bellinger. She married (1) **David Famme**; (2) **Daniel Chappell**.
+	347	iv	William Dudley6 Bellinger. He married **Jamie Dawn Sutton**.

Generation 6

190. Gertrude Lydia (Gertie; Pat)6 Davis. She married (1) **Joseph H. Zentner**; (2) **(---) Hooker**; (3) **(---) Theron**; (4) **Albert Norrborn**. Children (4):

| | 348 | i | Eric Theron7 Norrborn. He married **Rebecca E. Cunningham**. |

191. Viola (Vi) Rose6 Davis. She married **Donald L. Bell**. Children:

| | 349 | i | Ronald L.7 Bell. He married, divorced **Diane M. (---)**. |
| + | 350 | ii | Patricia A.7 Bell. She married **Abraham John Miller**. |

196. Harald William Davis6 Mack. He married **Marit Hansen**. Children:

| + | 351 | i | Asbjørn7 Mack. He married unknown. |
| | 352 | ii | Merete7 Mack. |

197. Henriette Laura (Etti)6 Astrup. She married **Johan Wilhelm Fremming Egilsrud.** Children:

+	353	i	Elisabeth (Lisbeth)7 Egilsrud. She married Albrecht Vogler.
	354	ii	Edith Wilhelmina7 Egilsrud.
+	355	iii	Eli7 Egilsrud. She married Egil Arentz Helland.

198. Alf6 Astrup. He married **Sigfried (Didi) Aass-Jacobsen.** Children:

+	356	i	Kirsten7 Astrup. She married Robertus van Prattenburg.
+	357	ii	Sidsel7 Astrup. She married Robert Nellemann.
	358	iii	Nils Alfssen7 Astrup.

200. Ebbe Carsten6 Astrup. He married **Bergljot Harlem.** Children:

	359	i	Signy7 Astrup. She married Per Kransted.
	360	ii	Edith7 Astrup. She married Kare Svartveit.
	361	iii	Ellen7 Astrup.
	362	iv	Nils7 Astrup.

201. Laura Elisabeth Secord6 Meier. She married **Sverre Ellingsen.** Children:

| | 363 | i | Elisabeth Secord7 Ellingsen. |
| | 364 | ii | Lars Fin7 Ellingsen. |

202. Agnes Klerck6 Meier. She married (1) **Sigurd Johannessen;** (2) **Henrik Aggerholm.** Children (1):

| + | 365 | i | Anne Lise Klerck7 Johannessen. She married Torleif (Hansen) Gange. |
| | 366 | ii | Karen Klerck7 Johannessen. She married Hjort Jensen. |

203. Ludvig Christian6 Meier. He married **Karin Leganger Anisdahl.** Children:

	367	i	Nanna7 Meier.
	368	ii	Ulla7 Meier.
	369	iii	Elisabeth7 Meier.
	370	iv	Kristen7 Meier.

371 v Anne7 Meier.

204. Johan Rieber6 Mack. He married **Ilse Margarethe Kauschke.**
Children:
+ 372 i **Janeke7 Mack.** She married **James Veitch Paton.**
373 ii **Bente7 Mack.**
374 iii **Vibeke7 Mack.**
375 iv **Ilse Merete7 Mack.**

206. Erik Klerck6 Mack. He married (1) **Nina Skappel Jensen;** (2)
Ingrid Solberg. Children:
376 i **Hans Petter7 Mack.**
377 ii **Beate7 Mack.**

207. Edith Elisabeth6 Mack. She married **Karsten Mageli.** Children:
+ 378 i **Laila Kristine7 Mageli.** She married **Harald Bøhn.**
+ 379 ii **Eldrid Ingebjorg7 Mageli.** She married **Audun Ruud.**

208. Gunnar Fredrik6 Mack. He married **Randi Bjelke.** Children:
+ 380 i **Jan Fredrik7 Mack.** He married **Eva (---).**
+ 381 ii **Ellen Elisabeth7 Mack.** She married **Frank Johnson.**

209. Stanley (Stan) Stebbins6 Smith. He married **Sara Dorothea (Thea) Dougherty.** Children:
+ 382 i **Sandra7 Smith.** She married (1) **Bradley Roger Jacobs;** (2) **Thomas A. Di Nanni.**
+ 383 ii **David Donahue (Lt.Col)7 Smith.** He married **Linda Joyce Borbe.**

211. Helen Elizabeth (Betty)6 Smith. She married (1), divorced
Donald Milton Sandberg; (2) **Robert (Bob) Frederic Straub.**
Children (1):
+ 384 i **Suzanne S.7 Sandberg.** She married (1) **Dennis Pollak;** (2) **B.J. Richardson.**
+ 385 ii **Elizabeth S. (Betsy) (Dr.)7 Sandberg.** She married (1) **Philip Rustad;** (2) **David Siitari.**
+ 386 iii **Robert Kenton7 Sandberg.** He married **Diana Heinrich.**

+ 387   iv   **William Donald (Bill)7 Sandberg.** He married **Jeanine Theresa Vogt.**

+ 388   v   **Martha7 Sandberg.** She married **Greg Yarber.**

212. **Alice Adair6 Smith.** She married (1) **Jay Leland Kevern;** (2) unknown. Children (1):

+ 389   i   **Randall7 Kevern.** He married **Cindy (---).**

215. **William Moland6 Smith.** He married **Elaine Adair Akre.**
Children:

    390   i   **David Alan7 Smith.** He married **Susan Garberg.**

+ 391   ii   **Joan Adair7 Smith.** She married **Merrill Francis Haukos.**

+ 392   iii   **Michael Steven7 Smith.** He married **Deborah Kay Fischer.**

+ 393   iv   **Diane Carol7 Smith.** She married **Dennis Harold Berneking.**

216. **James Secord6 Smith.** He married **Laura Catherine Bourland.**
Children:

    394   i   **Larry James7 Smith**

+ 395   ii   **Barbara Jean7 Smith.** She married **Dennis William Maher.**

+ 396   iii   **Janet Marie7 Smith.** She married **Donald Wayne Kellen.**

+ 397   iv   **Gary Arthur7 Smith.** He married **Loretta Irene Wyman.**

217. **Betty Jane6 Smith.** She married (1) divorced **Gabe Winters (Capt.) Potter;** (2) **Billy R. King.** Children (1):

    398   i   **Michael Allen7 Potter.**

    399   ii   **James R.7 Potter.** He married **Nancy (---).**

    Children (2):

    400   i   **Billy Dewayne7 King.**

218. **Francis Eugene (Pete)6 Smith..** He married **Lorraine M. Asplund.**
Children:

+ 401   i   **John J.7 Smith.** He married **Gayle Lee (---).**

    402   ii   **Francis Eric (Frank)7 Smith.**

    403   iii   **James (Jim)7 Smith..**

+ 404   iv   **Ann E.**7 **Smith.** She married **Robert V. (Bob) Johnston.**

219. Lillian S.6 **Strasburg.** She married **Arthur F. McCluskey.**
Children:
+ 405   i   **James**7 **McCluskey.** He married **Vicky Strasburg.**

220. Lawrence F.6 **Strasburg.** He married **Mildred V. Thompson.**
Children:
+ 406   i   **Janet M.**7 **Strasburg.** She married (1) **Tony Anderson;** (2) **Brody J. Granberg.**

221. Beverly Vesta Smith6 **Pew.** She married **Bill Andersen.** Children:
+ 407   i   **Wesley**7 **Andersen.** He married **Jan (---).**

222. Stanley Garrett Smith6 **Pew.** He married **R. Schultz.** Children:
+ 408   i   **Steven Wayne**7 **Pew.** He married **Judy (---).**
   409   ii   **Larry Douglas**7 **Pew.**

223. Shirley Nyota Smith6 **Pew.** She married (1) **James G. (Jim) Schubin;** (2) **Alfred Barbero.** Children (1):
   410   i   **Nyota**7 **Schubin.** She married **Carvet M. Wiles.**
+ 411   ii   **Valarie**7 **Schubin.** She married (1) **Gregg Campbell;** (2) unknown.

224. Lois Beverly6 **Smith.** She married **Herman Mayse.** Children:
   412   i   **Donna Lee**7 **Mayse.**

227. William Albert6 **Lunn.** He married **Marian Elizabeth Grebe.**
Children:
   413   i   **Robert Allen**7 **Lunn.** He married **Annette Loiselle.**

229. LaRhea Kathryn6 **Lunn.** She married (1) **Frank Wilson Newton;** (2) **Herbert N. Young.** Children (1):
+ 414   i   **Nola Naldeen**7 **Newton.** She married **Richard R. Raymond.**

234. Braton6 **Wallin.** He married **Emily Keith Frazer.** Children:
   415   i   **Milbrey Keith**7 **Wallin.**

237. Helen Zelma6 Marshall. She married **Henry Allen (Red) Gammel.** Children:

   416   i   **Marsha Kaye7 Gammel.**

238. Mary Ilene6 Marshall. She married **George A. McKinley** Children:

   417   i   **Stephen George7 McKinley.**

241. Gerald Edward (Lt.)6 Nearhood. He married **Theresa Ann Wetovick.** Children:

   418   i   **Gerald E. (Dr.)7 Nearhood.**
   419   ii   **Robert (Randy)7 Nearhood.**
   420   iii   **Katherine7 Nearhood.**

243. Corrine Bess (Corkie)6 Nearhood. She married **Edward F. (Jeep) Micek.** Children:

   421   i   **(---)7 Micek.**
+   422   ii   **William E.7 Micek.** He married **Chris (---).**

245. Marjory Jean (Margie)6 Nearhood. She married **Walter Francis Frey.** Children:

+   423   i   **Donald Joseph (Dr.)7 Frey.** He married **Sandra K. Battershaw.**
+   424   ii   **Patricia (Pat) Louise7 Frey.** She married **Robert (Bob) D. McKenzie.**
+   425   iii   **Michael (Mike) Lee7 Frey.** He married **Ellen J. Larson.**
+   426   iv   **James Francis7 Frey**He married **Joleen M. Philmalee.**
+   427   v   **John Henry7 Frey.** He married **Susan (Sue) M. Nelson.**

247. Patricia Elizabeth6 Downs. She married **Bernard Willis Gibb.** Children:

   428   i   **Bernard Willis7 Gibb.**

250. Roberto Edgard6 Secord Contreras. He married **Michelle M. (---).** Children:

   429   i   **Mishelle7 Secord.**

252. **Madeline Charlotte**6 **Secord Contreras.** She married **Karim Hadweh.** Children:

430	i	**Margarita**7 **Hadweh.**
431	ii	**Albert**7 **Hadweh.**

257. **Anna Maria**6 **Secord.** She married **Gert Gucciti.** Children:

432	i	**Jessica Adriana**7 **Gucciti.**
433	ii	**Vanessa Marie**7 **Gucciti.**
434	iii	**Andrea Christine**7 **Gucciti.**

258. **Christine Ingersoll**6 **Secord.** She married **Cesar Hernandez.** Children:

435	i	**Rebecca Christine**7 **Hernandez.**
436	ii	**Natalie Isabella**7 **Hernandez.**
437	iii	**Pedro Cesar**7 **Hernandez.**

260. **Nancy Jeannette**6 **Secord.** She married, divorced **Roberto Enriquez.** Children:

438	i	**Mark Cameron**7 **Enriquez.**
439	ii	**Melanie Rachel**7 **Enriquez.**

265. **Linda**6 **Deaton.** She married (1), divorced **Eugene Bittner;** (2) **Eddy Allen.** Children (1):

440	i	**Todd**7 **Bittner.**

266. **Steven**6 **Dillman.** He married **Lianne Lance.** Children:

441	i	**Joseph**7 **Dillman.**
442	ii	**Emily**7 **Dillman.**

268. **Bette Ann**6 **Yates.** She married **Howard Merle Sidwell.** Children:

443	i	**Susan Ann**7 **Sidwell.**

271. **Margaret Madeline**6 **Riley.** She married **George Joseph Rathbone Mountford.** Children:

444	i	**Dennis John**7 **Mountford.**

272. **Riley James**6 **Bracken.** He married **Mabel Alvilda Ellefson.** Children:

445	i	**Laurel Gail**7 **Bracken.**
446	ii	**James Keith**7 **Bracken.**

273. William Ernest[6] **Bracken.** He married **Fern Margaret Butler.**
Children:
    447   i   **Bonnie Jewelle**[7] **Bracken.**

274. David William[6] **Gossman.** He married **Eleanor Roulston.**
Children:
    448   i   **Gary Lee**[7] **Gossman.**

275. Jeanne Dorothy[6] **Gossman.** She married **Paul Dennis Madigan.**
Children:
    449   i   **Michael Dennis**[7] **Madigan.**
    450   ii   **Melinda Kathleen**[7] **Madigan.**

276. Kathryn Burns[6] **Gossman.** She married **Jerry Riebsamen.**
Children:
    451   i   **Craig DeLyle**[7] **Riebsamen.**

277. Jillian Ann[6] **Lamprey.** She married **Philip Ferber.** Children:
    452   i   **John**[7] **Ferber.** He married unknown.
    453   ii   **Wendy**[7] **Ferber.** She married **(---) Molnar.**

279. Peter Francis Gauntlett[6] **Fladgate.** He married **Jeanette Ruth Woodford.** Children:
    454   i   **James Gauntlett**[7] **Fladgate.**

281. Barbara Phyllis[6] **Hemmans.** She married **Jon Edward Turvey.**
Children:
    455   i   **Michael Anthony**[7] **Turvey.**
    456   ii   **Farrell Rae**[7] **Turvey.**

283. Ellen Jacqueline (Jackie)[6] **Carthew.** She married **Alfred Marinelli.**
Children:
    457   i   **Sharon Lynne**[7] **Martinelli.** She married **Edwin Albert James Ironside.**
    458   ii   **Kevin Patrick**[7] **Martinelli.** He married **Kim Cooney.**

284. James Morden[6] **Carthew.** He married (1) **Aileen Martin;** (2) **Caroline Gardner.** Children (1):

+   459   i   Leonard Morden7 Carthew. He married Sylvie
                      Ladouceur.
+   460   ii   Robert Albert7 Carthew. He married Laurie
                      Topolinsky.

285. Richard Peter6 Carthew. He married (1) Marjorie Burger; (2)
Claudia (---). Children (1):
     461   i   Marlene Marjorie Mae7 Carthew. She married
                      unknown.
     462   ii   Timothy Richard7 Carthew. He married Sandra (--
                      -).
     463   iii   Troy Peter7 Carthew.

287. Anne Marie6 Carthew. She married Neil Heynemans. Children:
     464   i   Darryl Peter7 Heynemans.

288. James Alexander6 Sutherland. He married Cheryl Lynn
Daskaluk. Children:
     465   i   Erinn Anne7 Sutherland. She married Arthur
                      Malcolm Blackburn.
     466   ii   Iain Alexander7 Sutherland.

289. Jean Anne6 Sutherland. She married Emmerson Joseph
McLaughlin. Children:
     467   i   Shannon Elizabeth7 McLaughlin.
     468   ii   Brian Michael7 McLaughlin.

292. Richard John Albert6 Mitchell. He married (1) Sherry Gardiner;
(2) Leslie Bulmer. Children (2):
     469   i   Megan7 Mitchell.

293. Peter Richard6 Mitchell. He married Dawna Hyde. Children:
     470   i   Adam Richard7 Mitchell.

296. Suzanne6 Braithwaite. She married (1) Orval Thompson; (2)
James Wylie. Children (1):
     471   i   Shelby7 Thompson.
     472   ii   Cesilee7 Thompson.
Children (2):
     473   i   Lanny McDonald7 Wylie.

297. **Dianne**6 **Braithwaite.** She married (1) **Robert Froese**; (2) **Malcolm Burrows**; (3) **Denis Shackle.** Children (2):

474	i	**Daniel**7 **Burrows.**
475	ii	**Michael**7 **Burrows.**

Children (3):

476	i	**Angela**7 **Shackle.**

298. **Bruce George Ross**6 **Davidson.** He married (1) **Heather Chadwick**; (2) **Katherine Godden.** Children (1):

477	i	**Niall**7 **Davidson.**
478	ii	**Colin**7 **Davidson.**

Children (2):

479	i	**Morgan**7 **Davidson.**

299. **John Thomas (Dr.)**6 **Davidson.** He married **Judith (Dr.) Hall.** Children:

480	i	**Christopher Ross**7 **Davidson.**
481	ii	**Caroline Louise**7 **Davidson.**
482	iii	**Andrew James**7 **Davidson.**

300. **Jane Anne**6 **Davidson.** She married **Joseph (Dr.) Niedoba.** Children:

483	i	**Emilie**7 **Niedoba.**
484	ii	**Kate**7 **Niedoba.**

301. **Roger Alan**6 **Mitchell.** He married **Coletta Ritter.** Children:

485	i	**Paige**7 **Mitchell.**
486	ii	**Chelsea**7 **Mitchell.**

302. **Caroline Winnifred**6 **Mitchell.** She married **Roderick (Roy) John McCormick.** Children:

487	i	**Taryn Kelly**7 **McCormick.**
488	ii	**Matthew F. John**7 **McCormick.**

304. **Elizabeth Gay**6 **Mitchell.** She married **Archibald W. McIntosh.** Children:

489	i	**Christopher Anthony**7 **McIntosh.**
490	ii	**Ryan William**7 **McIntosh.**

305. Victoria Isabel6 **Carthew.** She married **Joseph Edward Campbell.** Children:

491	i	**Stephen William**7 **Campbell.**
492	ii	**David Edward**7 **Campbell.**
493	iii	**Natalie Teresa**7 **Campbell.**

306. Audrey Marilyn6 **Carthew.** She married **John Bennett (Dr.) Dickinson.** Children:

494	i	**Jennifer Leigh**7 **Dickinson.**
495	ii	**Laura Joanne**7 **Dickinson.**
496	iii	**Michael John**7 **Dickinson.**
497	iv	**Robyn Michelle**7 **Dickinson.**

307. Richard William (Dr.)6 **Carthew.** He married **Janet MacDermid.** Children:

| 498 | i | **Robert William MacDermid**7 **Carthew.** |
| 499 | ii | **Daniel Gregory MacDermid**7 **Carthew.** |

314. Laura Secord6 **Giles.** She married **David C. Somers.** Children:

| + | 500 | i | **David Craig**7 **Somers.** He married **Maru (---).** |
| | 501 | ii | **Pamela Rae**7 **Somers.** She married, divorced **Rolf (---).** |

315. Susan Gladys6 **Giles.** She married **Gerald A. (Gerry) Alexander.** Children:

+	502	i	**Cynthia**7 **Alexander.** She married **Rick Giasson.**
+	503	ii	**Richard Lee**7 **Alexander.** He married **Karen (---).**
+	504	iii	**Sandra Rae**7 **Alexander.** She married **Robert Marshall.**

316. Michael Charles6 **Giles.** He married (1) divorced **Linda Devicq;** (2) **Anita Willis.** Children (1):

| 505 | i | **Crispen David**7 **Giles.** |

317. Nancy Rae6 **Giles.** She married (1) unknown; (2) divorced **Donald Titus.** Children (1):

| 506 | i | **Unknown**7 **(---).** |

Children (2):

| 507 | i | **(---)**7 **Titus.** |
| 508 | ii | **Lyle**7 **Titus.** |

509   iii   **Gregory7 Titus.**

318. **Mary Patricia6 Giles.** She married (1) **Doug Merrit**; (2) **Brett Anderson.** Children (1):
510   i   **Catherine Ruth7 Giles.**
Children (2):
511   i   **Laura Secord7 Giles.**

320. **William Mark6 Giles.** He married **Donna Sharpe.** Children:
512   i   **Laura7 Giles.**

322. **Matthew Dean Stonechild6 Giles.** He married **Mary (---).** Children:
513   i   **Marrissa Rose Stonechild7 Giles.**

325. **Mary Elizabeth6 Keene.** She married **Stuart Robertson.** Children:
514   i   **James7 Robertson.**
515   ii   **Sydney7 Robertson.**

329. **Elizabeth6 Eakins.** She married **James Bruwer.** Children:
516   i   **Mary7 Bruwer.**
517   ii   **Gray7 Bruwer.**

330. **Jane6 Dimock.** She married **Brian Mahoney.** Children:
518   i   **Kathleen7 Mahoney.**
519   ii   **James7 Mahoney.**
520   iii   **Jacqueline7 Mahoney.**

331. **Susan6 Dimock.** She married **Steven John Mulligan.** Children:
521   i   **Scott7 Mulligan.**
+ 522   ii   **Sheree7 Mulligan.** She married **Joel Plante.**
523   iii   **Lisa7 Mulligan.**

333. **Alicia6 Thomas.** She married **Pierre Clement.** Children:
524   i   **Angelica Lauri Julie7 Clement.**
525   ii   **Antony Oliver7 Clement.**

336. **Richard William6 Thomas.** He married **Kirsten Maxwell.** Children:

526   i   Jasper Maxwell7 Thomas.

340. Douglas Arnold6 Blaney. He married **Deborah Ann Double.**
Children:
527   i   **Devon7 Blaney.**
528   ii   **Erin7 Blaney.**

343. Susan Mary6 Winslow. She married **Murray Kropf.** Children:
529   i   **Peter James7 Kropf.**

345. Pamela Gale6 Bellinger. She married **Brian Carnell.** Children:
530   i   **Leah Dawn7 Carnell.**
+   531   ii   **Megan7 Carnell.** She married unknown.

346. Debra Anne6 Bellinger. She married (1) **David Famme;** (2) **Daniel Chappell.** Children (1):
532   i   **Gregory Scott7 Famme.**
533   ii   **Adam7 Famme.**

347. William Dudley6 Bellinger. He married **Jamie Dawn Sutton.**
Children:
+   534   i   **Erin Nicole7 Bellinger.** She married **Darren Lehman.**
+   535   ii   **Darrell William7 Bellinger.** He married unknown.

Generation 7

350. Patricia A.7 Bell. She married **Abraham John Miller.** Children:
+   536   i   **Darla8 Miller.** She married **Rick Keever.**
+   537   ii   **Kathy8 Miller.** She married **Rod Lincoln.**

351. Asbjørn7 Mack. He married unknown. Children:
538   i   **Cathrine Emily8 Mack.**

353. Elisabeth (Lisbeth)7 Egilsrud. She married **Albrecht Vogler.**
Children:
539   i   **Ingvar Johan Egilsrud8 Vogler.**
540   ii   **Øystein Albrecht Egilsrud8 Vogler.**

355. Eli7 Egilsrud. She married **Egil Arentz Helland.** Children:

541	i	Ellinor Egilsrud₈ Helland.
542	ii	Harald Egilsrud₈ Helland.
543	iii	Astrid Egilsrud₈ Helland.
+ 544	iv	Berit Egilsrud₈ Helland. She married unknown.
545	v	Inger-Helene M.A.₈ Helland Arentz.

356. Kirsten₇ Astrup. She married **Robertus van Prattenburg.**
Children:

546	i	Cecilie Dorothea₈ van Prattenburg.
547	ii	Benedicte Cornelia₈ van Prattenburg.

357. Sidsel₇ Astrup. She married **Robert Nellemann.** Children:

548	i	Lena₈ Nellemann.
549	ii	Gitti₈ Nellemann.
550	iii	Robert Kirli₈ Nellemann.
551	iv	Steven Axel₈ Nellemann.
552	v	Mark Astrup₈ Nellemann.
553	vi	Liv₈ Nellemann.

365. Anne Lise Klerck₇ Johannessen. She married **Torleif (Hansen) Gange.** Children:

+ 554	i	Bjørn₈ Gange. He married **Caroline M. Acheka.**
+ 555	ii	Finn₈ Gange. He married (1) **Randi Bergsvensen;** (2) **Toril Naustvold.**
+ 556	iii	Unn₈ Gange. She married **Tom Roger Hammer.**
+ 557	iv	Eva Klerck₈ Gange. She married **Henning Kramer Dahl.**

372. Janeke₇ Mack. She married **James Veitch Paton.** Children:

558	i	Johan Mack₈ Paton.

378. Laila Kristine₇ Mageli. She married **Harald Bøhn.** Children:

+ 559	i	Astrid Bøhn₈ Mageli. She married unknown.
560	ii	Håvard Bøhn₈ Mageli.
561	iii	Åshild Bøhn₈ Mageli.
562	iv	Gjertrud Bøhn₈ Mageli.

379. Eldrid Ingebjorg₇ Mageli. She married, divorced **Audun Ruud.**
Children:

563   i   **Ingvild Ruud**8 **Mageli.**

564   ii   **Eskild Ruud**8 **Mageli.**

565   iii   **Tiril Ruud**8 **Mageli.**

380. Jan Fredrik7 **Mack.** He married **Eva (---).** Children:

566   i   **Fredrik**8 **Mack.**

567   ii   **Helene**8 **Mack.**

381. Ellen Elisabeth7 **Mack.** She married **Frank Johnson.** Children:

568   i   **Sarah**8 **Johnson.**

569   ii   **Karin**8 **Johnson.**

570   iii   **Stewart**8 **Johnson.**

382. Sandra7 **Smith.** She married (1) **Bradley Roger Jacobs;** (2) **Thomas A. Di Nanni.** Children:

571   i   **Stephanie Ann**8 **Jacobs.** She married (1), divorced **Edwin Wernicke;** (2), divorced **Roger Pavek;** (3) **Rick Neville.**

+ 572   ii   **Lisa Alayne**8 **Jacobs.** She married **Kenneth Robert Anderson.**

573   iii   **Kimberley Sue**8 **Jacobs.** She married (1) divorced **Milan Thiemann;** (2) **Jeff Lee.**

+ 574   iv   **Brian**8 **Jacobs.** He married **Diane Marie Altringer.**

383. David Donahue (Lt.Col)7 **Smith.** He married **Linda Joyce Borbe.** Children:

575   i   **Thomas Stebbins**8 **Smith.**

576   ii   **Jamie Stevens**8 **Smith.** She married (1) divorced **Scott Allen (Capt.) Frerking;** (2) **Scott Colbert Bollinger.**

384. Suzanne S.7 **Sandberg.** She married (1) divorced **Dennis Pollak;** (2), divorced **B.J. Richardson.** Children:

+ 577   i   **Michael**8 **Pollak.** He married **Rebecca (---).**

578   ii   **David**8 **Pollak.**

385. Elizabeth S. (Betsy) (Dr.)7 **Sandberg.** She married (1), divorced **Philip Rustad;** (2) **David Siitari.** Children (1):

+ 579   i   **Kathryn Elizabeth (Katie)**8 **Rustad.** She married **Andrew Falvey.**

+ 580   ii   **Stephanie**8 **Rustad**. She married **Brian Loveland**.
Children (2):
     581   i   **William**8 **Siitari**.
     582   ii   **Alison**8 **Siitari**.
     583   iii   **Erica**8 **Siitari**.
     584   iv   **Andrew**8 **Siitari**.

386. **Robert Kenton**7 **Sandberg**. He married **Diana Heinrich**. Children:
     585   i   **Michael Brendan (Mike)**8 **Sandberg**.
     586   ii   **Christopher James (Chris)**8 **Sandberg**.

387. **William Donald (Bill)**7 **Sandberg**. He married **Jeanine Theresa Vogt**. Children:
     587   i   **Victoria**8 **Sandberg**.
     588   ii   **Alexandra**8 **Sandberg**.

388. **Martha**7 **Sandberg**. She married **Greg Yarber**. Children:
     589   i   **Christopher Paul**8 **Yarber**. He married **Jennifer Lee Kreitzer**.
     590   ii   **Brian James**8 **Yarber**.

389. **Randall**7 **Kevern**. He married **Cindy (---)**. Children:
     591   i   **Laurie**8 **Kevern**. She married **Patrick Thompson**.
     592   ii   **Glenniss**8 **Kevern**. She married **William (Bill) Bradow**.
     593   iii   **Amy**8 **Kevern**. She married **Daniel Beske**.

391. **Joan Adair**7 **Smith**. She married **Merrill Francis Haukos**.
Children:
     594   i   **Rebecca Ann**8 **Haukos**.
     595   ii   **Robert Norris**8 **Haukos**.

392. **Michael Steven**7 **Smith**. He married **Deborah Kay Fischer**.
Children:
     596   i   **Matthew Michael**8 **Smith**.
     597   ii   **Sarah Rose**8 **Smith**.
     598   iii   **Adam William**8 **Smith**.

393. **Diane Carol**7 **Smith**. She married **Dennis Harold Berneking**.
Children:

599	i	Kristi Diane8 Berneking. She married Jered R. Gruby.
600	ii	Dallas D.8 Berneking.

395. Barbara Jean7 Smith. She married, divorced **Dennis William Maher.** Children:

+	601	i	Jennifer Marie8 Maher. She married Kevin Anderson.
	602	ii	Jonathan James8 Maher. He married Lorena Pana.
+	603	iii	Patrick Leigh8 Maher. He married Melanie Schenkel.

396. Janet Marie7 Smith. She married **Donald Wayne Kellen.** Children:

604	i	Christopher Lee (Chris)8 Kellen.
605	ii	Jason Dane8 Kellen.
606	iii	Robin Ray8 Kellen.
607	iv	Amber Lynne8 Kellen.

397. Gary Arthur7 Smith. He married **Loretta Irene Wyman.** Children:

608	i	Brandon James8 Smith.
609	ii	Kyle William8 Smith.

401. John J.7 Smith. He married, divorced **Gayle Lee (---).** Children:

610	i	Samuel A. (Sam)8 Smith.
611	ii	Abbey L.8 Smith.

404. Ann E.7 Smith. She married **Robert V. (Bob) Johnston.** Children:

612	i	Mary E.8 Johnston.
613	ii	Eric J.8 Johnston.

405. James7 McCluskey. He married **Vicky Strasburg.** Children:

614	i	Kelly8 McCluskey.

406. Janet M.7 Strasburg. She married (1) **Tony Anderson;** (2) **Brody J. Granberg.** Children:

+	615	i	Steven8 Anderson. He married Courtney Whitson.

407. Wesley7 Andersen. He married **Jan (---).** Children:

616   i   Adam8 Anderson.

617   ii   Mackenzie8 Anderson.

408. **Steven Wayne7 Pew.** He married **Judy (---).** Children:

618   i   **Christopher8 Pew.**

411. **Valarie7 Schubin.** She married (1), divorced **Gregg Campbell**; (2) unknown. Children (1):

619   i   **Susan8 Campbell.** She married **Nathan Elder.**

620   ii   **Traci8 Campbell.** She married **Adam Hlebakos.**

414. **Nola Naldeen7 Newton.** She married **Richard R. Raymond.** Children:

621   i   **Lanette A.8 Raymond.**

622   ii   **Lisa Laree8 Raymond.**

623   iii   **Fina Richelle8 Raymond.**

422. **William E.7 Micek.** He married **Chris (---).** Children:

624   i   **Nicole8 Micek.**

625   ii   **Kent8 Micek.**

423. **Donald Joseph (Dr.)7 Frey.** He married **Sandra K. Battershaw.** Children:

+   626   i   **Caree Anne8 Frey.** She married **Tim Cielocha.**

627   ii   **Sherry Lynne8 Frey.**

+   628   iii   **Joseph Alan8 Frey.** He married **Laura Koepke.**

629   iv   **Katherine Marie (Katie)8 Frey.** She married **Brandon Gutzman.**

424. **Patricia (Pat) Louise7 Frey.** She married **Robert (Bob) D. McKenzie.** Children:

630   i   **Scott A.8 McKenzie.** He married **Jan (---).**

+   631   ii   **Marc Robert8 McKenzie.** He married **Kathy (---).**

632   iii   **Michael W.8 McKenzie.**

425. **Michael (Mike) Lee7 Frey.** He married **Ellen J. Larson.** Children:

+   633   i   **Christine8 Frey.** She married **Chris Mollhoff.**

+   634   ii   **Kimberly A.8 Frey.** She married **Eric Youngdahl.**

+   635   iii   **Craig8 Frey.** He married **Amy Ranks.**

+ 636 iv Justin D.⁸ Frey. He married **Brenda Dozler**.

426. James Francis⁷ Frey. He married **Joleen M. Philmalee**. Children:
+ 637 i **Jamie⁸ Frey**. He married **Kris Wright**.
+ 638 ii **Eric J.⁸ Frey**. He married **Kara L. Schaefer**.
639 iii **Kelli M.⁸ Frey**. She married **Weston Ray**.
640 iv **Melissa⁸ Frey**.

427. John Henry⁷ Frey. He married **Susan (Sue) M. Nelson**. Children:
641 i **Jaclyn⁸ Frey**.

459. Leonard Morden⁷ Carthew. He married **Sylvie Ladouceur**. Children:
642 i **Tyler Frank Morden⁸ Carthew**.
643 ii **Ryan James⁸ Carthew**.

460. Robert Albert⁷ Carthew. He married, divorced **Laurie Topolinsky**. Children:
+ 644 i **Alisha Joy Topolinsky⁸ Carthew**. She married unknown.
645 ii **Ashley Mari Topolinsky⁸ Carthew**.

500. David Craig⁷ Somers. He married **Maru (---)**. Children:
646 i **Laura⁸ Somers**.
647 ii **Daniella⁸ Somers**.
648 iii **Marie⁸ Somers**.

502. Cynthia⁷ Alexander. She married **Rick Giasson**. Children:
649 i **Josh⁸ Giasson**.
650 ii **Laura⁸ Giasson**.
651 iii **Jessica⁸ Giasson**.

503. Richard Lee⁷ Alexander. He married **Karen (---)**. Children:
652 i **Stephanie⁸ Alexander**.
653 ii **Tessa⁸ Alexander**.

504. Sandra Rae⁷ Alexander. She married **Robert Marshall**. Children:
654 i **Curtis⁸ Marshall**.
655 ii **Eric⁸ Marshall**.

522. Sheree7 Mulligan. She married **Joel Plante.** Children:

656	i	**Raiden8 Mulligan-Plante.**

531. Megan7 Carnell. She married unknown. Children:

657	i	**Emma Dawn8 Carnell.**

534. Erin Nicole7 Bellinger. She married **Darren Lehman.** Children:

658	i	**Jordyn Catherine8 Lehman.**
659	ii	**Taylor Dawn8 Lehman.**

535. Darrell William7 Bellinger. He married unknown. Children:

660	i	**Caden Dallan8 Bellinger.**

Generation 8

536. Darla8 Miller. She married **Rick Keever.** Children:

661	i	**Jacob A. (Jak)9 Keever.** He married unknown.
662	ii	**Heather Kay9 Keever.**
663	iii	**Karissa D.9 Keever.**

537. Kathy8 Miller. She married **Rod Lincoln.** Children:

664	i	**Justin9 Lincoln.**
665	ii	**Travis9 Lincoln.**

544. Berit Egilsrud8 Helland. She married unknown. Children:

666	i	**Lone9 Helland.**

554. Bjørn8 Gange. He married **Caroline M. Acheka.** Children:

667	i	**Farid9 Acheka.**
668	ii	**Arvid Acheka9 Gange.**

555. Finn8 Gange. He married (1) **Randi Bergsvensen;** (2) **Toril Naustvold.** Children (1):

669	i	**Katinka Bergsvendsen9 Gange.**

Children (2):

670	i	**Torstein9 Gange.**
671	ii	**Finn Andreas9 Gange.**

556. **Unn8 Gange**. She married **Tom Roger Hammer**. Children:
    672   i   **Lise Berit9 Hammer**.
    673   ii   **Tom Jarle9 Hammer**.

557. **Eva Klerck8 Gange**. She married **Henning Kramer Dahl**. Children:
    674   i   **Johanne Klerck9 Kramer-Dahl**.

559. **Astrid Bøhn8 Mageli**. She married unknown. Children:
    675   i   **Vlljar9 (---)**.
    676   ii   **Sigurd9 (---)**.

572. **Lisa Alayne8 Jacobs**. She married **Kenneth Robert Anderson**. Children:
    677   i   **Nicole Jermaine9 Anderson**.
    678   ii   **Kirstin Ashley9 Anderson**.

574. **Brian8 Jacobs**. He married **Diane Marie Altringer**. Children:
    679   i   **Angela Marie9 Jacobs**.

577. **Michael8 Pollak**. He married, divorced **Rebecca (---)**. Children:
    680   i   **Nathan9 Pollak**.
    681   ii   **Marcus9 Pollak**.

579. **Kathryn Elizabeth (Katie)8 Rustad**. She married **Andrew Falvey**. Children:
    682   i   **Freya Flynn9 Falvey**.

580. **Stephanie8 Rustad**. She married **Brian Loveland**. Children:
    683   i   **Joshua Alden9 Loveland**.
    684   ii   **Nathanael Brian9 Loveland**.
    685   iii   **LilyAnna9 Loveland**.

601. **Jennifer Marie8 Maher**. She married, divorced **Kevin Anderson**. Children:
    686   i   **Sean9 Anderson**.
    687   ii   **Jacob9 Anderson**.
    688   iii   **Alexis9 Anderson**.
    689   iv   **Brett9 Anderson**.

603. Patrick Leigh[8] Maher. He married **Melanie Schenkel.** Children:

690   i   **Alexander James[9] Maher.**

615. Steven[8] Anderson. He married **Courtney Whitson.** Children:

691   i   **Kellan[9] Anderson.**
692   ii   **Chloe[9] Anderson.**

626. Caree Anne[8] Frey. She married **Tim Cielocha.** Children:

693   i   **Haylee[9] Cielocha.**
694   ii   **Trenton[9] Cielocha.**
695   iii   **Tyson[9] Cielocha.**

628. Joseph Alan[8] Frey. He married on 16 Aug 2003 **Laura Koepke.** Children:

696   i   **Henry[9] Frey.**
697   ii   **Max[9] Frey.**
698   iii   **Charles[9] Frey.**

631. Marc Robert[8] McKenzie. He married **Kathy (---).** Children:

699   i   **Kayla[9] McKenzie.**

633. Christine[8] Frey. She married **Chris Mollhoff.** Children:

700   i   **Tyra[9] Mollhoff.**
701   ii   **Tony[9] Mollhoff.**
702   iii   **Cami[9] Mollhoff.**

634. Kimberly A.[8] Frey. She married **Eric Youngdahl.** Children:

703   i   **Tanner[9] Youngdahl.**
704   ii   **Cooper[9] Youngdahl.**

635. Craig[8] Frey. He married **Amy Ranks.** Children:

705   i   **Zak[9] Frey.**

636. Justin D.[8] Frey. He married **Brenda Dozler.** Children:

706   i   **Lucas[9] Frey.**

637. Jamie[8] Frey. He married **Kris Wright.** Children:

707   i   **Lauren[9] Frey.**

708	ii	Kaleb[9] Frey.

638. Eric J.[8] Frey. He married **Kara L. Schaefer.** Children:

709	i	Ava[9] Frey.
710	ii	Norah[9] Frey.

644. Alisha Joy Topolinsky[8] Carthew. She married unknown. Children:

711	i	Damien[9] (---).
712	ii	Dianne[9] (---).

So, today, there are over 700 descendants of Laura Ingersoll Secord, and over 130 surviving surnames. The only remaining line of 'Secord' surnames were born in Guatemala. Laura's great-grandson, Dr. Clayton (Carlos) Forsythe Secord was a medical missionary from 1900 to 1928 in Chichicastenango, Guatemala, married a local lady and had five surviving sons there; his descendants are now scattered across Guatemala, California, Georgia and Australia.

There are two extant all-female lines of Laura Ingersoll Secord descendants remaining. However, these ladies live in Norway and are direct descendants of Laura's eldest daughter, Mary Lawrence Secord Trumble. As a result, mtDNA analysis from Laura's direct descendant lines has now been made possible, based on current genealogy (above) and current state-of-the-art genetics. There are also two different locks of hair purported to be from Laura herself, in two collections of personal effects; however, it is unclear whether her mtDNA can be established without hair roots.

ALL-FEMALE LINE For LAURA SECORD

Laura Ingersoll
(1775-1868)

Mary Lawrence
Secord
(1799-1876)

Elizabeth Trumble
(1817-1893)

Laura Mary Davis
(1847-1932)

Edith Mack
(1874-1960)
+ Laura (mama)
+ Henriette (1900- ?)

Henriette Laura (Etti) Astrup
(1900 - ?)
CHILDREN:
Elisabeth Egilsrud (1931-)
Edith Wilhelmina Egilsrud (1933-)
Eli Egilsrud (1936-)

mtDNA without exhumation

239

Family Grave Markers in
Woodlawn Cemetery, Guelph

Sec. N, 25-2, Lot 397:
In loving memory of HARRIET SECORD relict of the late D.W.
SMITH, born Feb 10, 1803, died Jan 20, 1892. Also their daughter
LAURA LOUISA born Sep 11, 1825, died Jan 7, 1904.
Them also which sleep in Jesus will God bring with Him when
He comes. Thess. 4:14.

Sec. N, 25-1, Lot 398:
MARY AUGUSTA, daughter of DAVID & HARRIET SMITH,
born Nov 9, 1828, died Apr 16, 1911.
We believe that Jesus died and rose again.

Sec. N, 25-3, Lot 397:
Sacred to the memory of LAURA CLARKE wife of WILLIAM
CLARKE M.D. who departed this life Aug 18, 1852 in the 38th
year of her age. Believe in the word of the Lord.
Also their daughter LAURA SECORD CLARKE U.E.L. in her 94th
year, grand-daughter of LAURA & JAMES SECORD of
Chippawa, Ont.

Sec. O, 14-15, Lot 194:
Erected to the Memory of HANNAH wife of EDWARD
CARTHEW, Guelph, who died Nov 21, 1877, aged 59 years.
Blessed are the peace makers for they shall see God. Math.
5:VIII.
If we believe that Jesus died and rose again then so those also
which sleep in Jesus will God bring with him. 1st Thse. 4:XIII.

Sec. O, 14-14, Lot 194:
Sacred to the Memory of EDWARD CARTHEW who died April
8, 1879, aged 70 years.
Thus remained a rest for the people of God. Heb. IV:9.

CHARLOTTE SECORD is also buried here. She died Oct. 16,
1880 and is buried with no grave marker in Lot 397.

Bibliography

---, "Medical Missionary Work in Guatemala", The American Journal of Clinical Medicine, Volume 19, p. 102-103.

---, "Vast Indian Horde to Unite Central American Republics", The Toronto World, Monday 25 Aug 1913, p.2.

Auchinleck, Gilbert, "A history of the war between Great Britain and the United States of America, during the years 1812, 1813, & 1814", Anglo-American Magazine, Toronto, Volume III, No. 5, November 1853 (book), pp. 466-468.

Auchinleck, Gilbert, "A history of the war between Great Britain and the United States of America, during the years 1812, 1813, & 1814", Toronto, W.G. Chewett, 1862, vii, 408 pp. (repr. London, 1972).

Babcock, Louis L., "The War of 1812 on the Niagara Frontier", Buffalo, NY: The Buffalo Historical Society, 1927.

Barnett, Jody, "Women's Literary Club of St. Catharines Fonds", http://hdl.handle.net/10464/2719 , 2009, 2pp.

Bassett, John M. & Petrie, A. Roy, "Laura Secord", Fitzhenry & Whiteside, 2002, 64pp., ISBN 1-55041-490-9.

Boyko-Head, Christine, "The Myth of Laura Secord in Nineteenth Century Artistic (Re)presentations to Twentieth century Popular Culture", v.221, Ph.D. Thesis, McMaster University, December 1994.

Boyko-Head, Christine, "Laura Secord Meets the Candyman: The Image of Laura Secord in Popular Culture", in Slippery Pastimes, ed. Jean Nicks & Jeannette Sloniowski, Wilfrid Laurier University Press, 2002, pp. 61-80.

British Canadian compiler, "The Tour of H.R.H. The Prince of Wales through British America and the United States", John Lovell, London, 1860, 271pp.

Bryce, George (Rev., Prof.), "A Study in Canadian Patriotism, Laura Secord", Manitoba Free Press Co., Winnipeg, 1907, 16pp.

Bull, William Perkins, "From Brock to Currie", Toronto, Perkins Bull Foundation, G.J. McLeod Ltd., 1935.

Canniff, William, "History of the Province of Ontario (Upper Canada)", Toronto, A.H. Hovey, 1872.

Canniff, William, "History of the Settlement of Upper Canada (Ontario)", Toronto, 1869, 369 pp. In 1872 he published "History of the province of Ontario" (2nd ed., Toronto, 1874).

Carnochan, J., "Laura Secord monument at Lundy's Lane." Niagara Historical Society, Publication No. 25, 1913, 10 pp.

Carthew, C. W., "Genealogy of The Canadian Branch of the Carthew Family", Aug 1993, 9pp.

Coates, Colin M. & Morgan, Cecilia, "Heroines and History. Representations of Madeleine de Vercheres and Laura Secord", University of Toronto Press, 2002, 368 pp., ISBN 0-8020-8330-7.

Coffin, William F., "1812, the War and its Moral; a Canadian chronicle", John Lovell, Montreal, 1864, 296 pp. [The fictional assistance of a cow for Laura Secord's walk is first introduced here.] ISBN 1-1044-0788-4

Cotton, Henry, "The Succession of Prelates and Members of the Cathedral Bodies of Ireland", John Charles & Son, Dublin, 1878, 141 pp.

Crook, Connie B., "Laura Secord's Brave Walk", Second Story Press, Toronto, ON, 2000, 24 pp., ISBN 1-896764-34-7.

Cruikshank, Ernest A., "Documentary History of the Campaign upon the Niagara Frontier in 1813", Welland, ON, 1902, pp. 127-128.

Cruikshank, Ernest A., et al., "Story of Laura Secord", Lundy's Lane Historical Society Document, 1892.

Cruikshank, Ernest A., "The Fight at the Beechwoods", Welland Historical Society papers, 1895.

Cruikshank, Ernest A., "Laura Secord's Walk to Warn FitzGibbon", Niagara Historical Society, Publication No. 36, 1924, pp. 33-39.

Currie, Emma A., "The Story of Laura Secord and Canadian Reminiscences", Toronto, Briggs, 1900.

Curzon, Sarah A., "Memoir of Laura Secord. Laura Secord and Other Poems", Toronto, C. Blackett Robinson, 1887.

Curzon, Sarah A., "The Story of Laura Secord, 1813", Lundy's Lane Historical Society, 1891 (repr. 1898).

Dahlquist, Anna Marie, "Trailblazers for Translators: The Chichicastenango Twelve", William Carey Library, Oct 1, 1995 - 159 pp.

D'Este, A.F. (compiler), "Documents, selected from several others, showing the services rendered by Colonel FitzGibbon, while serving in Upper Canada, between the years 1812 and 1837", Windsor, England, 1859.

Dove, Stephen C., " Local Believers, Foreign Missionaries, and the Creation of Guatemalan Protestantism, 1882-1944", D.Phil. Dissertation, U. Texas, Austin, 2012, 382+xii pp.

Dunnville Weekly Chronicle, "What Laura Secord Did", 1935.

Edgar, Matilda, "Ten Years of Upper Canada in peace and War, 1805-1815", Toronto, Briggs, 1890.

Errington, Elizabeth J., "Wives and Mothers School Mistresses and Scullery Maids, Working Women in Upper Canada, 1790-1840", Montreal, McGill-Queens University Press, 1995, 375 pp. ISBN 0-7735-1310-8.

FitzGibbon, Mary A., "A Veteran of 1812: The Life of James FitzGibbon", Montreal, Briggs, 1894, 347 pp.

Garrard-Burnett, Virginia, "Protestantism in Guatemala: Living in the New Jerusalem", University of Texas Press, 1998, 248 pp.

Green, Ernest, "Some Graves in Lundy's Lane", Niagara Historical Society, Publication No. 22, 1912, p. 50.

Hansen, Solveig Mack & Mack, Rolf, "Slekten Mack I Norge", 1968, 76pp.

Hemmings, David F., "Disappearing History of Niagara", Niagara-on-the-Lake, Bygones Publishing, 2010, 374pp.

Herrington, W. S., "Heroines of Canadian history", Toronto, Briggs, 1910, 5 pp.

Historic Sites & Monuments Board of Canada, "Laura Secord, 1775-1868. Commemoration of the National Historic Significance of Laura Secord (1775-1868)", May 25, 2006, Queenston, Ontario, 4 pp.

Hitchcock, Mary L., "The Genealogy of the Hitchcock Family", Carpenter & Morehouse Press, 1894, 556pp.

Hitsman, J. Mackay, "The Incredible War of 1812", Toronto, University of Toronto Press, 1965.

Hodgins, J. George, "The Geography and History of British America and of the Other Colonies of the Emire", Toronto, Maclear, 1857.

Hughes, Alun, "Laura Secord's Key and the Schoolbook Scandal", The Historical Society of St. Catharines, December 2009 Newsletter, 2 pp.

Hughes, Alun, "The American Surrender at Beaverdams", The Historical Society of St. Catharines, September 2010, 10 pp.

Hughes, Alun, "Laura Secord and the Prince of Wales", The Historical Society of St. Catharines, March 2012, 10pp.

Hume, Blanche, "Laura Secord", Toronto, ON: Ryerson Press, 1928, 32 pp.

Ingersoll, J.H., "The Ancestry of Laura Ingersoll Secord", Ontario Historical Society Paper, 1926, 363 pp.

Ingram, George, "The Story of Laura Secord Revisited", Ontario History, Vol. LV11, No. 2, 1965, 8 pp.

Keefer, Frank H., "Beaverdams", Thorold Post Printers, 1914, 17pp.

Kellogg, John Harvey, "The Medical Missionary", Paper by Dr. C.F. Secord, 'The Indians of Central America' in Contributions & Selections, International Health and Temperance Association, 1912, p.72-74.

Lossing, Benson J., "The pictorial field-book of the War of 1812", New York, 1869, 621 pp.

Mack, Laura Mary Davis, "To My Children", Private Communication, 1928, 15 pp.

Mail & Empire, Toronto, newspaper, Dec 1931. Numerous subjective articles on Laura Secord debunking and support.

Mair, Charles, "A Ballad for Brave Women", in the Toronto Week, 21 June 1888.

Marchar, Agnes, "Laura Secord. Lays of the True North and Other Canadian Poems", Toronto, The Ciopp, Clarke Co. Ltd., 1899.

McKenzie, Ruth, "Laura Secord. The legend and the lady", Toronto, McClelland and Stewart. 1971, 142 pp., ISBN 0-7710-5800-4

McKenzie, Ruth, "Biography of Laura Secord", The Dictionary of Canadian Biography Online at Libraries and Archives Canada, 1 pp.

McKenzie, Ruth, "Biography of James FitzGibbon", The Dictionary of Canadian Biography Online at Libraries and Archives Canada, Volume IX, 1861-1870, 1 pp.

McLeod, C., "Legendary Canadian Women", Hantsport, N.S.: Lancelot Press, 1983.

McMaster University Library, William Ready Division of Archives and Research Collections: Secord family fonds, consisting of mortgages, indentures, quit claims, tax notices, genealogical trees, wills, deeds of land, and other miscellaneous documents.

Miller, Robert J., "Origins of 46 Paxton Lane", 2 February 2007, Niagara Historical Society Collection, 11 pp.

Miller, Robert J., "Review of 137 Four Mile Creek Road", 13 November 2003, Niagara Historical Society Collection, 17 pp & 3 research document attachments.

Moir, John S., "An Early Record of Laura Secord's Walk", Ontario History, 1959, Vol. 51, No. 2, 2 pp.

Montgomery, L. M., & MacGregor, M. E. M., et al., "Courageous women", Toronto, ON: McClelland & Stewart, 1934.

Mutrie, R. Robert, "The Niagara Settlers Land Records", from Abstracts of Deeds Registers (1796-1865) in: https://sites.google.com/site/niagarasettlers2/

Niagara Historical Society, "Laura Ingersoll Secord", No. 25, Niagara, 1913, 11pp.

Niagara Mail (Niagara, Ontario) reported on Laura Secord's contribution as a heroine, 8 August 1860.

Niagara Mail (Niagara, Ontario) reported on the Prince's gift to Mrs Secord, 27 March 1861 & 3 April 1861.

Niagara Mail (Niagara, Ontario), Obituary: "Laura Secord", after 17 October 1868.

Niles' Weekly Register, "Battle of the Beaver Dams", Baltimore, MD, March–September1816, pp. 119–21.

Public Archives of Canada.
(i)   The Laura and James Secord petitions are in:
        RG 5, A 1, vol. 46, pp.22844–45 (1820);
        RG5, A 1, 108, pp.61567–68 (1831);
        RG5 C1, vol. 52, no. 3157 (C-13561, microfilm);
        RG5, C1, vol. 59, no. 222 (C-13563, microfilm);
        MG24, I, 75, 1. R3457-0-9-E (C-15614 or C-15618, microfilms).
(ii)   The FitzGibbon certificates are in:
        RG 5, A 1, vol. 46, p.22847 (1820);
        RG5, A 1, vol. 84, pp.45661–63 (1827);
        RG5, C1, 82, no.2880, pp. 31886-91 (incl. 1837 certificate and
        Charles B. Secord's petition in 1842) (C-13568, microfilm).
(iii)   Laura Secord's memorial to the Prince of Wales in 1860 in:
        RG 7, G-23, 1, file 2.
(iv)   Official reports of the battle of Beaver Dams are in:
        RG 8, I (C series), 679, pp.132–41 (C-3172, C-3173, microfilms).
(v)   Laura Secord image woodcut, cat. 14/10/36. Other nos. 1936-
        229 PIC 00001; ICON75405; MIKAN 2909442.

(vi)   Ruth McKenzie fonds:
         MG31, D 135, boxes 1 & 2 only; R5343-0-2-E, including material
         on Laura Secord (volumes 1-2, 0.225 m) and related
         correspondence, and notes, photocopies of archival papers,
         press releases, book reviews and manuscripts.

Public Archives of Ontario
         Misc. 1933, is "The story of Laura Ingersoll Secord, wife of
         Captain James Secord, as related by Laura Secord Clark, grand-
         daughter of Laura Secord to Mrs. George S. Henry."

Ripley, Charles Stedman, "The Ingersolls of Hampshire", Alfred
Mudge & Son, Boston, 1893, 107pp.

Robertson, John Ross, "Laura Ingersoll Secord's Heroic Walk from
Queenston to DeCew Falls, 22nd June 1813", Canadian Prints of the
Toronto Public Reference Library. [Artist: Jacob Cotton, 1917.]

Robertson, John Ross, "History of Freemasonry in Canada", Part 1, p.
502.

Robinson, Helen Caistor, "Laura: A Portrait of Laura Secord", Toronto,
Dundurn Press, 1981, 240 pp.

Secord, Charles B., The Church magazine, 11/18 April 1845, a letter
relating his mother's deed in 1813.

Seibel, George A., "The Niagara Portage Road. A History of the
Portage on the West Bank of the Niagara River", The City of Niagara
Falls, 1990, xi, 371 pp.

Shepperd, George, "Plunder, Profit, and Paroles: A Social History of the
War of 1812 in Upper Canada", 1994, Montreal, McGill-Queens
University Press, 147 pp., ISBN 0-7735-1137-7

Sinclair, James Sr., "History of the Town of Ingersoll", 1924, 44pp.

Tate, Marsha Ann, "Looking for Laura Secord on the Web: Using a
famous figure from the War of 1812 as a Model for Evaluating
Historical Web Sites", The History Teacher, Feb 2005, Vol. 38, No. 2, 8
pp.

Taylor, Charles J., "History of Great Barrington, Massachusetts", Clark
W. Bryan & Co., 1882, 516pp.

Thompson, Elizabeth J., "Laura Ingersoll Secord," Niagara Historical Society, Publication No. 25, Niagara-on-the-Lake, Ontario, 1912, p. 10.

Thompson, John H., "Jubilee History of Thorold Township and Town", Thorold, The Thorold & Beaver Dams Historical Society, 1897-8.

Tolan, Eva Elliott, Niagara Falls newspaper, "Reminders of The Past – Chippawa" 28 Mar, 4 Apr 11 Apr 1953; and "-Laura Secord", 19 Jun 1954.

United States National Archives, "A court of inquiry into the affair called the Battle of the Beaver Dams, February, 1815." Washington, DC. (From a microfilmed copy, now located in The St. Catharines [Ontario] Public Library.)

Wallace, William S., "A History of the Canadian People", 1930, Copp Clark, xiii, 404 pp. [omitted Laura Secord in the Beaver Dams entry, infuriating her many supporters.]

Wallace, William Stewart, "The Story of Laura Secord: a study in historical evidence", Toronto, Macmillan, 1932.

Wetherall, J.E. & Jeffreys, Charles W., "Handbook to Nelson's Pictures of Canadian History", Toronto, Thomas Nelson & Sons, 1927.

Williams, Fred, "A Vindication of Laura Secord", Mail and Empire, Toronto, 23 June 1934. [The 1820 certificate from FitzGibbon newly found by Henry Cartwright Secord.]

Wilner, Merton M., "Niagara Frontier. A Narrative and Documentary History", Chicago, S.J. Clarke Publishing, Vol. 1, 1931.

Wood, William (Col.), "Review of 'The Story of Laura Secord: a study in historical evidence' by W.S. Wallace", Canadian Historical Review, March 1932, pp. 65-66.

Zaslow, Morris, "The Defended Border, Upper Canada, the War of 1812", Macmillan Co., 1964

Index